Verses and Prayers Compiled
by Florence Hobart Perin in 1907

The Optimist's

good

morning

journal

With Updated Text and Scriptures
Compiled by Lorie Grant DeWorken in 2023

Published in 2023
MindtheMargins, LLC

DEDICATIONS

Provided by FLORENCE HOBART PERIN in the last century...

To my mother and father

And by LORIE GRANT DEWORKEN in this one...

To my parents:
I am forever grateful for your faith and optimism
and even more that you instilled both in me!

To my children, BSQ,
and to my husband, Pete:
I love you more than you'll ever know
and I'm so grateful for our many good mornings!

Original Preface

Once family devotions were general, now they are rare. There are reasons for the change. One reason is that the simplicity of the old family life is gone. It is not easy to get all the members of the family together at any one time in the day. A part of this is due to less leisure now than formerly. Men must catch trains in the morning. In the evening they are distracted by manifold social engagements.

Yet the need of spiritual adjustment is ever the same. Rapid transit, the telephone, the telegraph, do not take the place of God. Indeed the more rapid pace involved in these modern pace-makers, renders the more necessary some pause in the day for prayer, some upward look, when for a moment the soul may find an open way between itself and God. But how and when? Why not the breakfast table? Surely one or two minutes may be spared. Thirty seconds of silence, then the reading of a noble sentiment from some one who has been thinking for us—another pause—and a few words of prayer, framed by some one with more leisure than we have, but who puts us in the mood of prayer and so starts us right upon the duties of the day, this will bring the needed readjustment.

Such is the plan and purpose of this little book. It is made for busy men and women, who *need* to begin the day with God. The quotations for each day are brief, but they are gleaned from the great Masters of thought. The prayers are from devout men of all the denominations.

As the title will have suggested, both quotations and prayers are generally in the spirit of a truly optimistic faith. However life may look in the middle of the night, it is a good thing to start out to do the work of the day with hope and courage. I shall be glad if I can feel that this little book has helped some busy people to begin the day in this spirit. I shall be particularly glad if I can feel that it has helped a little to keep the candles lighted on the family altar.

—FLORENCE HOBART PERIN.

Foreword

Mrs. Perin's original intent for this sweet book was for the family. I truly hope it will still be used in that way today, but I also hope anyone might find solace, hope, and inspiration in these pages whether they are reading through this book as a family or as an individual. The need for books like this one is the same now as it was in Mrs. Perin's day. Our lives are no less busy—probably more so. Family life is no longer simple, often far from it. Work and school and social lives—or even more often social media—keep us busier and busier.

But just as she reminds us, none of today's preoccupations or responsibilities take the place of God. Instead, they should be reminders of how much we need Him—now more than ever. Taking time each day to *be* with Him, to gain much-needed perspective on this world and His kingdom, is so very important. I hope that this book will be a useful tool for you in taking that time this year.

With the exception of the poetry, I took the liberty of modernizing most of the narrative text and prayers to eliminate Thees, Thous, and similar outdated language for ease of reading. As I read through the original book and inevitably did the "translation" in my head, it seemed that making that adjustment for other readers might make an "old" book more relatable and personal, especially for those readers who might not consider reading a book full of Thees and Thous otherwise.

The journaling portions on each page are intended for recording thoughts from/for each day or to record short notes across multiple years to see how God may use these pages in different ways at different times in your life—if you choose to go through this book more than once, which I hope you do!

During the many hours spent putting this book together, I've been pleasantly surprised that after more than 116 years so many of its sentiments are still incredibly impactful and useful for our lives now. And then I wonder how I can be surprised at all when I know full well the God I serve. His truth and His love are for all time and all people. It's no wonder at all that the words and thoughts placed in this book more than a century ago are still just as powerful today!

I hope these pages, including the addition of scripture to further underscore each day's themes, will help you to approach each and every morning with optimism and faith in the amazing God we serve and an eagerness to realize and share all the promise and love He holds for us. With this book, I pray you'll have good mornings with God all year long!

—LORIE GRANT DeWORKEN.

The Optimist's

good

morning

January 1

Forget the former things; do not dwell on the past.
See, I am doing a new thing!
Now it springs up; do you not perceive it?
I am making a way in the wilderness and
streams in the wasteland.

ISAIAH 43:18-19 (NLT)

Throughout the year, why not keep sweet? No frown ever made a heart glad; no complaint ever made a dark day bright; no bitter word ever lightened a burden or made a rough road smooth; no grumbling ever introduced sunshine into a home. What the world needs is the resolute step, the look of cheer, the smiling countenance, and the kindly word. Keep sweet! —GEORGE L. PERIN.

God of the years, our Heavenly Father, whatever the message of the old year may have been, whether of darkness or light, joy or sorrow, we stand this morning waiting expectantly and confidently for some message with glad tidings. May we therefore enter upon the New Year in the mood of hope and good cheer, brushing from our faces every sign of care, let us go forth into the New Year with the spirit of a child who puts his hand into the hand of a Father to be led into a field where the flowers blossom and the birds sing. Not for today only do we pray for sweetness and light, but let us be glad and happy every day. You are with us today, You will be with us through all the journey of the year. May our own daily gladness be born of the conviction that You are always near. Amen. —GEORGE L. PERIN.

January 2

The Lord is my strength and my shield;
my heart trusts in him, and he helps me.

PSALM 28:7a (NIV)

To keep my health!
To do my work!
To live!
To see to it I grow and gain and give!
Never to look behind me for an hour!
To wait in weakness and to walk in power
But always fronting forward to the light,
Always, and always facing toward the right.
Robbed, starved, defeated, fallen, wide astray—
On, with what strength I have!
Back to the way!

—CHARLOTTE PERKINS GILMAN.

With this new day, O God, let some new strength be mine, to walk in patience, the way appointed for me. Let me be strong to battle with the ills that shall beset me, to toil with faith and honest heart, to keep myself untainted and make my life helpful to my fellowmen. Help me to be forgetful of myself, but thoughtful to do no evil to any man. Your hand is strong and mine is weak. I need Your guidance, let Your strength be mine, that though I stumble I may not fall nor fail. And when the day is done, may happy memories be mine. Amen. —ALMON GUNNISON.

January 3

In him was life, and that life was the light of all mankind. The light shines in the darkness, and the darkness has not overcome it.   JOHN 1:4-5 (NLT)

> Build on resolve, and not upon regret,
> The structure of Thy future. Do not grope
> Among the shadows of old sins, but let
> Thine own soul's light shine on the path of hope
> And dissipate the darkness. Waste no tears
> Upon the blotted record of lost years,
> But turn the leaf, and smile, oh, smile, to see
> The fair white pages that remain to thee.
>
> —ELLA WHEELER WILCOX.

O All-persuasive God, who speaks within the souls of men in language which the heart interprets as its own! Enlarge our trust in that better self which beckons us, that we may be led out of the lingering darkness of regret, out of the shadow of embittered memory into the brightness of a new resolve where we may see Your face. Smile upon us in the smiling day; in the joy of strength renewed, and opportunity reborn; in the beauty of the promise each hour whispers to us as it passes by. So fill us with Yourself that each new day shall mean new life led by the glory of those hopes which do not fade at evening. Amen.   —CHARLES A. KNICKERBOCKER.

January 4

But the plans of the Lord stand firm forever,
the purposes of his heart through all generations.

PSALM 33:11 (NLT)

We of our age are part, and every thrill that wakes
The tremulous air of Life its motion in us makes.

The imitative mass mere empty echo gives
As walls and rocks return the sound that they receive.

But as the bell, that high in some cathedral swings,
Stirred by whatever thrill, with its own music rings,

So finer souls give forth, to each vibrating tone
Impinging on their life, a music of their own.

—W. W. STORY.

O living and loving One, brighter than the morning and fairer than the day, from You we come, to You we turn, who are more than Father and Mother to us all. Our times are in Your hand. You, who has set the sun and stars in the sky, has appointed our place and part in this human world. May Your light lead and Your love win us into the harmonies of law and grace, that we may become responsive to every touch of nature, every whisper of truth, every appeal of humanity. So prepare us to serve our generation in the spirit of Him who has taught us to do Your will on earth as it is done in heaven. Amen. —CHARLES G. AMES.

January 5

Do your best to present yourself to God as one approved, a worker who does not need to be ashamed and who correctly handles the word of truth.

2 TIMOTHY 2:14-16 (NLT)

All such as worked for love, not wages—some
Who, painting for a perfect tint did drain
Their hearts, or some to save their country slain,
Or many who for truth braved martyrdom,
Or more who, in what common days may come,
Have toiled in hope, beyond the hope of gain,
Of doing something well—all such would fain
Speak thus: These gifts more free than flowers from
The earth are given. Good world, if to our need
Ye offer bread and shelt'ring roof unsought,
As guests our thanks we give, but not for greed,
As if our gifts were bartered for and bought;
And if, perchance, good world, ye offer nought,
Ah, well, that were of life the lesser meed.

—J. S. JACKSON.

Father in Heaven, we thank You, as we enter upon another day, for strength with which to work. We thank You for our tasks; for our opportunities to work for You and for those we love, we thank You. May we know the joy, when night shall come, of having accomplished something worthy. Help us to see in that satisfaction a part of our pay. Make each of us faithful in his place; and help the humblest worker to understand that consecration and not rank is the all-important thing. Above all, may we not forget that living is giving, and may our desire either for rest or gain keep us from no helpful act. May we follow Him who came to minister, and live as sons and daughters of God. Amen.

—FRANK W. WHIPPEN.

January 6

Yet you, Lord, are our Father.
We are the clay, you are the potter;
we are all the work of your hand.

ISAIAH 64:8 (NLT)

The sculptor molds his clay
   with reverent hand,
That clay thro' which his fancy
   flashes free—
Quick with an answer
   to his soul's demand,
And pliant to his fingers' minstrelsy!
Could ever bronze or marble so respond
In wordless echo of the being's will?

Naught but the clay, as to a rapture fond
Could he with fire of genius thus infill!
And so the common people are the clay,
Swift molded by Divine Deific hand,
Until transfigured, in the glorious day,
The statue of humanity shall stand!
It knows no tinsel crown,
   this masterpiece.
But all the sovereignty of God's release!

—MARY HANAFORD FORD.

Heavenly Father, we are of Your plain common people: we feel ourselves of very little worth. For what can we do of ourselves? But, if You will graciously use us, shaping us to Your ends as the potter his clay, it may be that we shall serve some worthy purpose. We therefore yield ourselves to You, and beg You to use us this day. Make us pliant to Your purposes, make us a help to someone who needs us today. So take us into partnership with Yourself, and so may this day be a day of delight, and our plain common lives be made rich with the Glory of service. Amen.

—C. H. WHEELER.

January 7

And I, too, sing the song of all creation,
A brave sky and a glad wind blowing by,
A clear trail and an hour for meditation,
A long day and the joy to make it fly,
A hard task and the muscle to achieve it,
A fierce noon and a well-contented gloom,
A good strife and no great regret to leave it,
A still night—and the far red lights of home.

—H. H. BASHFORD.

Almighty God, we thank You that You are our Father, and that You love us as though You had no other children; we adore You for the beautiful world in which You have placed us; for trees and birds and flowers and sky, for friends and music and books and all the ten thousand mercies which crown our lives. We thank You too, for hard tasks and severe disciplines, for everything that is intended to make us strong and brave and true. You are the Lord of the day and of the night also. Give us grace to trust You and to believe in Your motherly solicitude at all times. May Your goodness lead us to repentance and to joyous unselfish living and may we so improve our opportunities for service that we shall make others think of Him who went about doing good and trusted in His Father with a perfect trust. Amen.

—DILLON BRONSON.

January 8

I wait for the Lord, my whole being waits,
and in his word I put my hope.

PSALM 130:5 (NIV)

Have we not all, amid life's petty strife,
Some pure ideal of a noble life
That once seemed possible? Did we not hear
The flutter of its wings and feel it near,
And just within our reach? It was. And yet
We lost it in this daily jar and fret.
But still our place is kept and it will wait,
Ready for us to fill it, soon or late.
No star is ever lost we once have seen:
We always may be what we might have been.

—ADELAIDE A. PROCTER.

O God, whose goodness is new to us every morning and fresh every evening, we bless You for Your patient and unforgetting care of all of us. Though we transgress Your beneficent laws and frequently lose sight of our cherished ideals, our hunger and thirst for righteousness never dies, for we partake of Your Divine Nature. O that we might always be animated with Your spirit of disinterested Love. We thank You this day for the inspiration of light and joy of our gifted poets and pray that we may meet the daily trials of life with a sweet and courageous spirit, remembering that "no star we have ever seen will cease to shine." Amen.

—WILLIAM G. BABCOCK.

January 9

Your sun will never set again,
and your moon will wane no more;
the Lord will be your everlasting light,
and your days of sorrow will end.

ISAIAH 60:20 (NIV)

The future is lighted for us with the radiant colors of hope. Strife and sorrow shall disappear. Peace and love shall reign supreme. The dream of poets, the lesson of priest and prophet, the inspiration of the great musician, is confirmed in the light of modern knowledge; and, as we gird ourselves for the work of life, we may look forward to the time when in the truest sense the kingdoms of this world shall become the kingdom of Christ, and He shall reign forever and ever, King of Kings, and Lord of Lords. —JOHN FISKE.

All-wise and all-loving Father, we invoke Your aid at the opening of a glad, new day. For the past we thank You, remembering that each day yielded its blessings. We rejoice that the victories of yesterday are the promise of larger successes today. Whenever during the day, we shall be conscious of our littleness, give us at that moment the vision of our possible largeness. Teach us, however tumultuous be the outward conditions, to maintain the inward calm. Today may Your love work its miracle upon our pain and pleasure. So through faithful, hopeful work may we find Your kingdom nearer at this day's close. Amen. —A. EUGENE BARTLETT.

January 10

Always be full of joy in the Lord.
I say it again—rejoice!

PHILIPPIANS 4:4 (NLT)

Blessings on the man who smiles! I do not mean the man who smiles for effect, nor the one who smiles when the world smiles. I mean the man whose smile is born of an inner radiance, the man who smiles when the clouds lower, when fortune frowns, when the tides are adverse. Such a man not only makes a new world for himself, but he multiplies himself an hundred fold in the strength and courage of other men.

—GEORGE L. PERIN.

Blessed are You, O Lord, our Father in heaven and on the earth! Give to us of Your blessedness that all this day we may rejoice in You. Incline our hearts to see Your goodness and wisdom. Make the gladness of our hearts constant that it may illumine our presence, so that those who walk with us may walk in Your light and give You thanks. Make Your joy our strength, whether expressed in storm or sunshine, that we may consent to Your will cheerfully. We ask these and all gifts in the name of Him who would have His joy abide in us, that our joy may be fulfilled. Amen.

—ALEXANDER MCKENZIE.

January 11

Talk happiness! The world is sad enough,
Without your woes. No path is wholly rough;
Look for the places that are smooth and clear
And speak of those who rest the weary ear
Of earth, so hurt by one continuous strain
Of human discontent and grief and pain.

Talk health! The dreary, never changing tale
Of mortal maladies is worn and stale.
You cannot charm or interest or please,
By harping on that minor chord, disease.
Say you are well, or all is well with you,
And God shall hear your words and make them true.

—ELLA WHEELER WILCOX.

Heavenly Father, by whose mercy we are permitted to greet another day, we offer You this morning our grateful praise for all the blessings of this life. We take from You with thankful heart the gift of health, conscious that we shall never know how rich the gift until we lose it. Now, while it is ours, may we use it with abounding joy for the good of those we may meet this day. To be able to bring light where there is darkness, hope where there is despair, comfort where there is sorrow, and so to be the children of our Father who is in Heaven, for this we pray, with the pardon of our sins, in Jesus' name. Amen.

—FRANCIS H. ROWLEY.

January 12

So now I am giving you a new commandment: Love each other. Just as I have loved you, you should love each other. Your love for one another will prove to the world that you are my disciples.   JOHN 13:34-35 (NLT)

> The crest and crowning of all good,
> Life's final star, is Brotherhood;
> For it will bring again to Earth
> Her long-lost Poesy and Mirth;
> Will send new light on every face,
> A kingly power upon the race,
> And till it comes, we men are slaves,
> And travel downward to the dust of graves.
> Come clear the way, then, clear the way;
> Blind creeds and kings have had their day,
> Our hope is in the aftermath—
> Our hope is in heroic men,
> Star-led to build the world again.
> To this event the ages ran;
> Make way for Brotherhood—make way for Man.
>
> —EDWIN MARKHAM.

O Lord, make us like You. There can be no greater ambition, no loftier desire, no holier purpose, for You hold the secret of Brotherhood. Like You, the only begotten of the Father, the essence of love, the joy of angels, the hope of the world, make us like You, O Christ. Let Your light be our light; your service our joy; Your peace our inheritance. Touch our lips that we may say no unkind word; touch our hearts that we may feel no wrong desires. May our living be for the world's good, our acts precious helps to Your kingdom, our all consecrated to Your blessed service. May we be satisfied when we awake with Your likeness. Amen.   —WILLIAM H. MAIN.

January 13

For you have been called to live in freedom, my brothers and sisters. But don't use your freedom to satisfy your sinful nature. Instead, use your freedom to serve one another in love.

GALATIANS 5:13 (NLT)

If there be some weaker one,
Give me strength to help him on;
If a blinder soul there be,
Let me guide him nearer Thee.
Make my mortal dreams come true
With the work I fain would do;
Clothe with life the weak intent,
Let me be the thing I meant;
Let me find in Thine employ
Peace that dearer is than joy!

—JOHN GREENLEAF WHITTIER.

Heavenly Father! We humbly beseech You to breathe upon us Your Holy Spirit, that we may be Your true disciples, that we may be quick to see our brother's need, and quicker to relieve it. If he has lost his way, may we be aided to show it to him clearly. May we see our brother in the Master's "prodigal," and find in every needy soul our sphere of service. Forgive our weak excuses, and make the flickering embers burn to fervent heat, that the ideal You have given in Your Word may command every power of our lives. For Jesus' sake, Amen. —GEORGE WHITAKER.

January 14

He said, "My grace is all you need. My power works best in weakness." So now I am glad to boast about my weaknesses, so that the power of Christ can work through me. That's why I take pleasure in my weaknesses, and in the insults, hardships, persecutions, and troubles that I suffer for Christ. For when I am weak, then I am strong.   2 CORINTHIANS 12:9-10 (NLT)

A German allegory tells of two little girls. They had been playing together in a strange garden, and soon one ran in to her mother full of disappointment. "The garden's a sad place, mother."

"Why, my child?"

"I've been all around, and every rose-tree has cruel, long thorns upon it!"

Then the second child came in breathless.

"O Mother, the garden's a beautiful place!"

"How so, my child?"

"Why, I've been all around, and every thorn-bush has lovely roses growing on it!"

And the mother wondered at the difference in the two children.

—ANONYMOUS.

Divine Spirit and Soul of this day! We rejoice in its accomplished and its prophetic beauty and wealth which even our undisciplined hearts and minds may readily perceive, but may we increase the joy of its activities and its whole divine meaning by a deeper appreciation of its ministry to the disciplined life we bear. If there shall be fortunes in its passing which we would not choose, if there shall be encountered any experiences we would shun, may we remember that our reverses only emphasize our successes, that our sorrows intensify our joys, that even the humiliation and shame of the "far country" add divine meaning to the Father's House where wait the sandals and robes and rings for the comfort and beauty that are yet to be. May we learn that the thorn protects the rose, that the flaming sword turning in all directions protects the Tree of Life in every Eden of the world. May we remember that every great and good fortune of life is guarded by a seeming hostility which bears in its soul the secret of a lasting benevolence appointed for our own good. Amen.   —E. L. REXFORD.

January 15

We are haunted by an ideal life, and it is because we have within us the beginning and the possibility of it. God is our continual incitement because we are His children. So the ideal life is in our blood and never will be still. We feel the thing we ought to be beating beneath the thing we are. Every time we see a man who has attained our ideal a little more fully than we have it wakens our languid blood and fills us with new longings. —PHILLIPS BROOKS.

O God, we thank You each morning for ideals which appeal to us with such persistence that we have no peace unless we pursue them. Even in our seeming indifference we are ill at ease, because Your voice calling to us disturbs our fancied content. We are not satisfied with ourselves nor with our attainments. "We shall be satisfied only when we wake in Your likeness." Weary though we often are in our service yet we thank You that You relentlessly pursue us with even greater and higher demands. Help us in our onward and upward plodding. Revive our failing spirits. Lead us ever on. Help us to realize that "in our patience we shall win our souls." We pray as followers of Jesus Christ. Amen.

—THEODORE A. FISCHER.

January 16

My old self has been crucified with Christ. It is no longer I who live, but Christ lives in me. So I live in this earthly body by trusting in the Son of God, who loved me and gave himself for me. GALATIANS 2:20 (NLT)

> O Singer of today, this glorious hour
> Is all for you and me—what shall it give
> To us, and ask of fate—what splendid power
> In brain and hand, what glorious right to live
> Among our fellows and to war with sin?
> What quickening of the pulse as we aspire
> To claim our right, and risk earth's joys to win,
> To conquer self, and force it through the fire!
> Give us this force, dear God, and evermore
> Give us a deepening love of all our fellowmen;
> Give us new insight—courage to explore
> With all the tenderness of human ken
> The lowliest heart that beats in human kind,
> Its glory and its soul to seek and find!
>
> —WILLIAM ORDWAY PARTRIDGE.

O Soul of all souls! Baptize us afresh this morning into the lustral waters that we may devoutly thank You that You are and that You do clearly reveal Yourself to Christian souls through Your Son, as the Father of the great brotherhood of mankind. So wait upon us that we shall go forth to this day's duties resolved upon so living as to render the morning glad, the noon redolent with merciful activity, and the evening full of praise. Thus quickened and enlarged the night will afford rest and recuperation fitting us to welcome the morrow, still hoping, loving, progressing, obedient to the sainted call, "Up higher," being incessantly recompensed with the coveted refrain, "Well done." Amen. —S. H. MCCOLLESTER.

January 17

Do everything without complaining and arguing,
so that no one can criticize you.

PHILIPPIANS 2:14-15a (NLT)

There is one topic peremptorily forbidden to all well-bred, to all rational mortals, namely, their distempers. If you have not slept or if you have slept, or if you have headache, or sciatica, or leprosy or thunder stroke, I beseech you, by all angels, to hold your peace, and not pollute the morning, to which all the housemates bring serene and pleasant thoughts, by corruption and groans.

—RALPH WALDO EMERSON.

Our Father, when we remember the multitude of Your mercies our hearts are filled with peace and praise and we are ashamed to murmur and complain. Turn our thoughts toward the love and joy that this day holds for us; its opportunities, its privileges and victories. Let the morning light dispel the shadows on our faces and the fears in our hearts. You have glorified us and will glorify us again. Help us to be grateful for the rose that smiles amidst the thorns and the light that ever shines behind the clouds. Grant that the spirit of trust may prevail in us and send us on our way with power to conquer. Amen.   —ABRAM CONKLIN.

January 18

Send out your light and your truth;
　let them guide me.
Let them lead me to your holy mountain,
　to the place where you live.
There I will go to the altar of God,
　to God—the source of all my joy.

PSALM 43:3-4 (NLT)

Simplicity is a state of mind. It dwells in the main intention of our lives. A man is simple when his chief care is the wish to be what he ought to be, that is, honestly and naturally human. And this is neither so easy nor so impossible as one might think. At bottom it consists in putting our acts and aspirations in accordance with the law of our being, and consequently with the Eternal Intention which willed that we should be at all. Let a flower be a flower, a swallow a swallow, a rock a rock, and let a man be a man, and not a fox, a hare, a hog, or a bird of prey; this is the sum of the whole matter.

—CHARLES WAGNER.

Dear Heavenly Father, we rejoice in the awakening of body and soul to new activities. We thank You for the gift of divinity in the soul and for opportunity to give it expression. We would be true to ourselves, knowing we can thus alone be true to You. O God, hush the voice of evil passion. Quicken every noble aspiration. Grant the vision of Your holy love that Your image within us may remain clear in the turmoil of our life. We pray You stir the heart and mind that both may grow up to the full stature of man as it was in Jesus, our Savior. Amen.

—L. WARD BRIGHAM.

January 19

> I pray that the eyes of your heart may be enlightened in order that you may know the hope to which he has called you, the riches of his glorious inheritance in his holy people, and his incomparably great power for us who believe.
>
> EPHESIANS 1:18-19a (NIV)

God has put the keys to His kingdom into your own hands. Your intelligence is a key, your affection is a key, your conscience is a key. With these keys you are to unlock the great doors of life, and gain access to its heavenly treasures.

—JAMES M. PULLMAN.

Master of life, as You have opened our eyes to see the sun, open the eyes of our hearts to see the splendor of Your law. And even as You do bring to birth, through the marriage of our eye and the sun, all the beauty of this visible world, so through the union between our hearts and Your holy will, create a world rejoicing in the beauty of truth and justice and peace. Lead us this day deeper into the mystery of Your life and our life and make us interpreters of life to our fellows, through Him who by His death opened for us the book of life, Jesus Christ our Lord. Amen.

—HENRY S. NASH.

January 20

A noiseless, patient spider,
I mark'd how on a little promontory it stood isolated,
Mark'd how to explore the vacant, vast surrounding,
It launch'd forth filament, filament, filament, out of itself,
Ever unreeling them, ever tirelessly speeding them.
And you, O my soul, where you stand,
Surrounded, detached, in measureless oceans of space,
Ceaselessly musing, venturing, throwing,
   seeking the spheres to connect them,
Till the bridge you will need be form'd, till the ductile anchor hold,
Till the gossamer threads you fling catch somewhere O my soul.

—WALT WHITMAN.

O Infinite Spirit, we are glad of all human relationships. We are thankful for all companionship with nature. We rejoice in the fellowship with books, yet like the child who grows tired with every plaything and every childish task and lonely for a mother's love, we look to You with an infinite longing. In our effort to solve the problems of life, we throw our web of life hither and thither, but it will not hold. Only when at last we have thrown the thread of faith to You, shall the ductile anchor hold. Our Heavenly Father, as we go forth into this day, may we not leave You for any dream or phantom, but may we walk with You all day long, and find in You the answer to every longing and the solution of every problem. Though we may not see, we may trust and wait. Amen. —GEORGE L. PERIN.

January 21

There are "friends" who destroy each other,
but a real friend sticks closer than a brother.

PROVERBS 18:24 (NLT)

Do not think of your faults, still less of others' faults; in every person who comes near you, look for what is good and strong; honor that; rejoice in it; and as you can, try to imitate it; and your faults will drop off like dead leaves when their time comes.

—RUSKIN.

With a clear sky, a bright sun, and a gentle breeze, you will have friends in plenty; but let fortune frown, and the firmament be overcast, and then your friends will prove like the strings of the lute, of which you will tighten ten before you find one that will bear the stretch and keep the pitch.　　　　　　　　　　—GOTTHOLD.

Dear Father, may the new day bring some fresh and inspiring thought of You. May it give some tender communion with the universe, kindling into beauty as Your smile shines through. May we make and keep a few dear friends. May some good book enrich the passing hours. May love flow through all acts, and the star of hope shine in all shadows. And trusting You supremely, may we humbly do our best that good may abound on earth. Amen.　　　　　　—JOSEPH H. CROOKER.

January 22

"You are the light of the world. A town built on a hill cannot be hidden. Neither do people light a lamp and put it under a bowl. Instead they put it on its stand, and it gives light to everyone in the house."   MATTHEW 5:13-15 (NIV)

The power of mere activity is often overrated. It is not what the best men do, but what they are, that constitutes their truest benefaction to their fellowmen. The things that men do get their value, after all, from the way in which they are able to show the existence of character which can comfort and help mankind.... It is the lives, like the stars, which simply pour down on us the calm light of their bright and faithful being, up to which we look and out of which we gather the deepest calm and courage.   —PHILLIPS BROOKS.

You know, dear Father, how often we wish to do many things which are beyond our power. Help us to believe that You do accept the wish when we cannot do the deed. But we thank You that we can do some things, though they are not large nor many. We know that as we grow in faith, in patience, in courage, in love, we radiate light and peace and power to those who are around us. As we begin a new day, we are uplifted by the thought that we have been called into being because You desire the love of children, and because we are to co-work with You by loving and serving all whom we can reach. Always, we believe, You are ready to help us. Always You are brooding over us to draw us nearer to You, and to give us light and strength to be fellow-workers with You. In this new day, may we speak some word and do some work which will please You and give us joy as we lie down to sleep. Amen.

—HENRY BLANCHARD.

January 23

We pride ourselves, in weighing worth and merit,
Too much in virtues that we but inherit.
Some punctual grandsire makes us hate delay
And we are proud to keep our oath and day.
But our ancestral follies and abuses
We still indulge in, and make for them excuses.
Let him be proud, dared man be proud at all,
Who stands where all his fathers used to fall,
Holding their virtues fast and passing on
Still higher good through his own victories won.

—ISAAC OGDEN RANKIN.

This morning, the sun shines by his own inherent worth. The clouds often intercept his influence but he shines on the back of them and finds a way through the slightest cleft to tip them with glory. He always reveals himself—his inner self—and makes all purer and more beautiful. May we so shine! The world needs the divinity there is in us. We are a part of You. You are our deeper self. The Nazarean prophet relied entirely upon his inner life and found ancient good uncouth. Whatever clouds intercept our influence, teach us to reveal what conscience dictates, what intuition illumines, what reason shows, to purify our time, and all unrighteousness, wrong thinking and useless and hurtful custom. To this end, give us purity, courage, and nobility. Amen. —WILLIAM S. MORGAN.

January 24

The greatest among you will be your servant. For those who exalt themselves will be humbled, and those who humble themselves will be exalted.

MATTHEW 23:11-12 (NIV)

My faith begins where your religion ends,
In service to mankind. This single thread
Is given to guide us through the maze of
   life.
You start at one end, I the other; you,
With eyes fixed only upon God, begin
With lofty faith, and, seeking but to
   know
And do His will who guides the universe,
You find the slender and mysterious
   thread

Leads down to earth, with God's divine
   command
To help your fellowmen; but this to me
Is something strangely vague. I see alone
The fellowmen, the suffering fellowmen.
Yet, with a cup of water in my hand
For all who thirst, who knows but I one
      day,
Following faithfully the slender thread,
May reach its other end, and kneel at last
With you in heaven at the feet of God?

—ALICE WELLINGTON ROLLINS.

Our Father in heaven, author of life and light, justice and mercy, liberty and love, we hail with joy and gratitude this newborn day, token of Your presence, good will and continued care. Help us with high ideals, pure thoughts and noble endeavors to hallow Your name, trusting where we cannot prove, proving where we cannot trust, by a willing service to our fellowmen, ever advancing by faith, by works, with a strong heart, a firm step, a generous hand, a sunny smile, and a cheering voice, until we all come into the measure of the stature of the fulness of Christ; and Your will be done on earth as it is in heaven. Amen.

—HENRY N. COUDEN.

January 25

Whatever you do, work at it with all your heart, as working for the Lord, not for human masters, since you know that you will receive an inheritance from the Lord as a reward. It is the Lord Christ you are serving.

COLOSSIANS 3:23-24 (NIV)

If you would have sunlight in your home, see that you have work in it: that you work yourself and set others to work. Nothing makes moroseness and heavy-heartedness in a house so fast as idleness. The very children gloom and sulk if they are left with nothing to do. Every day there is the light of something conquered in the eyes of those who work. In such a house, if there be also the good temper of love, sunshine never ceases. For in it the great law of humanity is obeyed, a law which is also God's law. For what said Christ, "My Father is working and I work." Sunlight comes with work. —STOPFORD A. BROOKE.

O God, who is the source of light and life, we pause in Your presence at the opening of the day, that in the light of Your countenance we may see ourselves as we are and as we ought to be, and receive the inspiration to consecrated effort and worthy achievement. We thank You that You have done so much for us and yet left so much for us to do. May we think how important are these lives we are going to live today; that no matter how small we are, this universe in all its majesty can never be complete without our effort, and You, Almighty God, are waiting with infinite patience for us to do our part. Thus shall our work, however humble, be glorified by a Godlike temper and a Christlike faith. Amen. —FREDERICK A. BISBEE.

January 26

Jesus looked at them intently and said,
"Humanly speaking, it is impossible.
But with God everything is possible."

MATTHEW 19:26 (NLT)

All that is, at all,
Lasts ever, past recall:
Earth changes, but thy soul and God stand sure;
What entered into thee,
That was, is and shall be.

*　　*　　*　　*　　*

He fixed thee 'mid this dance
Of plastic circumstance,
This Present, thou, forsooth, wouldst fain arrest;
Machinery just meant
To give thy soul its bent,
Try thee, and turn thee forth, sufficiently impressed.

—ROBERT BROWNING.

We thank You, O Father, for the yet unwrought possibilities of this day. Show us Your purpose; or, if it please You, withhold the entire plan, yet may our faith claim a divine sanction for each hour's work as a part of the fulfilment of Your purpose. We pray for strength and patience to have our souls rightly impressed by the cares, the joys, and disappointments of life. Make the things of the body only incidental to us. Save us from all but the best things. Give us the happiness of harmony with You. Grant these things through the power of Your spirit, and in the name of Your perfect Son, the vision of whom transforms our lives. Amen.　　　—GEORGE W. OWEN.

January 27

But let us who live in the light be clearheaded, protected by the armor of faith and love, and wearing as our helmet the confidence of our salvation.

1 THESSALONIANS 5:8 (NLT)

Beloved, let us love so well,
Our work shall still be better for our love
And still our love be sweeter for our work.

—ELIZABETH BARRETT BROWNING.

If your name is to live at all, it is so much more to have it live in people's hearts than only in their brains! I don't know that one's eyes fill with tears when he thinks of the famous inventor of logarithms, but a song of Burns or a hymn of Charles Wesley goes straight to your heart and you can't help loving both of them, the sinner as well as the saint.　　　　—OLIVER WENDELL HOLMES.

Our Father, who is in heaven, help us to hold You in our hearts this day, that we may live for You, from the love of You. Forgive us that we do not always have a thankful spirit. Strengthen our wills to do good work, as in Your sight, with clean hands and heart. Help us now as we pray, and flood the morning with the sunshine of Your face, that we may be glad all the day long, and bring other lives into the brightness of Your light. Save us from a partial mind, that we may love all Your little ones with the same love of Him who said "Of such is the Kingdom of Heaven." Amen.

—C. W. HOLDEN.

January 28

... but those who hope in the LORD will renew their strength.
They will soar on wings like eagles; they will run and not grow weary,
they will walk and not be faint.

ISAIAH 40:31 (NIV)

All thoughts of ill; all evil deeds.
That have their root in thoughts of ill;
Whatever hinders or impedes
The noble action of the will;
All these must first be trampled down
Beneath our feet if we would gain
In the bright fields of fair renown
The right of eminent domain.
We have not wings, we cannot soar;
But we have feet to scale and climb
By slow degrees, by more and more,
The cloudy summits of our time.

—HENRY W. LONGFELLOW.

We bless You, Lord, for the new day and for the new chance which it offers to our wayward lives. Forgive the evil in them, and make the good efficient. Let the tides of Your spirit bring to us cleansing, refreshment and power. In the day's business may we be brave, cheerful and considerate. Grant us a clear vision of the path of honor and the will to choose it at whatever cost. We wait upon You for renewal of our strength; for uplift as on eagle's wings; for unwearied running upon Your larger errands, if You would ordain us to such high employ; but most of all, for grace to walk life's common ways without fainting. So at evening You will send Your peace. Amen.

—EDWARD M. CHAPMAN.

January 29

> But may all who seek you rejoice and be glad in you;
>> may those who long for your saving help always say, "The LORD is great!"
>
> PSALM 40:16 (NIV)

Don't you touch the edge of the great gladness that is in the world, now and then, in spite of your own little single worries? Well, that's what God means; and the worry is the interruption. He never means that.... If you are glad for one minute in the day, that is His minute; the minute He means, and works for.

—MRS. A. D. T. WHITNEY.

Dear Father, You have made us fit for joy. Help us today to grasp our birthright of gladness. For those things which must be borne in sorrow give us submission. Let us taste the salt tonic of our tears and feel the strength born of struggle and the peace wrested from trial. Make us glad that friendly hands meet our own; that kindness is always sweet and sympathy divine. Teach us to lay hold on the radiance of each hour, that the morning bow of promise may become our evening glory and prophesy another glad new day. As children find content and joy by looking into their father's face so we turn to You. Amen. —EFFIE MCCOLLUM JONES.

January 30

Lift up your eyes to the heavens, look at the earth beneath;
  the heavens will vanish like smoke,
    the earth will wear out like a garment and its inhabitants die like flies.
But my salvation will last forever, my righteousness will never fail.

ISAIAH 51:6 (NIV)

Still must I climb if I would rest;
The bird soars upward to his nest;
The young leaf on the tree-top high
Cradles itself within the sky.

I cannot in the valley stay:
The great horizons stretch away;
The very cliffs that wall me round
Are ladders unto higher ground.

I am not glad till I have known
Life that can lift me from mine own;
A loftier level must be won.
A mightier strength to lean upon.

—LUCY LARCOM.

Heavenly Father, as the bird that soars first looks upward, we turn our souls to You, seeking inspiration that in the duties of today we may live to the full height of the faculties You have given. Help us to know what is right and to follow it day by day continually. Grant that our toils this day may be acts of service as sacramental as our prayer. In our weakness, grant us Your strength that we may pass from glory to glory till we are transformed at last into the perfect image of Your spirit. And when our work on earth is ended, when the clods of the valley are sweet to our weary frame, take us home to You. Amen. —NATHANIEL S. SAGE.

January 31

Only a frown! Yet it pressed a sting
Into the day which had been so glad;
The red rose turned to a scentless thing:
The bird-song ceased with discordant ring;
And a heart was heavy and sad.

Only a smile! yet it cast a spell
Over the sky which had been so gray;
The rain made music wherever it fell;
The wind sang the song of the marriage-bell;
And a heart was light and gay.

—ANONYMOUS.

With our tribute of praise, O Father, we would begin this day; this day, which, with all its bounties, is Your gift. Prepare us, we beseech You, for the experiences of the hours as they open before us. Gratefully remembering that we are Your children, may our duties weigh with such sacredness upon our hearts that we may shun the evil way as unworthy of those so richly endowed and blessed. Write, we pray You, Your law within us; and may our love of You make it so easy and so joyous to obey that we shall continually grow into the likeness of Him whose mission it is to fill the world with blessedness and peace. Amen.   —CHARLES W. TOMLINSON.

February 1

Carry each other's burdens, and in this way you will fulfill the law of Christ.

GALATIANS 6:2 (NIV)

Father, I will not ask for wealth or fame,
Though once they would have joyed my carnal sense.
I shudder not to bear a hated name,
Wanting all wealth, myself my sole defence.
But give me, Lord, eyes to behold the truth;
A seeing sense that knows the eternal right;
A heart with pity filled, and gentlest ruth;
A manly faith that makes all darkness light;
Give me the power to labor for mankind;
Make me the mouth of such as cannot speak;
Eyes let me be to groping man and blind;
A conscience to the base; and to the weak
Let me be hands and feet; and to the foolish, mind;
And lead still farther on such as Thy Kingdom seek.

—THEODORE PARKER.

Heavenly Father, we speak to You this morning out of a sense of rest and trust. We would begin the day with You and keep in Your company to its close. Whether we work or pray, will You rule our spirits? Conscious in this moment of freedom, that we shall soon be pressed and absorbed by our own cares, we pray, Father, that we may keep in mind the privilege and joy of bearing each other's burdens and so fulfilling the law of Christ. Nor ever permit us to fall away from perfect faith in Your purpose. Work in us and through us to usher in the morning when Truth shall spring out of the earth and Righteousness shall come down from heaven. Amen.

—ISAAC M. ATWOOD.

February 2

Do not grieve, for the joy of the Lord is your strength.

NEHEMIAH 8:10b (NIV)

As when good news is come to one in grief, straightway he forgets his former grief, and no longer attends to anything except the good news which he has heard, so do you, also, having received a renewal of your soul through the beholding of these good things. Put on therefore gladness that always has favor before God, and is acceptable to Him, and delight yourself in it; for every man that is glad does the things that are good, and thinks good thoughts, despising grief.

—MARIUS THE EPICUREAN.

O Lord, we know there are a thousand reasons why we should be glad. We cannot always forget our sorrows and our failures; there are manifold sources of temporary vexation and annoyance and harassing care, but in the face of Your overmastering Providence and Love we cannot long be vexed nor sad. If tears have dimmed our eyes let us brush away the tears. If troubles and cares have burdened our hearts let us rise triumphant over them all and for this day be glad; and in our gladness let us find our strength. Amen.

—GEORGE L. PERIN.

February 3

No one should seek their own good, but the good of others.

1 CORINTHIANS 10:24 (NIV)

Do not dare to be so absorbed in your own life, so wrapped up in listening to the sound of your own hurrying wheels, that all this vast pathetic music, made up of the mingled joy and sorrow of your fellowmen, shall not find out your heart and claim it and make you rejoice to give yourself for them.... Be sure that ambition and charity will both grow mean unless they are both inspired and exalted by religion. Energy, love, and faith—these make the perfect man.   —PHILLIPS BROOKS.

O You who are not far from any one of us, but are the Source and Sustainer of our life, gratefully do we acknowledge the Mercy that has given us this new day with its certain opportunity for living the glad, true life. Directed by You, may this be for us a day of progress. May its duties be performed with alacrity and cheerfulness, its lessons learned with humility, its temptations met with resolute will, its crosses with patient hope. We thank You for the life of the Master who has shown us that if we would live Your divine life, ours must be one of continual service and constant progression. If, tried by the seeming drudgery of duties daily repeated, we long for the end of our labors or dream of an idle heaven, O forgive our weakness, and help us trustingly to obey Your voice as it whispers, "Up and on, this is not your rest." Thus let the day close on hours well spent, and Your joy and peace fill our hearts. Amen.

—JOHN MURRAY ATWOOD.

February 4

Surely, Lord, you bless the righteous;
you surround them with your favor as with a shield.

PSALM 5:12 (NIV)

Who are you that complains of your life of toil? Complain not. Look up, my wearied brother; see your fellow-workmen there, in God's eternity; surviving there, they alone surviving; sacred band of the Immortals, celestial body-guard of the empire of mankind. To you, Heaven, though severe, is as that Spartan mother, saying while she gave her son his shield, "With it, my son, or upon it." You too shall return home in honor; to your far distant Home, in honor; doubt it not—if in the battle you keep your shield! You, in the Eternities, and deepest death-kingdoms, are not an alien; you everywhere are a denizen. Complain not.　　　　—THOMAS CARLYLE.

O God of goodness and grace, who turns Your smiling countenance upon the upturned faces of Your children, help us to find in the light of another day the continued proof of Your fatherly care and tender mercy. Since You are so well disposed towards us, give us courage to attempt anything which the duties of this day require, remembering that You cannot ask anything beyond our strength, or withhold from us the blessing of Your Divine approval. Living under Your smile, help us to be strong and calm and confident, delighting Your heart by our faith in You and our love for our fellowmen. Amen.　　　　—SAMUEL C. BUSHNELL.

February 5

See what great love the Father has lavished on us, that we should be called children of God! And that is what we are!

1 JOHN 3:1a (NIV)

This goodly frame, the earth, seems to me a sterile promontory; this most excellent canopy, the air, look you, this brave o'er-hanging firmament, this majestical roof fretted with golden fire, why, it appears no other thing to me than a foul and pestilent congregation of vapors. What a piece of work is a man! How noble in reason! How infinite in faculty! In form and moving how express and admirable! In action how like an angel! In apprehension how like a god! —SHAKESPEARE.

Our Father in Heaven, we pray that this may be a bright and happy day in each of our lives. May there be sunshine in our hearts because they are attuned to Yours. Going about our daily tasks, Your spirit within us, may we make our little portion of the earth not a sterile promontory but a rich garden abounding in the fruits of the spirit, and may we, by Your grace, be enabled to dispel some of the pestilent vapors of worldliness and doubt. In all things, may we remember our divine parentage and conform our lives more and more to the pattern shown us by Your dear Son, Jesus Christ, in whose name we pray. Amen. —FRANCIS E. CLARK.

February 6

> Feed the hungry,
> and help those in trouble.
> Then your light will shine out from the darkness,
> and the darkness around you will be as bright as noon.
>
> ISAIAH 58:10 (NLT)

There was a merchant once, who on the way
Meeting one fatherless and lamed, did stay
To draw the thorn which pricked his foot, and passed;
And 'twas forgot; and the man died at last.
But in a dream the Prince of Khojand spies
That man again, walking in Paradise.
Walking and talking in that blessed land,
And what he said the prince could understand;
For he said this, plucking the heavenly posies;
"Wonderful! One thorn made me many roses!"

—EDWIN ARNOLD.

Dear Father in Heaven, with our life refreshed and renewed by sleep, we would face the duties of the day with strong hope and a ready courage. Forbid that these shall in any degree be diminished by any difficulty or perplexity that may arise. We pray for wisdom and love. Grant us that interest in others that shall impel us to help those who are in need. And may our desire to minister move us not only to dress the wounds of those whom the thorns have injured, but to clear the paths, along which men must pass, of those conditions and influences which inevitably maim and blight. May we serve You faithfully and with gladness this day! Amen.

—HARRY L. CANFIELD.

February 7

I rise before dawn and cry for help;
I have put my hope in your word.

PSALM 119:147 (NIV)

Quicksand years that whirl me I know not whither,
Your schemes, politics fail, lines give way, substances mock and elude me,
Only the theme I sing, the great and strong-possess'd soul, eludes not,
One's self must never give way—that is the final substance—that out of
all is sure,
Out of politics, triumphs, battles, life, what at last finally remains?
When shows break up what but One's self is sure?

—WALT WHITMAN.

O You, who beholdest all the souls of men, in our vision of another new day, help us to see as You see; to be conscious not of our own need and desert alone, but also of the deserts and needs of all those with whom we have to do; shaping our prayer and directing the effort that follows after all true prayer in accordance with this wider outlook. O You, who fashions the hearts of all, who observes all their works, we would strengthen and purify our hearts that they may be fit to be fashioned by You to noble ends, and set to some good service; and we would do our daily work as in the sight of one who knows and loves all honest, thorough workers, great or humble, wise or simple. Amen. —AUGUSTUS MENDON LORD.

February 8

> Jesus answered, "I am the way and the truth and the life.
> No one comes to the Father except through me."
>
> JOHN 14:6 (NIV)

Truth should be the first lesson of the child and the last aspiration of Manhood; for it has been well said that the inquiry of truth, which is the love-making of it, the knowledge of truth, which is the presence of it, and the belief of truth, which is the enjoying of it, is the sovereign good of human nature.

> We search the world for truth; we cull
> The good, the pure, the beautiful,
> From graven stone and written scroll,
> From all old flower-fields of the soul.
>
> —JOHN GREENLEAF WHITTIER.

Our Heavenly Father, we acknowledge You as the Author and Giver of all truth. We bless You that You have attuned our souls to its music, and that when with conscious life we touch its strings covering the universe we feel harmony with the Divine. We thank You for the truths of our sonship in You and for the assurances of Your Fatherhood. We bless You for Jesus who was the truth made life, and who is our daily guide to its blessings. We thank You for the truth of immortality, with its encouragement to eager life today and its assurances of endless joyful tomorrows. Make us seekers of truth, lovers of truth and examples of truth as it is in Jesus our Savior. Amen.

> —FRED A. DILLINGHAM.

February 9

The heavens declare the glory of God; the skies proclaim the work of his hands.
Day after day they pour forth speech; night after night they reveal knowledge.
They have no speech, they use no words; no sound is heard from them.
Yet their voice goes out into all the earth, their words to the ends of the world.

PSALM 19:1-4 (NIV)

All things are engaged in writing their history. The planet, the pebble, goes attended by its shadow. The rolling rock leaves its scratches on the mountain; the river, its channel in the soil; the animal, its bones in the stratum; the fern and leaf, their modest epitaph in the coal. The falling drop makes its sculpture in the sand or the stone. Not a foot steps into the snow or along the ground, but prints, in characters more or less lasting, a map of its march. Every act of the man inscribes itself in the memory of his fellows, and in his own manners and face. The air is full of sounds, the sky of tokens, the ground is all memoranda and signatures, and every object covered over with hints which speak to the intelligent. —RALPH WALDO EMERSON.

Our Father, who is in Heaven and in every manifestation of living nature, we turn our thoughts to You with the rising of each new sun. We hear Your voice in the singing of every summer bird. We realize Your presence in the shifting shadows of the clouds. In the arching blue above us we realize something of the depth and breadth of the love that arches over the horizon of our life and stretches like the radiant bow of promise from the green hills of childhood to the sombre mountains of old age. We beseech You to give us thoughts so beautiful and ennobling that even amid the sods and clods of life's daily drudgery we can always face the morning light of some new hope which comes like the old song sung in the new land. Amen.

—JOHN KIMBALL.

February 10

Devote yourselves to prayer with an alert mind and a thankful heart.

COLOSSIANS 4:2 (NLT)

First, when I feel that I am become cold and indisposed to prayer, by reason of other business and thoughts, I take my book of psalms and run into my chamber, or, if day and season serve, into the church to the multitude, and begin to repeat to myself—just as children used—the ten commandments, the creed, and, according as I have time, some sayings of Christ or of Paul, or some Psalms. Therefore, it is well to let prayer be the first employment in the early morning, and the last in the evening. Avoid diligently those false and deceptive thoughts which say, Wait a little, I will pray an hour hence; I must first perform this or that. For with such thoughts a man quits prayer for business that lays hold of and entangles him, so that he comes not to pray the whole day long. —MARTIN LUTHER.

O Lord, our Heavenly Father, who keeps covenant and loving kindness with Your servants, who walk humbly with You, and who have been attentive to the prayers of our fathers when they lifted up their hearts and their hands to You, teach us to pray, and to love to pray. Visit us in the night season and before the morning watch. Touch our spirits with the flame of Your Spirit, before the day's business lays hold upon us and entangles us, through Jesus Christ, our Lord. Amen. —REUBEN KIDNER.

February 11

Is there anyplace I can go to avoid your Spirit? To be out of your sight?
If I climb to the sky, you're there! If I go underground, you're there!
If I flew on morning's wings to the far western horizon,
You'd find me in a minute—you're already there waiting!

PSALM 139:7-10 (MSG)

In one of Dean Stanley's sermons to children, preached at Westminster Abbey, he told the following story: "There was a little girl living with her grandfather. She was a good child, but he was not a very good man; and one day, when the little child came back from school, he had put in writing over the bed, 'God is nowhere,' for he did not believe in the good God, and he tried to make the little child believe the same. What did the little girl do? She had no eyes to see, no ears to hear, what her grandfather tried to teach her. She was very small. She could only read words of one syllable at a time; she rose above the bad meaning which he tried to put in her mind; she rose, as we all ought to rise, above the temptation of our time; she rose into a higher and better world; she rose because her little mind could not do otherwise, and she read the words, not 'God is nowhere,' but 'God is now here.' That is what we all should strive to do. Out of words which have no sense or which have bad sense, our eyes, our minds, ought to be able to read a better sense." —WILLIAM MOODIE.

O You, Invisible Presence, there can be no place where You are not. You, our Father, are in heaven and on earth and everywhere. You are in the order of the rock, the beauty of the flower, the light of the sun and stars, and goodness in the human soul. Teach us to be conscious of Your nearness to us, and so may we never be afraid. In the light of Your countenance, may we see duty and truth, and recognize more easily the good in one another. Amen. —ALVA ROY SCOTT.

February 12

I thank my God every time I remember you.

PHILIPPIANS 1:3 (NIV)

ABRAHAM LINCOLN BORN 1809
Chosen for large designs, he had the art
Of winning with his humour, and he went
Straight to his mark, which was the human heart;
Wise, too, for what he could not break he bent.

Upon his back a more than Atlas-load—
The burden of the Commonwealth was laid;
He stooped, and rose up to it, though the road
Shot suddenly downwards, not a whit dismayed.

Hold, warriors, counsellors, kings! All now give place
To this dear benefactor of the race.

—RICHARD H. STODDARD.

Almighty Father, we thank You today for the gracious memory of Your servant who lived and died for the sake of a free and united nation. We thank You more that we have his life inwrought into the very fabric of the life of the nation. We had in him "a hiding place from the wind and a covert from the tempest, a river of water in a dry place and the shadow of a great rock in a weary land." We gratefully join in praise with the thousands who found help and cheer in the shadow of his strength. And now we humbly beseech You, help us in some small way this day to be a helper to the helpless, a friend to the needy, sunshine to those whose day will be gray and gloomy, the shadow of a great rock to those who are buffeted by the world's storms. Thus shall we prove our gratitude to You for the gift of Your servant whom we honor today, and thus shall we honor You. We ask and offer all in the name of Your Son Jesus Christ. Amen.

—AVERY A. SHAW.

February 13

You have searched me, Lord, and you know me.

You know when I sit and when I rise; you perceive my thoughts from afar.

You discern my going out and my lying down; you are familiar with all my ways.

Before a word is on my tongue you, Lord, know it completely.

PSALM 139:1-4 (NIV)

Let us learn to be content with what we have. Let us get rid of our false estimates, set up all the higher ideals—a quiet home; vines of our own planting; a few books full of the inspiration of a genius; a few friends worthy of being loved, and able to love us in return; a hundred innocent pleasures that bring no pain or remorse; a devotion to the right that will never swerve; a simple religion empty of all bigotry, full of trust and hope and love—and to such a philosophy this world will give up all the empty joy it has. —DAVID SWING.

O gracious Spirit of Life, our Father, at the beginning of this new day we wait for a moment before You with uncovered heads and with reverent spirits; You know us through and through, whatever man may think of us You know just what we are. In Your sight we need not pretend; we need not make believe, we need only be simple and genuine and brave and earnest. We need be glad in the possession of what we have. Help us this day to rightly value that which is good and honest. Let us for this day at least, put away all vanity and give ourselves unreservedly to Your service and the love of our fellow men. To this high end, may we have the sweet companionship of Jesus. Amen. —GEORGE L. PERIN.

February 14

Be still, and know that I am God;
I will be exalted among the nations,
I will be exalted in the earth.

PSALM 46:10 (NIV)

We go through life as some tourists go through Europe—so anxious to see the next sight, the next cathedral, the next picture, the next mountain peak, that we never stop to fill our sense with the beauty of the present one. Along all our pathways sweet flowers are blossoming, if we will only stop to pluck them and smell their fragrance. In every meadow, birds are warbling, calling to their mates, and soaring into the blue, if we will only stop our grumbling long enough to hear them.

—MINOT J. SAVAGE.

Give us, O God, the vision to see the way where duty lies and strength to walk in it, to ever keep the forward look and never to lose heart today because of the stumblings and fallings in the yesterdays that are forever gone. Let us remember that we are in Your hands and we are faithless to You and to ourselves if knowingly we fail to do Your work. Though we cannot see You, we now see our fellow men and we shall best serve You if, in love and patience, we help our fellows. Amen.

—ALMON GUNNISON.

February 15

Rejoice with those who rejoice; mourn with those who mourn.

ROMANS 12:15 (NIV)

May I reach
That purest Heaven—be to other souls
The cup of strength in some great agony,
Enkindle generous ardor, feed pure love,
Beget the smiles that have no cruelty,
Be that sweet presence of a good diffused,
And in diffusion ever more intense!
So shall I join the choir invisible,
Whose music is the gladness of the world.

—GEORGE ELIOT.

Our heavenly Father, we bless You for the gift of another day with all its opportunities for service. And we pray that our hearts may respond in sympathy with the heartbeats of those who love and toil and suffer around us today. May we learn to make their joys and sorrows our own. Do not let our unfeeling hands strike the heart-strings of others harshly, nor allow our feet to go crushing roses of love, without thought. Help us, we pray, to walk tenderly and reverently among our fellow men. May their hopes and noble endeavors ring within us the prayer bells of the soul. Make us thus to grow large and tender and noble through our helpful ministries. Amen.

—JOHN WESLEY CARTER.

February 16

And now these three remain: faith, hope and love.
But the greatest of these is love.

1 CORINTHIANS 13:13 (NIV)

Ah, love and love alone at last will solve
All the vast, threatening questions that distract
Mankind; that fellow-men in strife array,
And the whole world with fierce contentions rend.
Still keep your idle millions under arms—
Fed on the hard-earned substance of the poor—
Still watch each other with keen jealousy,
Still slaughter thousands on the field of war,
Or strive with statesman's craft to arbitrate;
Thread the sly mazes of diplomacy,
Try communistic cures for every ill,
And when all fails at last, for lack of love,
Try love—the mightiest of them all—and win!

—HENRY NEHEMIAH DODGE.

God of the light—within, without, who has lifted the curtain of night from our abodes, perfect now Your blessing unto us, and take the veil from all our hearts, and make clear to us Your holy presence. Filled with the everlasting light, may we look on each other, and on our work here below, and on the strifes and conditions of humanity, with a love and hope that are not of this world. May Faith, Hope and Love abide with us—and may we realize that the greatest of these is Love. Hasten the time when by love alone Your kingdom shall come, and Your will be done on earth as it is in heaven. Amen.

—WILLIAM B. EDDY.

February 17

The Lord is my shepherd, I lack nothing. He makes me lie down in green pastures, he leads me beside quiet waters, he refreshes my soul. He guides me along the right paths for his name's sake. Even though I walk through the darkest valley, I will fear no evil, for you are with me; your rod and your staff, they comfort me.

PSALM 23:1-4 (NIV)

If the day and night are such that you greet them with joy, and life emits a fragrance like flowers and sweet-scented herbs, is more starry, more immortal—that is your success. All nature is your congratulation and you have cause momentarily to bless yourself.   —HENRY DAVID THOREAU.

Father, I have found Your gift of life, a sweet and beautiful thing. It has known cloud and rain, but these have nourished it, and the darkness has sheltered it. It has felt driving storms, but these have strengthened it. It has known sunshine too. And now every day is a transfiguration and every night a benediction. Let thanksgiving be my prayer. What I need You will give. My hands You will touch with the soft petals of Your flowers; and the arms of Your strong care shall be about me. By the voices of brooks and rivers and winds and birds and little children You will speak to me, and in the deeper silences I shall hear Your still small voice. Father, I thank You. Amen.

—O. C. S. WALLACE.

February 18

I know that there is nothing better for people than to be happy and to do good while they live. That each of them may eat and drink, and find satisfaction in all their toil—this is the gift of God.　　　　ECCLESIASTES 3:12-13 (NIV)

Let us not care too much for what happens: Let us not leave our peace of mind at the mercy of events.　　　　—CHARLES G. AMES.

Let us lay hold of the happiness of today. Do we not go through life blindly, thinking that some fair tomorrow will bring us the gift we miss today?... Know you, my heart, if you are not happy today, you shall never be happy.

—ANNA ROBERTSON BROWN.

We thank You, our Father, that the Satisfaction of righteousness is present as well as future. Help us, we beseech You, to live this day so that earth shall seem like heaven. In the proof of our adequacy to the demands of duty may we find a delight that shall more than compensate us for any pleasure or profit surrendered for its sake. May the sense of Your approval sanctify our joys and comfort our sorrows. May we win love by deserving it, and find happiness in bestowing it. Through obedience to Your will may we add strength and spiritual beauty to our own character and carry into the evening shadows the sweet assurance that other lives have been enriched by our kind words and helpful deeds. We ask it as Your children. Amen.

—J. FRANK THOMPSON.

February 19

Give thanks to the Lord, for he is good.
His love endures forever.

PSALM 136:1 (NIV)

'Tis always morning somewhere, and above
The awakening continents from shore to shore.
Somewhere the birds are singing evermore.

—HENRY W. LONGFELLOW.

The inconveniences and the petty annoyances, the pains and the sorrows, do we ever forget them? Indeed, no; we grumble and groan continually. The blue sky and the sunshine, the everyday mercies and the wonderful blessings that we accept as a matter of course, do we remember to rejoice because of them? Only too seldom. On this one day, do let us be sincerely and expressedly thankful.   —ANONYMOUS.

Our Father, we rejoice to believe that Your love is the eternal sun which knows no eclipse and that in its pure shining, we Your children can go forward with brave hearts and radiant hopes, assured that Your wisdom has left nothing unfinished and that "Your goodness never fails." We greet this new day with newness of joy in Your Fatherhood as our personal right, and with ascending ideals of a service whose gracious light shall kindle other souls into a larger hopefulness and a deeper tenderness. We would fill this day with all sunny thoughts, with all cheering words and with all generous deeds, and thus the more effectually bring the divine light into the human and make clearer the outlines of a heaven on earth. Amen.   —ARNOLD S. YANTIS.

February 20

No blast of air or fire of sun
Puts out the light whereby we run
With girdled loins our lamplit race,
And each from each takes heart of grace
And spirit till his turn be done,
And light of face from each man's face
In whom the light of trust is one;
Since only souls that keep their place
By their own light, and watch things roll,
And stand, have light for any soul.

—ALGERNON CHARLES SWINBURNE.

O God, who covers Yourself with light as with a garment, even the true light which lights every man coming into the world, shine in us, putting to flight all the powers of darkness, and guilt of sin, and selfishness. Shine also through us to any that live in the shadow; and so fill us with Your radiant Spirit, that we may be a lamp unto a neighbor's feet and a light unto his path. And when this day is done may every face we have met be the brighter for our meeting, and every heart braver with new joy and cheer and grace and strength. For in You O Lord, is life, and Your life is the light of men. Amen.

—THEODORE PARKER.

February 21

Work with enthusiasm, as though you were working for the Lord
rather than for people.   EPHESIANS 6:7 (NLT)

The longer on this earth we live
And weigh the various qualities of men
The more we feel the high, stern-featured beauty
Of plain devotedness to duty,
Steadfast and still, nor paid with mortal praise,
But finding amplest recompense
For life's ungarlanded expense
In work done squarely and unwasted days.

—JAMES RUSSELL LOWELL.

Our dear Heavenly Father, we would greet You as this morning greets us. We thank You for the daily duty; that, amid this wondrous world, You have set somewhat for our doing. May we appreciate the honor. May we not grudge our best, even in the humblest tasks, since You appoint them. Strengthen us, we beseech You, if sometimes the heart fails, and the tired hands get laggard. Show us how the lowliest service becomes loftiest if done with the glorifying motive of pleasing You. Make us this day blithe in duty. When our heads find the pillow may Your peace enfold us; forgive our failures; and, for Jesus' sake, may we never cease endeavor. Amen.

—WAYLAND HOYT.

February 22

The king rejoices in your strength, LORD.
How great is his joy in the victories you give!

PSALM 21:1 (NLT)

GEORGE WASHINGTON BORN
Welcome to the day returning,
Dearer still as ages flow,
While the torch of faith is burning,
Long as Freedom's altars glow!
See the hero whom it gave us
Slumbering on a mother's breast;
For the arm he stretched to save us,
Be its morn forever blest.

—OLIVER WENDELL HOLMES.

Father of life, we thank You that You have been with the Fathers; that You have been with him whose birth this day we celebrate. You were willing to speak to them, and they were willing to hear You and answer You, "Here am I; send me." We thank You that the memory of this great man has come down to us; of him who was first in war, first in peace, and first in the hearts of his countrymen; and we ask that You will be with our countrymen today; that You will teach us Your law, that we may walk in Your ways; that this may be that happy nation whose God is the Lord. In all time of our trial, if we have sought You we have found You—in all time of our success You have won for us our victories—You have been with our counsellors. Father, today, tomorrow, and in days to come, in our memories and in our hopes be with us still, Our Father, who is in Heaven. Amen. —EDWARD EVERETT HALE.

February 23

Therefore, since we are surrounded by such a great cloud of witnesses, let us throw off everything that hinders and the sin that so easily entangles. And let us run with perseverance the race marked out for us, fixing our eyes on Jesus, the pioneer and perfecter of faith. HEBREWS 12:1-2a (NIV)

If you always remember that in all you do in soul or body God stands by as a witness, in all your prayers and your actions you will not err; and you shall have God dwelling with you. —EPICTETUS.

Faith acts on our souls as a moral tonic; it takes the fret and fever out of our lives; it gives the appetite and desire for noble living; it removes despondency; it gives energy, courage, hope, patience, and persistence; and in its highest manifestations it makes our lives a blending of power, sweetness, and peace. —JAMES M. PULLMAN.

Father of spirits! We yield ourselves to You. We will be afraid of neither sorrow nor death in a world where many saintly souls have sanctified them by a divine patience, and amid a Providence wherein no evil thing can dwell. Clinging unto You, we shall not perish with the fashion of this world that passes away. As sparks falling on the river, so shall the glories of our strength go out. But the graces of the holy soul shall be as the brightness of the firmament, and as the stars forever and ever. In You, O Lord, is our undying trust. Amen. —JAMES MARTINEAU.

February 24

Give careful thought to the paths for your feet
and be steadfast in all your ways.

PROVERBS 4:26 (NIV)

Be of good cheer, brave spirit; steadfastly serve that low whisper you have served; for know, God has a select family of sons now scattered wide thro' earth, and each alone, who are your spiritual kindred, and each one by constant service to that inward law, is weaving the sublime proportions of a true monarch's soul. Beauty and strength, the riches of a spotless memory, the eloquence of truth, the wisdom got by searching of a clear and loving eye that sees as God sees. These are their gifts, and time, who keeps God's word, brings on the day to seal the marriage of these minds with yours, your everlasting lovers. —RALPH WALDO EMERSON.

O God, who makes the outgoings of the morning and evening to rejoice, help us to welcome this new day as Your gift, to take up its duties with courage, and to follow the light which You shall give. Conscious of the meaning and purpose of life, undismayed by the failures of past days, and ever remembering that Your strength is made perfect in human weakness, may we consecrate ourselves anew to the glad service of life, knowing that in so doing we enter into fellowship with all who have been workers together with You, and into increasing likeness of soul to Your holy Son. May the beauty of the Lord our God be upon us, and may life become stronger and sweeter and richer, until at last we receive through grace the "well done!" of the Master. Amen. —HENRY M. KING.

February 25

Then your light will break forth like the dawn,
and your healing will quickly appear;
then your righteousness will go before you,
and the glory of the Lord will be your rear guard.

ISAIAH 58:8 (NIV)

There is no music in a rest, but there is the making of music in it. In our whole life melody, the music is broken off here and there by "rests," and we foolishly think we have come to the end of time. God sends a time of forced leisure—sickness, disappointed plans, frustrated efforts—and makes a sudden pause in the choral hymn of our lives, and we lament that our voices must be silent, and our part missing in the music which ever goes up to the ear of the Creator. How does the musician read the rest? See him beat time with unvarying count and catch up the next note true and steady, as if no breaking place had come in between. Not without design does God write the music of our lives. But be it ours to learn the time, and not be dismayed at the "rests." They are not to be slurred over, nor to be omitted, nor to destroy the melody, nor to change the key-note. If we look up, God Himself will beat the time for us. With the eye on Him we shall strike the next note full and clear.   —JOHN RUSKIN.

O God, help us to trust where we cannot see, and to feel that life is not necessarily a failure because we are shut out from its activities. Grant us in sickness such visions and such communion with You that disease of the body shall be transformed into a healer of the soul; and, as the crushed rose the sweeter fragrance emits, so may our sorrows chasten and refine us.

O Heavenly Father, grant that all our sickness and pain and disappointment may so sweeten our dispositions, purify our character and strengthen our souls that we shall bring heaven's sunlight into the lives of all whom we meet. Amen.

—MYRON W. HAYNES.

February 26

> Now that you have purified yourselves by obeying the truth so that you have sincere love for each other, love one another deeply, from the heart. For you have been born again, not of perishable seed, but of imperishable, through the living and enduring word of God.
>
> COLOSSIANS 3:1-2 (NIV)

Love is the greatest thing that God can give us, for Himself is love; and it is the greatest thing we can give to God, for it will also give ourselves, and carry with it all that is ours.

—JEREMY TAYLOR.

> High thoughts and noble in all lands
> Help me, my soul is fed by such;
> But ah, the touch of lips and hands,
> The human touch!
> Warm, vital, close, life's symbols dear,
> These need I most and now and here.

—RICHARD BURTON.

Our Father in Heaven, we bless You this morning for all Your care and love; You have made our houses homes, sweet, quiet dwelling-places. We thank You for sleep, for communion with one another in all holy and tender speech. We thank You for all our hopes; the worlds are nearer than we thought, heaven's fragrance attempers the winds of earth, we almost hear the upper song: may we listen for it, may our souls delight in sweet anticipations of immortal fellowship, and may we come out of these high reveries determined to work more, suffer more patiently, to accept every discipline more willingly, and to do all our little day's work as men whose citizenship is in heaven. Amen.

—JOSEPH PARKER.

February 27

So I find this law at work: Although I want to do good, evil is right there with me. For in my inner being I delight in God's law; but I see another law at work in me, waging war against the law of my mind and making me a prisoner of the law of sin at work within me.... Thanks be to God, who delivers me through Jesus Christ our Lord!   ROMANS 7:21-25 (NIV)

Flame of the spirit, and dust of the
   earth—
This is the making of man,
This is his problem of birth;
Born to all holiness, born to all crime,
Heir of both worlds, on the long slope
   of time
Climbing the path of God's plan;
Dust of the earth in his error and fear,
Weakness and malice and lust;

Yet, quivering up from the dust,
Flame of the spirit, unleaping and clear,
Yearning to God, since from God is its
   birth—
This is man's portion, to shape as he can,
Flame of the spirit, and dust of the
   earth—
This is the making of man.
            —PRISCILLA LEONARD.

O God, You are the Father of our spirits, but our spirits have come to us through ways of flesh. We are both spiritual and carnal. Our spirits seek You evermore, but our flesh turns away from You and strives to drag us down. Between our best and our worst is bitter conflict. Help us to the discovery that all that lives is in like conflict, and that there can be no virtue and no glory except in overcoming. Make us see that the spirit is stronger than the flesh because it is of God, and that in the obedience and inspiration of Jesus, Your Son and our Brother, we may at last be enthroned with Him. Amen.   —CEPHAS B. CRANE.

February 28

Indeed, there is no one on earth who is righteous,
no one who does what is right and never sins.

ECCLESIASTES 7:20 (NIV)

Neither let mistakes nor wrong directions, of which every man, in his studies and elsewhere, falls into many, discourage you. There is precious instruction to be got by finding we were wrong. Let a man try faithfully, manfully, to be right; he will grow daily more and more right. It is at bottom the condition on which all men have to cultivate themselves. —THOMAS CARLYLE.

Almighty God, our heavenly Father—in Your own loving way You do bless us when we do right; when we fall into mistakes so teach us by Your judgments that we become wise unto salvation. Help Your children to recognize their proneness to blunder, that they learn to walk circumspectly. When we fall into the wrong, grant that we lie prone not long but arise undismayed to greater effort. Bring to bear upon us the influences of the Holy Spirit, that we strive earnestly and devoutly to be right at the center of our being; that rightness be the fabric of our life. To You be all glory evermore. Amen. —EDWARD A. PERRY.

February 29

O people, the Lord has told you what is good,
and this is what he requires of you:
to do what is right, to love mercy,
and to walk humbly with your God.

MICAH 6:8 (NLT)

Henceforth I learn that to obey is best,
And love with fear the only God, to walk
As in His presence, ever to observe
His providence, and on Him sole
  depend,
Merciful over all His works, with good
Still overcoming evil, and by small
Accomplishing great things—by things
  deemed weak

Subverting worldly strong, and worldly
  wise
By simply meek, that suffering for
  Truth's sake
Is fortitude to highest victory,
And to the faithful death the gate of
  life—
Taught this by His example whom I now
Acknowledge my Redeemer ever blest.

—JOHN MILTON.

O Eternal One before whom from day to day we walk and on whom we ever depend, help us today to love whatever is good and beautiful and to follow obediently the commands of Your Spirit. May we overcome evil with good; and may we accomplish whatever tasks the hours as they pass demand of us, whether small or great, with such strength as may be vouchsafed us and with a wisdom begotten of meekness. If we must suffer for truth's sake may we manifest such humility and fortitude as shall be conducive to the highest success. Open for us hourly the gates of life, as those who endeavor to be faithful to their high calling. These favors we ask in the name of Him who redeems our lives from all evil and crowns us daily with His loving kindness. Amen. —EDWARD DAY.

March 1

There is no greater love than to lay down one's life for one's friends.

JOHN 15:13 (NLT)

All the strength of the world and all its beauty, all true joy, everything that consoles, that feeds hope, or throws a ray of light along our dark paths, everything that makes us see across our poor lives a splendid goal and a boundless future, comes to us from people of simplicity, those who have made another object of their desires than the passing satisfaction of selfishness and vanity, and have understood that the art of living is to know how to give one's life. —CHARLES WAGNER.

Heavenly Father, help us to be like You, as manifested in the person of Jesus Christ, Your Son! It was His will to do the will of His Father by living and dying for others. Teach us so to live. Help us to learn by positive personal experience that supremest joy comes only "in ministering unto others." Teach us what Jesus meant when He said: "I am among you as he that serves." Plant deeply within us His passion for a life of service. May our morning hours be gladdened and inspired by this divine purpose. Let Your holy will be done in us this day. Amen.

—CHARLES PARKHURST.

March 2

Commit to the Lord whatever you do,
and he will establish your plans.

PROVERBS 16:3 (NIV)

The year's at the spring
And day's at the morn;
Morning's at seven;
The hill-side's dew-pearled;
The lark's on the wing;
The snail's on the thorn;
God's in His heaven—
All's right with the world!

—ROBERT BROWNING.

Father in Heaven, refreshed and heartened by the night, we begin again with You the high adventure of our life. Add to the beauty of the world about us a finer spiritual beauty in our souls. Save us from our own undoing. If our thoughts are dark, shine in upon them with Your glory; if they be bright, make them to light the pathway of another. Have us wholesomely to forget ourselves, in the joy of Your good world, the promise of our imperfection and the trust in God that makes us not afraid. And when the duties of the day are done, dismiss us, Your well-meaning children, with a quiet mind to rest. Amen.   —ALBERT WELLMAN HITCHCOCK.

March 3

> But among you it will be different. Whoever wants to be a leader among you must be your servant, and whoever wants to be first among you must become your slave. MATTHEW 20:26–27 (NLT)

We will do something worth doing—that is the resolution for you and me.

—EDWARD EVERETT HALE.

We admire the man who embodies victorious efforts, the man who never wrongs his neighbor, who is prompt to help a friend, but who has those virile qualities necessary to win in the stern strife of actual life. —THEODORE ROOSEVELT.

Father of Lights in whom is no darkness at all, and in whose light we see light, help us to clearly see and never forget that only right deeds are worthy of a child of Yours. May we in no moment forget that to yield to the wrong is to bring upon us Your just condemnation and sow for us a sure reaping of sorrowful repentance. By doing the things we know to be right and worth doing, the things worthy of our true selves and of our Father and of our Master whose we are, may this day, through us, yield some benefit to other children of Yours, and bring to us the sweet reward of Your approval. Amen. —OSCAR F. SAFFORD.

March 4

All the days of the oppressed are wretched,
but the cheerful heart has a continual feast.

PROVERBS 15:15 (NIV)

It is worth a thousand pounds a year to have the habit of looking on the bright side of things. —SAMUEL JOHNSON.

Not by appointment do we meet delight and joy;
They wait not our expectancy;
But round some corner in the street of life,
They, on a sudden, greet us with a smile.

—GERALD MASSEY.

Our Father, at the beginning of a new day, refreshed by the night's rest, we turn to Your for strength for the day's task. We know not what the hours hold for us, but this we do know, that come what may, You will go with us to bless, to cheer; we shall not walk or work alone. As we faithfully and cheerfully perform our work, conscious of Your presence, there will come joys and smiles unexpected and unsought. This is Your way of teaching us faithfulness and endurance. May we soon learn, that if we would make the day happy and worth while, we must not seek our own pleasure and good, but that of our brethren. May we so live that when the night shadows are again upon us, there shall be no cause for shame or regret. In the Master's spirit! Amen.

—O. HOWARD PERKINS.

March 5

He gives strength to the weary
and increases the power of the weak.

ISAIAH 40:29 (NIV)

Not in dumb resignation we lift our hands on high;
Not like the nerveless fatalist, content to do and die.
Our faith springs, like the eagle's, who soars to meet the sun,
And cries exulting unto You, "Oh, Lord, Your will be done."

Your will! It bids the weak be strong; it bids the strong be just;
No lips to fawn, no hand to beg, no brow to seek the dust,
Wherever man oppresses men beneath the liberal sun,
O Lord, be there, Your arm made bare, Your righteous will be done.

—JOHN HAY.

It is with the beautiful assurance of Your love and kindness, our Father, that we draw close to You. It is Faith that seems to give us wings by which we rise above the darkness, into Your Presence of light and love. We feel our divine relationship to You, so that we lift up our hands to You, as the child to the parent. We are content to do Your will, because we know then just what it is to love You. Our Master taught us this great lesson by His own faith in You. To do Your will means strength to the weak, hope to the hopeless. To the sorrowing there can be seen, beyond the tear, the rainbow of Your promise. Thus, as we realize our sonship will we work to make all men feel their own power, and all become one in Your great love. May Your Kingdom come and Your will be done, in Christ our Lord. Amen. —C. E. FISHER.

March 6

As iron sharpens iron,

so a friend sharpens a friend.

PROVERBS 27:17 (NLT)

If you are my friend you cannot be indifferent to my faults of character, any more than you can be indifferent to my sickness or suffering. But, if you care to help me cure these faults, please let them alone! Please make much of my good qualities if you can discover any. And especially bless me with the encouraging sight of a better man than myself, and cheer me with a high example. I know that there are times when a sharp or gentle rebuke is in order, and that "faithful are the wounds of a friend." But the wiser doctors have lost their faith in blood-letting; and they know that clumsy surgery kills more than it cures. —CHARLES G. AMES.

In our prayer, our Heavenly Father, we desire to be consciously grateful for the opportunities this new day affords us of being helpful to each other. The inspiration so to act comes from You. You are the constant and never-failing Helper of Your children. May we be mindful of the fact that our noblest service to another may not be an alms, but a look of encouragement, a word of cheer. Enable us to be not too sensible of others' faults and failings. Assist us to see and magnify the good in other lives. To this end may we be to others such examples in conduct and character as we would have them be to us. We offer and ask all in the spirit of Jesus. Amen.

—LEROY W. COONS.

March 7

But I am trusting you, O Lord,
saying, "You are my God!"
My future is in your hands.

PSALM 31:14-15a (NLT)

The mariner of old said to Neptune in a great tempest, "O God! You may save me if You will, and if You will You may destroy me, but whether or no, I will steer my rudder true." —MONTAIGNE.

> I go to prove my soul
> I see my way as birds their trackless way.
> I shall arrive! What time, what circuit first,
> I ask not; but unless God send His hail
> Or blinding fire-balls, sleet or stifling snow,
> In some time, His good time, I shall arrive;
> He guides me and the bird. In His good time!

—ROBERT BROWNING.

Once more we face the day that can be dreadful only to our poor sight and trembling faith. For You have made flame and pain, the hurricane and quaking earth to be Your ministers of grace. Shall trust depart when shadows fall? You are "in the shadow keeping watch above Your own." As truly in severity as in gentleness, You are the All-Loving and All-Wise. Shall we fear to go anywhere? Lord, You are everywhere! Defend us only from the blindness and fear of ignorance and sin. Draw us nearer to You, this day, by any means in Your good pleasure, so that at last, truly knowing Your way, we shall rise above the worst that circumstances may do into joy unspeakable and peace unbroken. In the name of Him made perfect through suffering. Amen.

—HENRY B. TAYLOR.

March 8

Be still in the presence of the Lord,
and wait patiently for him to act.
Don't worry about evil people who prosper
or fret about their wicked schemes.

PSALM 37:7 (NLT)

We complain of the slow, dull life we are forced to lead, of our humble sphere of action, of our low position in the scale of society, of our having no room to make ourselves known, of our wasted energies, of our years of patience. So do we say that we have no Father who is directing our life, so do we say that God has forgotten us, so do we boldly judge what life is best for us, and so by our complaining do we lose the use and profit of the quiet years. —BISHOP HUNTINGTON.

Infinite and Holy One, by the tender mercies of Your great love show us this day the true life that is hid in You. Feed us with Your spirit that we hunger not. Make us strong and merciful in You. Help us to be simple, brave, and true. Give us to speak and live the truth. Make us content with life while ever dreaming of the more perfect day. Fix our lives in a great and brave integrity. Humble us in our pride, lift us from our despondency. Keep our hearts pure and our lips from speaking guile. Send us forth in perfect faith that here and now our lives may be patterned after that of Jesus without loss of influence over men. Make us not ashamed to be good and forgiving and gentle in all our ways. Amen. —FREDERICK W. BETTE.

March 9

The Lord gives his people strength.
The Lord blesses them with peace.

PSALM 29:11 (NLT)

Count each affliction, whether light or grave,
God's messenger sent down to you; do you
With courtesy receive him; rise and bow;
And, 'ere his shadow pass your threshold, crave
Permission first his heavenly foot to lave.

*   *   *   *   *

Grief should be
Like joy, majestic, equable, sedate,
Confirming, cleansing, raising, making free.
Strong to consume small troubles; to commend
Great thoughts, grave thoughts, thoughts lasting to the end.

—AUBREY DEVERE.

Our Father, we would learn to trust Your love, to live so that Your grace shall have in us its perfect work. Not the easy thing is what we ask, but strength for duty. Give us the confidence that You are by our side. Let Your strong touch be felt, Your blessed presence seen. In all the turmoil that rages within, without, grant us Your peace. In childish helplessness, grant us the Father's help. To grow like Jesus is our heart's desire. All things that Your great heart permits or sends, we would receive with gratitude, that so our wills and lives may be in harmony with Yours. And so day by day may something of the Saviour's glory shine through us and bless and brighten other lives in need. Amen.

—FRANK M. HOLT.

March 10

Look, the winter is past, and the rains are over and gone.
The flowers are springing up,
　　the season of singing birds has come,
　　and the cooing of turtledoves fills the air.

SONG OF SOLOMON 2:11-12 (NLT)

Dawn and its silence draw a silver sigh
Far in the east where early shadows lie
All flocked and folded like soft peaceful
　　sheep.
The spirit of the spring stirs in its sleep,
Breathes into life a misty floating sheen;
The willows dreamy drip of constant
　　green;
Exultant beats a bird-heart o'er a nest,
Where dim, vague stirrings 'neath the
　　tiny breast
Spell fresh the miracle of motherhood.
Ah, how the world is young! Ah, how 'tis
　　good!
To feel the new life flutter mystic wing;
Like to a lark to feel one's soul upspring,
Transpierce the very limit of the sky,
And toss its challenge to Eternity!

—MARY BALDWIN.

O God, our heavenly Father, make our hearts exultant, as the earth in the spring morning, with the radiance of Your Presence. Fill them with the joy and hopefulness of eternal youth, and cause them to be uplifted in gratitude and thankfulness to You. We have seen earthly faces so beaming with the light of love that we never shall forget them. We have spoken names that are so endeared to us that they will linger in our memory as long as we live. So, O Father, may it be with Your face and Your name. May Your face beaming upon us as the sun of righteousness win our love to holiness and virtue, making us fruitful of good works, and Your name be so woven in our affections that we shall cherish and hallow it forever. Amen. —EDGAR W. PREBLE.

March 11

> For even the Son of Man did not come to be served, but to serve, and to give his life as a ransom for many.   MARK 10:45 (NIV)

You must be serving something, someone, that needs your help in order to really appreciate the Divine care. It may be the parents' care of their children; the teacher and her scholars; the charity-worker and the poor, the friendless, the benighted; it may be friend helping friend—in some way the life of loving service must be there as something out of which God can help us think of and value the care which infinite love bestows upon us.   —JULIAN K. SMYTH.

Heavenly Father, with the opening of a new day we thank You for father love and mother love, for love of patriot and philanthropist, and for the love which that has called into being in our own hearts. Through this love and the service of mutual helpfulness to which we have been led thereby, You open our eyes to behold the world pervaded and overruled by a spirit of infinite goodness, society resting upon mutual services, and through that service mankind rising to a nobler and diviner civilization. Help us to be mindful of this heavenly vision, and so make our feet swift to run and our hands eager to work in the service of righteousness and mutual helpfulness. We ask in His name, who loving us, has taught us the divinity of service. Amen.

—LEGRAND POWERS.

March 12

Am I now trying to win the approval of human beings, or of God? Or am I trying to please people? If I were still trying to please people, I would not be a servant of Christ.   GALATIANS 1:10 (NIV)

Far better is it to dare mighty things, to win glorious triumphs even though checkered by failure, than to rank with those poor spirits who neither enjoy nor suffer much because they live in the gray twilight that knows neither victory nor defeat.

—THEODORE ROOSEVELT.

But only he whose judgment never strays
Beyond the threshold of the right,
  learns this—
Not always is it good to have one's wish;
What seemeth sweet full
  oft to bitter turns;

Fulfilled desire hath made mine eyes
  to weep.
Therefore, O reader of these lines, if thou
Would'st virtuous be,
  and held by others dear
Will ever for the power to do aright.

—LEONARDO DA VINCI.

God of the morning light, with the dawn of another day we come to You with prayer for help in the steadfastness of our manifold duties. The cares that oppress us, the burdens we carry, the obligations that fall upon us, are too much for our little strength without Your help. That help we crave from You, the only source of all-availing strength. Let us not be dismayed by the powers of this world or busy ourselves in vain ambitions seeking the praise of men, but may we seek that Divine approval which is of more worth than all the favors of earth. Make us brave and strong to follow in the way of Your appointment, and grant that we may so sincerely feel and act in the busy times of this day that when the evening comes no wasted hours may be laid to our charge. Amen.   —EDWARD M. BARNEY.

March 13

And we know that in all things God works for the good of those who love him, who have been called according to his purpose. ROMANS 8:28 (NIV)

You are in God's world; you are God's child. Those things you cannot change; the only peace and rest and happiness for you is to accept them and rejoice in them. When God speaks to you, you must not believe that it is the wind blowing or the torrent falling from the hill. You must know that it is God. You must gather up the whole power of meeting Him. You must be thankful that life is great and not little. You must listen as if listening were your life. And then, then only can come peace. All other sounds will be caught up into the prevailing richness of that voice of God. The lost proportions will be perfectly restored. Discord will cease; harmony will be complete.
—PHILLIPS BROOKS.

Almighty God! We thank You for the peace and comfort of the night; for the new day and all the hope and peace and promise that it brings to us. Help us that with glad faces and joyous hearts we may take up its every privilege and duty, doing in the spirit of the Master every good and helpful thing our hands find to do. And when the evening shall have come may we look back on a day of plenty, service, and peace, retiring to our rest with songs in our hearts and thanksgiving on our lips because Your blessings have been on this, as on all other days new every morning and fresh every evening. Amen.
—GEORGE MAYO GERRISH.

March 14

Let the heavens rejoice, let the earth be glad;
let the sea resound, and all that is in it.
Let the fields be jubilant, and everything in them;
let all the trees of the forest sing for joy.

PSALM 96:11-12 (NIV)

It is the first mild day of March:
Each minute sweeter than before,
The red-breast sings from the tall larch
That stands beside our door.

There is a blessing in the air,
Which seems a sense of joy to yield,
To the bare trees and mountain bare,
And grass in the green field.

—WILLIAM WORDSWORTH.

Our Father, we wake each morning refreshed and thankful for the joy of living; for the air we breathe, the things we see, the sounds of nature's sweetest harmonies and all the beauty which surrounds our earthly life. May the wonders of the earth speak to us in witness of Your love. Let springing-grass and opening flower remind us of the new life which is ours through the resurrection of our Lord. His blessing like the light of the sun runs everywhere, carrying with it morning and hope, springtime and gladness. The joy is in the song of the birds, the murmur of the waters, the children's laughter and the song of happy hearts. Attune our hearts to notes of praise and make us glad upon the earth until You bring us to perfect and unshadowed joys where we shall see You as You are and be like You. Amen. —J. W. STEPHAN.

March 15

Lift up your eyes and look to the heavens: Who created all these?
He who brings out the starry host one by one
   and calls forth each of them by name.
Because of his great power and mighty strength,
   not one of them is missing.

ISAIAH 40:26 (NIV)

As to equality and inequality, all the beauty and glory of life come from inequalities. If we were all Beethovens or Shakespeares or marvelous in any one direction, life would be unbearable. Who shall tell me if an Easter lily is the equal of a rose, or if either is equal to an oak or a pine? The question of equality is out of the court. The one thing we need to do is to cultivate the finest and sweetest things in us; and then, whether we are one of the California big trees or the violet in a valley, we shall help on the beauty and glory of the earth. —ROBERT COLLYER.

Our Heavenly Father, we thank You for the manifold beauties of Your universe, the revelations of Yourself to Your children. For those large wonders which stir men's minds and rouse their souls to awe, we thank You, but not less for the little things of life, filling their places well, and showing daily to the seeing eye that without them Your universe could not be complete. Help us to grasp the lesson that they teach. If You have given to us the great place, we thank You, but we thank You not less for the homely task, the humble duty, for it is all necessary to Your plan. Help us, day by day, with stronger purpose, larger consecration, to fill our place, to do Your will, in His name. Amen. —GEORGE F. FORTIER.

March 16

Look at the birds of the air; they do not sow or reap or store away in barns, and yet your heavenly Father feeds them. Are you not much more valuable than they? Can any one of you by worrying add a single hour to your life?

MATTHEW 6:26-27 (NIV)

There must be a way of taking worry rightly, so that it shall do us good and not harm. Worry, rightly taken, should train to quietness, humility, patience, gentleness, sympathy. It ought not to eventuate (though it naturally does) in making others suffer because we are uncomfortable; in making us a source of painful worry to others because we are worried ourselves. —A. H. K. BOYD.

Father of Love, Your blessing it is which gives us another day. Help us to put before its cares the spirit that will banish care, to find in its beginning the power that will make labors happy and its ending sweet, and so to open our hearts to Your light that no gloom of night shall linger 'round our way. If heaviness there be in ours or others' lives may every wholesome cheer make it less sore. If remembered faults and follies quench a better hope, send Your patience and Your will to be our courage and fresh resolve. Through all the noisy world may the secret music of Your law swell in our breasts and every step keep time with its glorious march. Amen.

—JOHN DAY.

March 17

Let the morning bring me word of your unfailing love,
    for I have put my trust in you.
Show me the way I should go,
    for to you I entrust my life.

PSALM 143:8 (NIV)

Therefore to whom turn I but to Thee, the ineffable Name?
Builder and maker, Thou, of houses not made with hands!
What, have fear of change from Thee who art ever the same!
Doubt that Thy power can fill the heart that Thy power expands!
There shall never be one lost good! What was, shall live as before;
The evil is null, is nought, is silence implying sound;
What was good, shall be good, with, for evil, so much good more;
On the earth the broken arcs; in the heaven, a perfect round.

—ROBERT BROWNING.

We thank You, O God, that each morning brings us fresh assurance of Your wisdom and goodness—that the days have taught us to believe in You and to trust You as our perfect Friend. We are glad that we can face the day in the faith that You are sufficient to the needs of the day—to all the needs of all Your children. In this trust, we beseech You, make us more and more to rejoice in life and its high privileges. Help us to go on our way with gladness and peace in our hearts—to worship You hourly by honest work, by faithful service, by kind words, by helpful deeds, and so, to find life good by doing something to make it good. Amen. —FLINT M. BISSELL.

March 18

The Lord directs the steps of the godly.
He delights in every detail of their lives.
Though they stumble, they will never fall,
for the Lord holds them by the hand.

PSALM 37:23-24 (NLT)

"If I were you," she said, "I should not worry. Just make up your mind to do better when you get another chance. One can't do more than that. That is what I shall think of: that God will give each of us another chance, and that each one of us will take it and do better—I and you and everyone. So there is no need to fret over failure, when one hopes one may be allowed to redeem that failure later on. Besides which life is very hard. Why, we ourselves recognize that. If there be a God, some intelligence greater than human intelligence, He will understand better than ourselves that life is very hard and difficult, and He will be astonished not because we are not better, but because we are not worse. At least, that would be my notion of a God. I should not worry if I were you. Just make up your mind to do better if you get the chance and be content with that."   —BEATRICE HARRADEN.

O Lord, how often we have failed—how weak and frail we are—we have groped and stumbled along the pathway of life and have been defeated over and over again. Yet in the light of Your providence and Your love in spite of all defeats, we take heart and face the day with hope. In Your economy no failure is ever final—we rejoice that You open before us another opportunity. Let us be brave and earnest to seize the opportunities of these passing hours. Amen.   —GEORGE L. PERIN.

March 19

To every life there comes a time supreme:
One day, one night, one morning, or one noon,
One freighted hour—one moment opportune,
One rift through which sublime fulfilments gleam;
One time when fate goes tiding with the stream,
One Once in balance 'twixt Too Late, Too Soon—
And ready for the passing instant's boon
That shall in favor tip the wavering beam.
Ah! Happy he who, knowing how to wait,
Knows also how to watch and how to stand
On life's broad deck alert, and at the prow,
To seize the happy moment big with fate
From Opportunity's extended hand
When the great clock of Destiny strikes Now!

—MARY ASHLEY TOWNSEND.

Our heavenly Father! You are the Author of all our days, and all our times and seasons are hid in the unfolding mystery of Your Thought and Purpose. It is not given to us to know what a day or an hour may bring forth, but the opportune moments come, ways are opened before us to larger life and usefulness and privilege and duty. May we, by faithfulness, and watchfulness, and the readiness of those on duty, be prepared for each divinely offered opportunity. Surrounded by blessings, may we live to bless. Ministered unto, may we minister. Grateful to You, may we show our gratitude by service. In Your name, Amen. —DWIGHT M. HODGE.

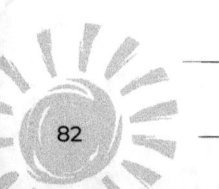

March 20

See, I will create new heavens and a new earth.
The former things will not be remembered,
nor will they come to mind.

ISAIAH 65:17 (NIV)

Put out of your thought the past whatever it may be; let go even the future with its golden dream and its high ideal; and concentrate your soul in this burning, present moment. For the man who is true to the present is true to his best; and the soul that wins the ground immediately before it, makes life a triumph.

—OZORA STEARNS DAVIS.

Almighty Giver of every good, we come to You amid the joys of a new morning, with its new blessings and opportunities. We would dedicate this day to Your service. We would forget the past and waste not our time in idle dreaming of tomorrow, but with consecrated zeal we would apply ourselves to the tasks You have appointed us for this present hour. Your hand is ever opened to let down the tokens of Your love. May all that is best within us rise up in answer, and may we be dedicated anew to our upbuilding in righteousness and the fulfilment of our duties to one another. May we this day follow the footsteps of the Christ and prove ourselves His faithful disciples! Amen.

—R. PERRY BUSH.

March 21

For where your treasure is, there your heart will be also.

MATTHEW 6:21 (NIV)

I believe that today is better than yesterday, and that tomorrow will be better than today.   —GEORGE F. HOAR.

Make yourselves nests of pleasant thoughts, bright fancies, faithful sayings; treasure-houses of precious and restful thoughts, which care cannot disturb nor poverty take away from you—houses built without hands for your souls to live in.

—JOHN RUSKIN.

Dear Father in heaven, around Your name cluster the most sacred and holy affections. Your name, indeed, is above every name infinite in love, and awakening in each heart a sense of filial gratitude. At this morning hour, therefore, we are mindful of the tie that binds us to You, that provides a nesting-place for pleasant and restful thoughts, that makes duty less irksome, home-love more tender, sacrifice more willing, and character more noble. In this spirit we pray, O Father, send us forth to the labor which awaits us, only to realize, under Your Providence, that this is the best day of our life, and full of assurance and rejoicing for a still better tomorrow. In the light of faith, hope and love do we ask and offer all. Amen.

—WILBURN D. POTTER.

March 22

For ever since the world was created, people have seen the earth and sky. Through everything God made, they can clearly see his invisible qualities—his eternal power and divine nature. So they have no excuse for not knowing God.

ROMANS 1:20 (NLT)

Scarce tangible may be the first glad sign,
Yet how it shakes us with a vernal thrill!
The voice of the south wind behind the
   hill;
Or an elusive bird-note faint and fine;
A flush at dawn along the wan sky-line;
A lyrical exuberance in the rill;
A something working its mysterious will
Both in majestic hole and tenuous vine!

It is the vernal spirit. In the earth
It throbs and pulses; quickens in the air;
And permeates all nature thro' and thro'.
In the expectant poignancy of birth
What raptures, what rare ecstasies we
   share—
Old—ah, how old!—and yet forever new!
—CLINTON SCOLLARD.

O God, how good You are! All Your works praise You. The world is filled with Your glory. This dawning Springtime brings You very near every responsive heart. You are the fountain of life. We see You in bursting bud and incipient bloom. We hear You in the rapture of birds and in the newfound gladness of sun-kissed rivulets. May we, the children of Your love, be new born into a deeper spirituality—a richer life! May the beauty of the Spirit breathing through our hearts call forth the latent goodness that slumbers there! Speak through us the music of Your love. Perfume us with the odors of Your heavenly grace, and may we walk this day in tune with You! Amen.

—JOSEPH COOPER.

March 23

Lazy people want much but get little, but those who work hard will prosper.

PROVERBS 13:4 (NLT)

Work is the grand cure of all the maladies and miseries that ever beset mankind—honest work, which you intend getting done.   —THOMAS CARLYLE.

Thank God every morning when you get up that you have something to do which must be done whether you like it or not. Being forced to work and forced to do your best will breed in you temperance, self-control, diligence, strength of will, content and a hundred virtues which the idle will never know.

—CHARLES KINGSLEY.

Kind Father and Friend, Your presence has watched over us all our days and has been a comfort in all our labors. We thank You for Your unwearied watching over us. May we at the dawn of this new day, come to our tasks with thanks in our hearts and a song on our lips. May all life's stern duties and its perplexities get grace and beauty from our hallowed thoughts and sanctified resolves. We would ask that Your free spirit be with us this day to give us hope and joy in our several tasks. May the sweet peace of mind of those who learn to labor and to wait crown all our efforts. Dear Father, forgive our failures and keep us ever Yours. Amen.   —CHARLES E. PETTY.

March 24

Whoever dwells in the shelter of the Most High
   will rest in the shadow of the Almighty.
I will say of the Lord, "He is my refuge and my fortress,
   my God, in whom I trust."

PSALM 91:1-2 (NIV)

Ah, the mis-takings and the mis-leavings; and all the ignorant beginning, when we can only lay up things for late wisdom to repent of!

Nothing really bad can ever happen.... I've meant right—and I mean right now. I'll do the best I can, and the Lord will take care of everybody.

—MRS. A. D. T. WHITNEY.

Lord, You come to us with light and life, forgive us for coming to You as aliens and beggars; daily You are our refuge and strength, and this should subtract our fear and multiply our confidence, comfort and consecration. Our needs are Your opportunity; we have more sunshine than we can use, more love than we can repay and more revelation than we can translate. O may this satisfy us early and strengthen us through all our days. Alone we are very weak, but we are never alone; all of life is a company affair, for You are with us; help us to be as truly Your children as You are our Father and Mother. Through our thinking, working and waiting may men see You and glorify You. O teach us to abide ever in Your love, and help us to work some helpful miracle by the gates of need, and to see the rainbow of prophecy through earth's tears and over its years. Amen.

—ALAN R. TILLINGHAST.

March 25

Join together in following my example, brothers and sisters, and just as you have us as a model, keep your eyes on those who live as we do.

PHILIPPIANS 3:17 (NIV)

'Tis the fine souls who serve us, and not what is called fine society.

—RALPH WALDO EMERSON.

We find what we look for in the world. I have always been looking for the nobler qualities in human beings, and I have always found them. There are great souls all along the highway of life, and there are great qualities even in the people who seem common and weak to us ordinarily.

—ELLA WHEELER WILCOX.

Gracious Father, we thank You for the power You have given us to labor for our own and others' advancement and happiness. As we begin this new day we trust in Your bounty and would draw on Your strength to sustain us in our toil. We thank You for the brave souls in every walk of life who have set us an example worthy to be followed. Many have been or are notable in the world for their fortitude, honor and achievements; many others have been known to us but have been unheralded by men, and from all these we have ourselves been made more capable and faithful. By Your grace may we be aided in emulating the good we see in others, and be able to make the world a little brighter because of Your gift to us of this day. Amen.

—FRANK S. RICE.

March 26

And so we know and rely on the love God has for us. God is love. Whoever lives in love lives in God, and God in them. This is how love is made complete among us so that we will have confidence on the day of judgment: In this world we are like Jesus. There is no fear in love. But perfect love drives out fear because fear has to do with punishment. The one who fears is not made perfect in love.

1 JOHN 4:16–18 (NIV)

An old, worn Harp that had been played
Till all its strings were loose and frayed,
Joy, Hate, and Fear, each one, assayed
To play. But each in turn had found
No sweet responsiveness of sound.

Then Love the Master-player came
With heaving breast and eyes aflame;
The Harp he took all undismayed,
Smote on its strings, still strange to song,
And brought forth music sweet and
strong.

—PAUL LAURENCE DUNBAR.

Heavenly Father, I pray that You will help me to love today. You are Love and if You shall fill my life there will be no room for hate and no room for fear, for "Perfect Love casts out fear." As the Master stilled the waves in Galilee, so speak peace to my soul, and bid all discord cease, that my whole life may be in tune with heaven, and may be one happy song. Love alone can bring harmony out of discord, love out of hate, trust out of fear, and music out of a worn-out, or a long unused or misused life. So let Love control the whole of my life for Jesus' sake. Amen.

—B. L. JENNINGS.

March 27

I pray that out of his glorious riches he may strengthen you with power through his Spirit in your inner being.　　EPHESIANS 3:16 (NIV)

No stream from its source
Flows seaward, how lonely soever its course,
But some land is gladdened. No star ever rose
Or set without influence somewhere. Who knows
What earth needs from earth's lowliest creature? No life
Can be pure in its purpose and strong in its strife,
And all life not be purer and stronger thereby.

　　　　　　　　　　　　　　　　—OWEN MEREDITH.

If I am this day to touch other lives helpfully so that they may be gladdened and strengthened for truer and nobler living, I shall need, my Father, not only a clear perception of myself in relation to that to which You call me, but also a clear vision of the Christ who would be felt through me, not only the impulse of a strong purpose but also the endowment of power by Your spirit of power. That this may be, do test my purpose by that of Your son and fashion my life by His teaching, keeping my heart open always toward You. Amen.　　　　　　—F. H. WHEELER.

March 28

God is our refuge and strength, always ready to help in times of trouble.
So we will not fear when earthquakes come
  and the mountains crumble into the sea.
Let the oceans roar and foam.
  Let the mountains tremble as the waters surge!

PSALM 46:1-3 (NLT)

I but open my eyes—and perfection, no more and no less,
In the kind I imagined, full-fronts me, and God is seen God,
In the star, in the stone, in the flesh, in the soul and the clod.
And thus looking within and around me, I ever renew
(With that stoop of the soul which in bending upraises it too)
The submission of man's nothing-perfect to God's all-complete,
And by each new obeisance in spirit, I climb to His feet.

—ROBERT BROWNING.

O Infinite Spirit, we cannot understand You, yet we feel Your presence within us and about us. We cannot unravel the mystery of Your life, not even of our own lives, yet we feel ourselves linked as by chains of steel to You. We are poor and ignorant and little and finite; You are great and strong and infinite, yet we cling to the thought that we are Your children. Even in Your infinity You stoop to listen to us. You care for us, love us. O Father of our Souls, may we cling to You today and every day. We do not ask You to explain Yourself, but we do ask that in storm and sunshine, in adversity and in prosperity, and in every emergency we may keep our anchorage to You unbroken, and feel Your presence with us. Amen.

—GEORGE L. PERIN.

March 29

Suppose you see a brother or sister who has no food or clothing, and you say, "Good-bye and have a good day; stay warm and eat well"—but then you don't give that person any food or clothing. What good does that do? So you see, faith by itself isn't enough. Unless it produces good deeds, it is dead and useless.

JAMES 2:15-17 (NLT)

I wonder why it is that we are not all kinder to each other than we are. How much the world needs it! How easily it is done! —HENRY DRUMMOND.

Let us awaken to the divine privilege of sharing the heartaches of our friends; of the meaning of good fellowship; of that independence of spirit that does not imitate; of courage and pride that can endure adversity with dignity, and without fear.

—ANONYMOUS.

Our Heavenly Father, help us through this new day to allow the impulses of our hearts to have fullest play. Help us to help each other, Lord, and of whatever grace or influence we have to bless and uplift our fellowmen to give generously and gladly. Help us scatter sunshine along our pathway, to speak the cheering word to discouraged hearts and to lend the helping hand to feeble or halting ones along the way. May we find our greatest happiness following in the footsteps of our Master, humbly serving our neighbor's needs, and doing good even at every wayside opportunity. Amen.

—JAMES F. ALBION.

March 30

For the Lord gives wisdom;
from his mouth come knowledge and understanding.

PROVERBS 2:6 (NIV)

Once to every man and nation comes the moment to decide,
In the strife of Truth with Falsehood, for the good or evil side;
Some great cause, God's new Messiah, offering each the bloom or blight,
Parts the goats upon the left hand, and the sheep upon the right,
And the choice goes by forever 'twixt that darkness and that light.

—JAMES RUSSELL LOWELL.

Almighty Father, we are before You, asking for strength this day, that for today's duty we may have the help of Your Infinite wisdom, as we know we have Your love, Our Father with His Children. Father, help us to look to You for strength and wisdom in every moment of doubt. We are not afraid, because we can come to You for counsel, and companionship. We can come to You for everything, and we find everything if we seek for it with all our heart and soul and strength. So today, Father, be with us to show each one of us here, the youngest or the oldest, the weakest or the strongest, what is the duty next his hand today, that we may enter into that work and go about our Father's business. Go with us and be with us as with Your own children. Amen.

—EDWARD EVERETT HALE.

March 31

I long to accomplish great and noble tasks, but it is my duty and joy to accomplish humble tasks as though they were great and noble.   —HELEN KELLER.

It is a fine notion of life to liken it to the loom. God puts on the warp in those circumstances in which we find ourselves, and which we cannot change. The weft is wrought by the shuttle of everyday life. It is made of very homely threads sometimes, common duties, unpromising and unwelcome tasks. But whoever tries to do each day's work in the spirit of patient loyalty to God is weaving the texture whose other side is fairer than the one he sees.   —ANONYMOUS.

Our Father in heaven, grant that we may be "faithful in that which is least," leaving to Your will whether we have the opportunity of being "faithful in much." May we understand that the value of our service is not so much in what we do as the spirit in which we do it. Help us to remember that no service is common in Your sight, if it is done for Your glory and the betterment of humanity; that in blessing others, we ourselves are blessed; that life is mostly made up of little things, but a character which is perfected by Thy grace and humble service is not a little thing, but a jewel to shine in Thy crown forever. Amen.   —E. T. CURNICK.

April 1

> You will go out in joy and be led forth in peace;
>
> the mountains and hills will burst into song before you,
>
> and all the trees of the field will clap their hands.
>
> ISAIAH 55:12 (NIV)

April is here!

There's a song in the maple, thrilling and new;

There's a flash of wings of heaven's own hue;

There's a veil of green on the nearer hills;

There's a burst of rapture in woodland rills;

There are stars in the meadow dropped here and there;

There's a breath of arbutus in the air;

There's a dash of rain, as if flung in jest;

There's an arch of color spanning the west;

April is here!

—EBEN E. REXFORD.

O God, ever-living and ever-acting, all Your works praise You, and Your saints bless You! We rejoice that You are bringing in this new springtime, and are preparing to pour out Your summer glory and bounty in garden and field and wood, that Your children may be richly blessed. As You are working mightily in nature today so will You work in us, Your children, that the blessed fruits of the Spirit may appear in all that we think and do and are? And may the spontaneous spring song of the woods find its counterpart in the perpetual gladness of our souls sunk deep in the love of Christ! Amen.

—HENRY IRVING CUSHMAN.

April 2

> Therefore, if anyone is in Christ, the new creation has come:
> The old has gone, the new is here!
>
> 2 CORINTHIANS 5:17 (NIV)

The sweetest sound our whole year round
'Tis the first robin of the spring!
The song of the full orchard choir,
Is not so fine a thing.

—EDMUND CLARENCE STEDMAN.

The grass comes, the flower laughs where lately lay the snow,
O'er the breezy hill top hoarsely calls the crow,
By the flowing river the alder catkins swing
And the sweet song sparrow cries, "Spring, it is Spring!"

—CELIA THAXTER.

Accept from a heart of gratitude, O God, thanksgiving and praises for the glad anticipation of the coming days of spring. May the awakening of nature, this living garment in which You have robed Your mysterious loveliness, be to each of Your children symbol of the new life which comes to those who put their trust in the risen Christ and of the higher life beyond where shadows are no more and light and gladness bless an eternity of joy. O, Father of lights, make every hour of this opening day rich and radiant with Your effulgent presence through Jesus Christ. Amen.

—KERR BOYCE TUPPER.

April 3

> What is mankind that you are mindful of them,
> human beings that you care for them?
> You have made them a little lower than the angels
> and crowned them with glory and honor.
>
> PSALM 8: 4–5 (NIV)

Within my earthly temple there's a crowd;
There's one of us that's humble, one that's proud,
There's one that's broken-hearted for his sins,
There's one that unrepentant sits and grins;
There's one that loves his neighbor as himself,
And one that cares for naught but fame and pelf.
From much corroding care I should be free
If I could once determine which is me.

—THEODORE MARTIN.

Our Heavenly Father, we thank You for our multiform life. You have made us a little lower than the angels and has crowned us with glory and honor, yet how little we know ourselves! We go astray; we fall from our high estate; like the moth we flutter around the blaze that burns us. When we would do good, evil is present with us. Yet through all complexity of thought and feeling, of passion and appetite, through all our wanderings and all our sins we thank You that there shines clearly the light of our own Divinity. We are Your children. Help us, we pray, to know ourselves at our best. May we not be betrayed in this day's journey by any siren voice. Let us go forth to the tasks of the day with the consciousness that until the evening shadows fall You will be with us. Amen.   —GEORGE L. PERIN.

April 4

But ask the animals, and they will teach you, or the birds in the sky, and they will tell you; or speak to the earth, and it will teach you, or let the fish in the sea inform you. Which of all these does not know that the hand of the LORD has done this? In his hand is the life of every creature and the breath of all mankind.

JOB 12:7-10 (NIV)

If we but knew the secret of that power
That opes the bud in early days of spring,
If we but knew what makes the robin sing
His wondrous song just at the matin
    hour,
If we but knew the priceless boon and
    dower
Of human life when man is truly king.
If we but understood the little thing
That vexes us just at the present hour,

If we but knew—ah, well, 'tis vain to sigh
And speculate on things beyond our ken!
We know that earth is fair and life is
    sweet,
And something tells us that we cannot
    die.
And if we live and love the good, ah! then
We face to face with truth some day
    must meet.

—CLARENCE HAWKES.

O Lord, we thank You for a day so sweet and fair as this, when the trees lift up their hands in a psalm of gratitude to You, and every little flower that opens its cup and every wandering bird seem filled by Your spirit, and grateful to You. We thank You for all your handwritings of revelation on the walls of the world, on the heavens above us and the ground beneath, and all the testimonies recorded there of Your presence, Your power, Your justice, and Your love. Amen. —THEODORE PARKER.

April 5

For we are co-workers in God's service; you are God's field, God's building.

1 CORINTHIANS 3:9 (NIV)

Yet we must give the children leave to use
Our garden tools, though they spoil tool and plant
In learning. So the Master may not scorn
Our awkwardness, as with these bungling hands
We try to unroot the ill, and plant with good
Life's barren soil: the child is learning use.
Perhaps the angels even are forbid
To laugh at us, or may not care to laugh,
With kind eyes pitying our little hurts.

—EDWARD ROWLAND SILL.

Our Father: You know how unskilled are these hands and hearts of ours. You know how much that we do, think, and speak often tends to retard the progress of that which we would promote. Give us, then, this day that wisdom which is from above, that no touch of our hand may mar the beauty of one of Your creations: no thought nor word wrong one of Your creatures. Help us to know that we are workers with God, and in this knowledge may we strive for that excellence of service that shall hasten the coming of that kingdom of peace, joy and righteousness which is life eternal. Amen. —FLORENCE KOLLOCK CROOKER.

April 6

Come near to God and he will come near to you.

JAMES 4:8a (NIV)

Plant flowers in the soul's front yard,
Set out new shade and blossom trees,
An' let the soul once froze an' hard,
Sprout crocuses of new idees.

Yes, clean yer house, an' clean yer shed,
An' clean yer barn in ev'ry part;
But brush the cobwebs from yer head,
An' sweep the snow banks from yer heart.

—SAM WALTER FOSS.

Gracious Father, help us gratefully to begin this day with You. We expect the day to bring its accustomed routine of cares and duties, and its round of petty irritations, but we confidently believe that You will help us in all our experiences. Let this morning's freshness, hope and vigor be ours through the whole day. Help us to put faith in the place of fear that all our efforts may be crowned with the success of helpfulness. May we go blithely about our business with kind words and cheerful faces that our day's work may be our day's worship. Amen. —AUGUSTUS B. CHURCH.

April 7

Though you have not seen him, you love him; and even though you do not see him now, you believe in him and are filled with an inexpressible and glorious joy, for you are receiving the end result of your faith, the salvation of your souls.

1 PETER 1:8-9 (NIV)

Ye seek for happiness—alas the day!
Ye find it not in luxury nor in gold,
Not in the fame nor in the envied sway,
For which O willing slaves to custom old,
Severe taskmistress, ye your hearts have sold.
Ye seek for peace, and, when ye die, to dream
No evil dreams; all mortal things are cold
And senseless then; if aught survive, I deem
It must be love and joy, for they immortal seem.

—SHELLEY.

O Eternal God who has given us life, help us to love Your will and to walk in Your way this day. If flowers chance to grow beside our path we would pluck them, but most of all would we rejoice in You alone, knowing that in Your will is perfect peace. Fill our souls with Your joy and strengthen us in the spirit of self-forgetfulness to spill it out into the lives of others. Give us hearts "roomy, radiant, and full of laughter," learned of "Jesus Christ, whom not having seen we love; on whom though now we see Him not, yet believing, we rejoice greatly with joy unspeakable and full of glory, receiving the end of our faith, even the salvation of our souls." Amen.   —WALTER HEALY.

April 8

> Whenever I bring clouds over the earth and the rainbow appears in the clouds, I will remember my covenant between me and you and all living creatures of every kind.
>
> GENESIS 9:14-15a (NIV)

A gush of bird song, a patter of dew,
A cloud and a rainbow's warning,
Suddenly sunshine and perfect blue—
An April day in the morning.
—HARRIET P. SPOFFORD.

There is something in the air
That's new and sweet and rare—
There's something too that's new,
In the color of the blue
That's in the morning sky,
Before the sun is high.
—NORA PERRY.

Infinite and Holy One, be with us in the beauty of this new day. May the dewy sweetness of the dawn You have given to us be regarded as a token of Your love for Your children. As an atmosphere of joy and peace may be the thought of Your consolation and Your care. The delicate tints of Your sky arching over us may we compare to the blue of a constancy that is divine, and which is freely shown to even the humblest and more erring of Your flock. Bless us and guide us on our pilgrim way, and inspire our hearts and our hands to perform well their daily task. In His name do we ask it. Amen.
—EDMUND Q. S. OSGOOD.

April 9

The voice of the Lord echoes above the sea.

The God of glory thunders.

The Lord thunders over the mighty sea.

The voice of the Lord is powerful; the voice of the Lord is majestic.

PSALM 29:3-4 (NLT)

As I have walked in Alabama my morning walk,

I have seen where the she-bird—the mocking-bird sat on her nest in the briers
hatching her brood,

I have seen the he-bird also,

I have paused to hear him near at hand inflating his throat and joyfully singing,

And while I paused it came to me that what he really sang for was not there only,

Nor for his mate nor for himself only, nor

All sent back by the echoes,

But subtle, clandestine, away beyond,

A charge transmitted and gift occult for those being born.

—WALT WHITMAN.

Great Spirit of Life, Our Father, in heaven, and in the earth, with what myriad voices
You do speak to us, sometimes with the voice of thunder and sometimes with the
voice of bird. Even the rocks and hills have their language. With every manifold voice
You tell us that we do not live nor work for a day only. The song and the word and
the work of today have larger relations. They pass over into other days. We pray this
morning that the thoughts we think, the words we speak, and the work we do may
be so true that they may be fit for another day. So may we begin now to realize the
meaning of Eternal Life. Amen. —GEORGE L. PERIN.

April 10

> But for you who fear my name, the Sun of Righteousness will rise with healing in his wings. And you will go free, leaping with joy like calves let out to pasture.
>
> MALACHI 4:2 (NLT)

If the stream had no quiet eddying place, could we so admire its cascade over the rocks? Were there no clouds, could we so hail the sky shining through them in its still calm purity?

The night is mother of the Day
The Winter of the Spring,
And ever upon old Decay
The greenest mosses cling.
Behind the cloud the starlight lurks,
Through showers the sunbeams fall:
For God, who loveth all His works,
Has left His Hope with all!

—JOHN GREENLEAF WHITTIER.

Our Father, with childhood's glowing morning face we would turn to You and be conscious that the brightness of life comes only to those upon whom the sun of righteousness shines with clear light. Full of trust, full of joy, we turn our faces towards the light and take up the labors of life with entire confidence in the Divine care and guidance that blesses the open vision, the faithful hand and the loving heart. We would follow our Master, feeling that we could choose no better way, and content if we be not called to suffer more than He in His life of service and sacrifice, while our hearts praise the giver of spiritual things with unceasing happy songs. Amen.

—RALPH EDWIN HORNE.

April 11

But he said to me, "My grace is sufficient for you, for my power is made perfect in weakness." Therefore I will boast all the more gladly about my weaknesses, so that Christ's power may rest on me. That is why, for Christ's sake, I delight in weaknesses, in insults, in hardships, in persecutions, in difficulties. For when I am weak, then I am strong.   2 CORINTHIANS 12:9-10 (NIV)

> Oh, the little birds sang east, and the little birds sang west,
> And I smiled to think God's greatness flowed around our
>   incompleteness—
> Round our restlessness, his nest.
>
> —ELIZABETH BARRETT BROWNING.

And I saw that there was an Ocean of Darkness and Death; but an infinite Ocean of Light and Love flowed over the Ocean of Darkness; and in that I saw the infinite Love of God.   —GEORGE FOX.

Father of Light, in whom is no darkness at all, to You we lift our longing eyes again. Shine away the darkness of our minds by the light of Your presence. Complete our incompleteness. Bring us out of our restlessness into Your rest. We thank You for our daily gifts—bread to feed the body, strength to sustain the soul, light to guide the feet. Help us to put away the mistakes of the past, remembering them only with the penitence that shall cause You to remember them no more. Help us all through this day to know ourselves surrounded by Your Infinite Love. Amen.

—A. GERTRUDE EARLE.

April 12

Let the message of Christ dwell among you richly as you teach and admonish one another with all wisdom through psalms, hymns, and songs from the Spirit, singing to God with gratitude in your hearts.

COLOSSIANS 3:16 (NIV)

Just as you now play a piece without the music and do not think what notes you strike, though once you picked them out by slow and patient toil, so, if you begin of set purpose, you will learn the law of kindness in utterance so perfectly that it will be second nature to you and make more music in your heart than all the songs the sweetest voice has ever sung. —FRANCIS E. WILLARD.

Father, we rejoice and will be glad all the day that You have made it possible for us and all Your children to learn the sweet song of true life and that You give us so many opportunities for its practice. O Lord, give us patience and kindness toward our fellowmen and trust in You, so that whether the lessons be easy or hard we may take them cheerfully, believing that You give us only that which is best. Grant that we may be earnest and faithful until our souls can sing the highest, purest and sweetest notes, until we are in harmony with All Good. Amen. —ABBIE E. DANFORTH.

April 13

He shielded him and cared for him; he guarded him as the apple of his eye,
  like an eagle that stirs up its nest and hovers over its young,
  that spreads its wings to catch them and carries them aloft.

DEUTERONOMY 32:10b-11 (NIV)

So many little faults we find:
We see them, for not blind
Is love—we see them; but if you and I
Remember them, perhaps, some by and by
They will not be
Faults then, grave faults to you and me,
But just odd ways, mistakes, or even less—
Remembrances to bless.

—GEORGE KLINGLE.

Our dear Father in Heaven: for this day help us to be good. All through the long night You have watched over us. Under Your wing have we been sheltered as the chickens under the wing of the mother. Now that light has come we will help You to keep this world sweet and bright and clean. Help us to be true to this our promise; we resolve to be patient, steadfast, cheerful, kindly, sturdy, and good. Our Father, we need You. We want to walk in You way. Help us, for we are Your children. Amen.

—WILLIAM CHANNING BROWN.

April 14

The man without a purpose is like a ship without a rudder; a waif, a nothing, no man. Have a purpose in life, if it is only to kill and divide and sell oxen well, but have a purpose; and having it, throw such strength of mind and muscle into your work as God has given you.   —THOMAS CARLYLE.

Neither a borrower nor a lender be;   This above all: to thine own self be true
For loan oft loses both itself and friend,   And it must follow, as the night the day,
And borrowing dulls the edge   Thou canst not then be false to any man.
    of husbandry.   —SHAKESPEARE.

Almighty God, at the commencement of this day's work may we look on high, and measure everything we are about to do by the scale of eternity. Keep us from all littleness; may we not be turned aside by things that are insignificant and unworthy. Help us, we beseech You, to make the glory of our life commensurate with the splendors of our privileges. May we live life in a great spirit, realizing that there is no duty so simple, no position so humble, but that we may show forth the grandeur of trust, and obedience toward You. May the great and holy purpose we cherish find its expression as we cooperate with the divine purpose. Amen.   —J. H. BARKER.

_____

_____

_____

_____

_____

_____

April 15

Every good and perfect gift is from above, coming down from the Father of the heavenly lights, who does not change like shifting shadows.

JAMES 1:17 (NIV)

> 'Twas one of those charmed days
> When the genius of God doth flow,
> The wind may alter twenty ways,
> A tempest cannot blow;
> It may blow north, it still is warm;
> Or south, it still is clear;
> Or east, it smells like a clover farm;
> Or west, no thunder fear.

—RALPH WALDO EMERSON.

Father of Lights, from whom comes every good and perfect gift, we thank You for the morning and for the sunshine. We rejoice in the light, but when it is hidden from us, we are thankful that in the upper air above our clouded morning it still fills Your heavens. You gave us good things while we slept, and now, refreshed by Your Spirit, may we go forth to our appointed tasks with cheerful obedience and joyful expectation. If trial and trouble await us, or if, in the heat of the day the burden seems too great, may we still be comforted, because we put our trust in You. Amen.

—GEORGE BATCHELOR.

April 16

But spring-wind,
  like a dancing psaltress, passes
Over its breast, to waken it, rare verdure
Buds tenderly upon rough banks between
The withered tree-roots
  and the cracks of frost,
Like a smile striving with a wrinkled face;
The grass grows bright,
  the boughs are swol'n with blooms
Like chrysalids impatient for the air,
The shining dors are busy, beetles run
Along the furrows; ants make their ado;
Above, birds fly in merry flocks, the lark
Soars up and up, shivering for very joy;
Afar the ocean sleeps; white fishing gulls
Flit where the sand is purple
  with its tribe
Of nested limpits; savage creatures seek
Their loves in wood and plain—
  and God renews
His ancient rapture.

—ROBERT BROWNING.

O Lord, who gives to mankind liberally, and upbraids not, we thank You for the blessings You bestow from day to day. We thank You for this material world, now clad in its garment of Northern beauty, for the great sun which all day pours down his light upon the waiting and the grateful world, and for the earth underneath our feet. We bless You for the grass, bread for the cattle, its harvest of use spread everywhere, and for the various beauty which here and there spangles all useful things which Your eye looks down upon. May we use this world of matter to build up the being that we are to a nobler stature of strength and of beauty. Amen.   —THEODORE PARKER.

April 17

Sing to the Lord a new song;
sing to the Lord, all the earth.
Sing to the Lord, praise his name;
proclaim his salvation day after day.

PSALM 96:1–2 (NIV)

O brothers all! Come near
And hear
A bird's
Melodious dreaming set to words,
    and flung
The spring's new leaves
    and tender buds among,
For very joy of life, and hope, and love
In a world made broad enough
For all God's creatures to be merry in,
With joyous clash and din,
And yet too small
For any greed at all!
Lo! Deep and sure
Is cut this truth in heaven's book of gold:
Out of one mother in the garden old
Were born the rich and poor.

—MAURICE THOMPSON.

Our Father, may we begin this day with a song in our hearts—a song as rich and full and free as the bird sings at the earliest dawning of the sun's light—a song so attuned with infinite life and hope and love that it must be sung. Giver of abundance unto the rich and poor alike, help our souls to mount unto the highest reaches of living thoughts and generous deeds, that we may give unto others as You give. Unfettered by unholy passions and freed from the spirit of greed, may we feel the unity of the bonds of a universal brotherhood, and be just and true, honest, and helpful in all our dealings with all men this day. Amen.

—HENRIETTA G. MOORE.

April 18

Long ago you laid the foundation of the earth
  and made the heavens with your hands.
They will perish, but you remain forever; they will wear out like old clothing.
You will change them like a garment and discard them.
But you are always the same; you will live forever.   PSALM 102:25-27 (NLT)

O spring, of hope and love and youth and gladness
Wing-winged emblem! Brightest, best and fairest!
Whence comest thou when with dark Winter's sadness
The tears that fade in sunny smiles thou sharest?
Sister of Joy! Thou art the child who wearest
Thy mother's dying smile, tender and sweet:
Thy mother Autumn, for whose grave thou bearest
Fresh flowers, and beams like flowers,
Disturbing not the leaves which are her winding-sheet.

—SHELLEY.

God unchanging, and still the creator of the seasons, we look up to You, as the spring-tide works out the miracle of the resurrection from the sleeping forms of the past season, in confidence and in trust that ever You will bless us with a nobler, holier, sweeter, more wholesome life, as the seasons come and go. The resources of trusting hearts are always reinforced and reinvigorated by contact with Your life, Your power, Your goodness and Your love. Out of the winter of our discontent, we enter the springtime of love, that leads us forward in confidence through the glad summer of growth to the soul's fruition and the place of rest and peace in our Father's Home beneath Your everlasting Love. Amen.   —FRANCIS A. GRAY.

April 19

His master replied, "Well done, good and faithful servant! You have been faithful with a few things; I will put you in charge of many things. Come and share your master's happiness!"   MATTHEW 25:21 (NIV)

One sound always comes to the ear that is open; it is the steady drum-beat of Duty. No music in it, perhaps—only a dry rub-a-dub. Ah, but that steady beat marks the time for the whole orchestra of earth and heaven! It says to you: "Do your work—do the duty nearest you!" Keep step to that drum-beat, and the dullest march is taking you home.   —GEORGE S. MERRIAM.

O great impelling Spirit, whom we see manifest in all the world, as we open our eyes to the light of another morning, may we be as responsive to Your influence as the sun and the flowers which brighten our way. May we be very sensitive to Your promptings as we go about our day's work. May we be very quick to do the things You would have us do. May we give ourselves to Your service without reserve. When again the night shades draw about us, may our hearts be filled with deepest gratitude for all the experiences of the day, and, deep within, may our spirits be conscious of Your approving benediction, "Well done, good and faithful servant; enter You into the joy of Thy Lord." Amen.   —FRANK LINCOLN MASSECK.

April 20

Each of you should use whatever gift you have received to serve others, as faithful stewards of God's grace in its various forms.

1 PETER 4:10 (NIV)

Thyself and thy belongings
Are not thine own so proper as to waste
Thyself upon thy virtues, they on thee.
Heaven doth with us as we with
   torches do
Not light them for themselves;
   for if our virtues
Did not go forth of us, 'twere all alike
As if we had them not. Spirits are not
   finely touched
But to fine issues, nor Nature never lends
The smallest scruple of her excellence
But like a thrifty goddess, she
   determines
Herself the glory of a creditor,
Both thanks and use.

—SHAKESPEARE.

Father, with faith and confidence in You we begin the day's duties, with a blithe song upon our lips, expressing the melody of our souls, thanking You for opportunities for work, and thought and love. We ask not for more blessings but to be more worthy of those we have, using and not abusing them. May our minds be open to Your truth, and hearts to Your love, and when received may we be almoners of both to the waiting world. May we keep by giving Your love abundantly, and grow through the glory of self-sacrifice. Give us the heart, O God, to sanctify our work and to lift it above drudgery into the divinest service, and give us strength to perform it. Amen.

—U. S. MILBURN.

April 21

Therefore, my dear brothers and sisters, stand firm. Let nothing move you. Always give yourselves fully to the work of the Lord, because you know that your labor in the Lord is not in vain.   1 CORINTHIANS 15:58 (NIV)

A man is simple where his chief care is the wish to be what he ought to be; that is honestly and naturally human. We may compare existence to raw material. What it is matters less than what it is made of; as the value of a work of art lies in the flowering of a workman's skill. True life is possible in social conditions the most diverse and with natural gifts the most unequal. It is not fortune or personal advantage, but our training them to account, that constitutes the value of life. Fame adds no more than does length of days; quality is the thing.   —CHARLES WAGNER.

Heavenly Father, our eyes are ever toward You. We do not pray for the things of the world. Teach us to walk in Your truth. Though our days be few, may our lives be hopeful and cheerful. Though our bodies be frail, may we be invincible in spirit. All Your children are immortal, but it is for us to attain the eternal life. May we know You through Jesus. Then days and hours and minutes will disappear in the liberty and glory and peace of the life eternal. Then poverty of worldly goods will be forgotten in the riches of the Spirit. Then the cares of the world that now is will be lost in the joy of the life that is to be. Amen.   —REIGNOLD K. MARVIN.

April 22

A little sun, a little rain,
A soft wind blowing from the west—
And woods and fields are sweet again
And warmth within the mountain's breast.

So simple is the earth we tread,
So quick with love and life her frame,
Ten thousand years have dawned and fled.
And still her magic is the same.

—STOPFORD A. BROOKE.

Gracious God, we thank You for the gift of sight whereby we behold the marvels of the outer world. But greater is our gratitude for the inner sight, the power to see things as they ought to be. If we but look deep enough, we find Your central laws ever at the heart of all life. With such insight, apparent confusion shall not bewilder us, life's cares shall not harden us, the world's show cannot dazzle us. Give us, we pray, unceasing ability to wonder and admire, which brings perpetual youth; to hope, to believe, to trust; to rest content in working with You, the Eternal One, Lord of the seasons, this is our heart's desire. Amen.   —EDWARD A. HORTON.

April 23

Two people are better off than one, for they can help each other succeed.
If one person falls, the other can reach out and help.
But someone who falls alone is in real trouble.

ECCLESIASTES 4:9–10 (NLT)

"What is the secret of your life?" asked Mrs. Browning of Charles Kingsley; "tell me, that I may make mine beautiful too."

He replied, "I had a friend."

Somewhere in her "Middlemarch," George Eliot puts it well: "There are natures in which, if they love us, we are conscious of having a sort of baptism and consecration; they bind us over to rectitude and purity by their pure belief about us; and our sins become the worst kind of sacrilege, which tears down the invisible altar of trust."

—WILLIAM C. GANNETT.

Our Heavenly Father, we thank You for all the sweet and sacred influences of life. Music comes with its invisible fingers to weave a magic charm around our souls—the home with its love is ours—but we thank You today for the sweet and saving influence of friendship—for the counsel and fellowship of those who are wise and good and faithful to us. We would not walk alone—we would find strength in the strength of others, and faith in other's faith. Let us cherish such fellowships and give back to those, who love us, love again. Amen.

—GEORGE L. PERIN.

April 24

Rejoice always, pray continually, give thanks in all circumstances; for this is God's will for you in Christ Jesus.

1 THESSALONIANS 5:16–18 (NIV)

Live in the sunshine,
   don't live in the gloom,
Carry some gladness
   the world to illume.
Live in the brightness,
   and take this to heart;
The world will seem gayer
   if you'll do your part.
Live on the housetop,
   not down in the cell;
Open air Christians live nobly and well.

Live where the joys are,
   and, scorning defeat,
Have a good-morrow
   for all whom you meet.
Live as a victor, and triumphing go
Through this queer world,
   beating down every foe.
Live in the sunshine,
   God meant it for you!
Live as the robins,
   and sing the day through.

—MARGARET SANGSTER.

O God, our heavenly Father, who gives us the sunshine of this new day, who is the God of life and light, we ask Your help and Your strength as we again go out to our separate duties and cares. Help us to fill this day with good deeds, to give cheer and comfort to all we meet. May our lips be clean. May our hearts be pure. And when the evening time comes, may it find us conscious that we have put no cloud upon the day, that we have walked through its hours true disciples of the Master who went about doing good. Amen.

—WILLIAM H. MORRISON.

April 25

Jesus replied: "'Love the Lord your God with all your heart and with all your soul and with all your mind.' This is the first and greatest commandment. And the second is like it: 'Love your neighbor as yourself.'" MATTHEW 22:37–39 (NIV)

To weigh the material in the scales of the personal, and measure life by the standard of love; to prize health as contagious happiness, wealth as potential service, reputation as latent influence, learning for the light it can shed, power for the help it can give, station for the good it can do—to choose in each case what is best on the whole, and accept cheerfully incidental evils involved; to put my whole self into all that I do, and indulge no single desire at the expense of myself as a whole; to crowd out fear by devotion to duty, and see present and future as one; to treat others as I would be treated, and myself as I would my best friend; and to recognize God's coming kingdom in every institution and person that helps men to love one another.

—WILLIAM DEWITT HYDE.

For the dear love that kept us
   through the night,
And gave our senses
   to sleep's gentle sway,
For the new miracle of dawning light,
Flushing the east with prophecies of day,
We thank Thee, O, our God!
For the fresh life that through
   our being flows,
With its full tide to strengthen
   and to bless,
For calm, sweet thoughts,
   upspringing from repose,

To bear to Thee their song
   of thankfulness,
We praise Thee, O, our God!
Thou knowest our needs,
   Thy fulness will supply
Our blindness—
   let Thy hand still lead us on,
Till, visited by the dayspring
   from on high,
Our prayer, one only,
   "Let Thy will be done,"
We breathe to Thee, O, God!
Amen.

—W. H. BURLEIGH.

April 26

Is it not possible, then, that the hindrances which arrest our progress, and the obstacles that lie broadly in our path, are the divinest agents of help which our Creator could give us? The painful struggles to overcome and remove them develop in us strength, courage, self-reliance, and heroism. They are the hammer and chisel that release the statue from the imprisoning marble—the plow and the harrow that break up the soil, and mellow it for the reception of the seed that shall yield an abundant harvest. Perfection lies that way.   —MARY A. LIVERMORE.

We seek Your face anew this day, O our Father, and ask that You will help us to live our lives in constant communion with You. Let us see You at every turn in the way. Let us find Your hand in all our duties, all our meditations, all our intercourse with men, all our doings and all our deeds. Help us to make You our counsellor every hour. Help us to undertake nought without Your blessings, to finish nought without Your benediction. Morning and evening may we turn in prayer to Your throne. At every meal may we seek Your grace and give You thanks. So may we find the blessing of them that abide in Your house. Amen.   —J. COLEMAN ADAMS.

April 27

For it is God who works in you to will and to act in order to
fulfill his good purpose.   PHILIPPIANS 2:13 (NIV)

I think the sweetest thought, the very central idea, of the revelation of the character
of God to me, is this: that He does everything out of His supreme will. There is no one
thing that I can say with more heartiness, or that has in it more echoes of joy, than
"Thy will be done." If anything works righteousness in me or in you, it is God. The
nature of God is fruitful in generosity. He is so good that He loves to do good, and
loves to make men good, and loves to make them happy by making them good. He
loves to be patient with them, and to wait for them, and to pour benevolence upon
them, because that is His nature.   —HENRY WARD BEECHER.

Father, we thank You for the blessing. We know what are our privileges, we know
what are our duties, and we are before You again to consecrate this day in all its glory
and beauty to You, the Father of perfect Love. You will be with us as we strive to be
with You. You will make us strong when we are weak. You will make us see where we
are in darkness. You will send us forth on Your infinite mission to the world. Boys or
girls, men or women, here we are, the living children of the living God, sent forward
by You to proclaim it that all may be one as Christ Jesus with You and You with Him,
that this world may be perfected into one, that men may know that You are Father
and what the Father has given us to do, that each one of us may lift up what has fallen
down, that each one may open the eyes that are blind and the ears that are deaf, that
each one of us may proclaim the gospel of Your perfect love. This is our prayer and
our hope, in Christ Jesus. Amen.   —EDWARD EVERETT HALE.

April 28

Brothers and sisters, I do not consider myself yet to have taken hold of it. But one thing I do: Forgetting what is behind and straining toward what is ahead, I press on toward the goal to win the prize for which God has called me heavenward in Christ Jesus.   PHILIPPIANS 3:13–14 (NIV)

With every rising of the sun,
Think of your life as just begun.

The past has shrived and buried deep,
All yesterdays; there let them sleep.

Nor seek to summon back one ghost
Of that innumerable host.

Concern yourself with but today.
Woo it, and teach it to obey

Your will and wish. Since time began
Today has been the friend of man;

But in his blindness and his sorrow,
He looks to yesterday and tomorrow.

You, and today! a soul sublime,
And the great pregnant hour of time,

With God himself to bind the twain!
Go forth, I say, attain, attain!
—ELLA WHEELER WILCOX.

Infinitely wise and loving Father, our minds and hearts reach out to You in this morning hour thankful that the rest of the night has prepared us for the work of the new day, and that the light brings the call to service. The past cannot be recalled, but today is ours. I and today, with God and in the Spirit of Jesus! Priceless privilege! Grant us, O Father, to use it for You, for humanity and in His name. Amen.

—SAMUEL GILBERT AYERS.

April 29

I will give you a new heart and put a new spirit in you;
I will remove from you your heart of stone and give you a heart of flesh.

EZEKIEL 36:26 (NIV)

Life is full of new beginnings. Some change may come, something is sure to come, to close one chapter and begin another. Life is planned just so... that there should be a break from former link and habit, often from imperfection and mistake, and a clear, clean start for the fulfilment of the best one has grown to, even in desire, unhampered by the poorest one has ever happened to be, or to get credit for.

—MRS. A. D. T. WHITNEY.

O, You who dwellest in the light, help Your children this morning to see the light of Your truth and feel the warmth of Your love. We thank You for the open doors of opportunity for helpful service; for the exhibition of kindness and for growth in the kingdom of Heaven. May we clearly see the way to the Eternal life and have strength to walk therein. May we so welcome Your truth that we shall be free from error and sin. May Your wisdom so guide our energies that we shall reach after greater perfection. May the evening of this day find us more in harmony with God than we now are. And may the evening of life find us rich in the treasures of heaven. Amen.

—ANDREW WILLSON.

April 30

Do not merely listen to the word, and so deceive yourselves.
Do what it says.   JAMES 1:22 (NIV)

True worth is in being, not seeming;
In doing each day that goes by,
Some little good—not in the dreaming
Of great things to do by and by,
For whatever men say in blindness,
And spite of the fancies of youth,
There's nothing so kingly as kindness,
And nothing so royal as truth.

We get back our mete as we measure:
We cannot do wrong and feel right;
Nor can we give pain and gain pleasure,
For justice avenges each slight.
The air for the wing of the sparrow,
The bush for the robin and wren,
But always the path that is narrow
And straight for the children of men.

—ALICE CARY.

Almighty Father, who with every morning does give us a new day and with each day some fresh duty, mercifully equip us for every task that awaits us! Give us eyes to see, and hearts to love the truth and right, and the disposition that makes every duty a delight, and the doing of good to others a sacred privilege. Save us this day from angry passions and low desires. Forgive us when we are selfish; recall us when we go astray; save us from wronging ourselves by thinking ill of others, and in all places and to all people give us the mind which was in Christ Jesus. Amen.

—JOHN CUCKSON.

May 1

O Lord, what a variety of things you have made!
   In wisdom you have made them all.
   The earth is full of your creatures.
   Here is the ocean, vast and wide, teeming with life of every kind,
      both large and small.   PSALM 104:24–25 (NIV)

To the Woods—Whoso goeth in your paths readeth the same cheerful lesson, whether he be a young child or a hundred years old, comes he in good fortune or in bad, ye say the same things, and from age to age. Ever the needles of the pine grow and fall, the acorns on the oak, the maples redden in autumn and at all times of the year the ground pine and the pyrola bud and root under foot. What is called fortune and what is called time by men, ye know them not. Men have not language to describe one moment of your life.   —RALPH WALDO EMERSON.

O God of Nature and of the human heart, we thank You for our human relations, but we thank You also for our kinship with the birds. We thank You for that instinct which makes us to sympathize with the mating of the bird lovers and for that music of the heart which makes us to love the song of the birds. We pray this morning for a life so simple and natural that we shall be able to enter into sympathetic relations with everything that lives—the flowers of the garden, and the field—the bees that sip the flowers' honey, and the bird that makes her nest among the trees. If You speak to men in the glory of the heavens, You speak also in the manifold voices of all Your loving creatures. May our ears be trained to hear You when You speak. Amen.

                    —GEORGE L. PERIN.

May 2

> The grasslands of the wilderness become a lush pasture,
> and the hillsides blossom with joy.
>
> PSALM 65:12 (NLT)

Hail bounteous May, that doth inspire
Mirth and youth, and warm desire;
Woods and groves are of thy dressing,
Hill and dale doth boast thy blessing,
Thus we salute thee with our early song,
And welcome thee and wish thee long.

—JOHN MILTON.

Almighty and All-loving Father, who makes all the earth to rejoice in the brightness of returning springtime, fill our hearts with like joy and renewal. Graciously awaken in us the life that the cold or care or trouble or sorrow of the world often has caused to fade and go out. As our eyes behold all this outward beauty and glory, give unto us that spiritual vision by which we behold the beauty and glory of divine things. Then when the springtime of our life passes with the summer and the summer ripens into the autumn, and our work is done, may we bring unto You the harvest of spiritual riches. Amen. —JAMES DENORMANDIE.

May 3

Fight the good fight for the true faith. Hold tightly to the eternal life to which God has called you, which you have declared so well before many witnesses.

1 TIMOTHY 6:12 (NLT)

Success!
It is won by a patient endeavor,
Energy's fire,
and the flame-glow of Will;
By grasping the chance with a
"Now, now or never!"
Urging on, on!
While the laggard stands still.

Success!
It is facing life's trials, undaunted;
Fighting the present—
forgetting the past:

By trusting to Fate,
though for years she has taunted,
And bearing Time's scars;
facing front, to the last!

Success! Would you win it
and wear its bright token?
Smile and step out to the drummer's
light lilt;
Fight on till the last inch of sword-blade
is broken.
Then do not say die.
Fight on with the hilt!

—MARY MARKWELL.

We thank You, Our Father, that You have enriched our being with those faculties which prompt to noble endeavor. We rejoice in our power, guided by Your free Spirit, both to overcome evil and to do good. Help us, dear Father, to recognize the great incentives of conscience and of duty, assured that in cheerful conformity thereto we shall find the sweetest zest of life. Increase our faith in You, O Lord. Enable us more clearly to realize that in the end truth and right will gain the victory. Thus may we be inspired to live brave, true and wholesome lives. May we fight the good fight of faith and win the crown of life promised to all those who follow the conquering Christ. In His name. Amen.

—HENRY W. RUGG.

May 4

The green grass is bowing;
The morning wind is in it;
'Tis a tune worth the knowing,
Though it change every minute.
'Tis a tune of the Spring;
Every year plays it over.
—RALPH WALDO EMERSON.

God does not send strange flowers
    every year.
When the spring winds blow
    o'er the pleasant places
The same dear things lift up
    the same fair faces.
The violet is here.
—MRS. A. D. T. WHITNEY.

O God, Father Almighty, who brings light out of darkness and at whose word night yields to day, we offer You glad worship and praise. We thank You for Your gifts which are beautiful and good; for flowers which renew old friendships and awaken new affections; for songs in which voices of all yesterdays sound through today's melodies; for rich memories of the past; for the joy of living now; for the hope of better days; for new expressions of abiding truth and fresh breathings of eternal love; for courage to do right and for confidence in righteousness. May we this day, mindful of earthly duty and of heavenly promise, humbly follow Him "who went about doing good" and "gave Himself a ransom for many." Amen. —W. I. WARD.

May 5

Love the Lord your God with all your heart and
with all your soul and with all your strength.

DEUTERONOMY 6:5 (NIV)

Bishop Brooks taught me no special creed or dogma; but he impressed upon my mind two great ideas—the fatherhood of God and the brotherhood of man, and made me feel that these truths underlie all creeds and forms of worship. God is love, God is our Father, we are His children; therefore the darkest clouds will break, and though right be worsted, wrong shall not triumph. He said: "There is one universal religion, Helen—the religion of love. Love your Heavenly Father with your whole heart and soul, love every child of God as much as ever you can, and remember that the possibilities of good are greater than the possibilities of evil; and you have the key to Heaven."   —HELEN KELLER.

Infinite Spirit! We shall not look upon You as a friend looks upon the face of his friend, but may we learn to see You in every form of life and beauty and service here in this great world of Nature and of Man. May we discover You in the midst of common things and then they shall no more be common, but all things shall be sacred and divine. May we see Your face in all human faces, clasp Your hand in all human hands, and when we have walked with a friend, or talked with those we love, may it be as a walk with You and a communion with You. May we not think of You as afar off but always near, making all things holy. May we realize that it is a diviner thing to serve the lowly who need our help than to praise the Infinite who needeth not. May the sense of Your presence in all things be the inspiration and interpretation of all days for us. Amen.   —E. L. REXFORD.

May 6

God saw all that he had made,
and it was very good.

GENESIS 1:31a (NIV)

The brown, brown woods of March
Are the green, green woods of May,
And they lift their arms with a freer swing
And shake out their pennons gay.
And the brown, dead world of March,
Is the living world of today;
Life throbs and flushes and flashes out
In the color and fragrance of May.

—ANONYMOUS.

Infinite Spirit of the winter and the summer and of the night and the morning, You have watched over and guarded, during its winter sleep and rest, this earth which You have made, and which You have made for a purpose—to be beautiful and fruitful in its season, to be a humble and obedient servant of Your will of goodness. And now, as the woods of May are radiant in the beauty of springtime, and ready to do Your will; so as we wake to the opportunity of this new day, may we rejoice in the privilege of living to You and doing Your will in the glad service of lives lived as the Master lived. Amen.   —GEORGE WALLACE PENNIMAN.

May 7

For we are not fighting against flesh-and-blood enemies, but against evil rulers and authorities of the unseen world, against mighty powers in this dark world, and against evil spirits in the heavenly places. Therefore, put on every piece of God's armor so you will be able to resist the enemy in the time of evil. Then after the battle you will still be standing firm.   EPHESIANS 6:12–13 (NLT)

> One who never turned his back, but marched breast forward,
> Never doubted clouds would break,
> Never dreamed, though right were worsted—wrong would triumph,
> Held we fall to rise, are baffled to fight better,
> Sleep to wake.
>
> —ROBERT BROWNING.

Our Father, in the heaven, we thank You for the birth of a new day. May we be full of gladness during its golden hours, may our hearts be tranquil with God's peace. A day is a part of Your eternity. You have set us in the battle, You are watching us in the fight; You are training us by well-accepted controversy. May nothing of Your purpose be lost because of the blinding details of the conflict. Strengthen our hearts to do the work of this day. Help us to be as grateful as we are dependent upon God. Inspire our whole life; help us quickly to learn why we are here, what we are to do while here, and the path that leads home when the work-day is over. In the name of the Christ! Amen.   —W. A. WOOD.

May 8

Then sing, ye birds, sing, sing a joyous song!
And let the young lambs bound
As to the tabor's sound!
We in thought will join your throng,
Ye that pipe and ye that play,
Ye that through your hearts today
Feel the gladness of the May!

—WILLIAM WORDSWORTH.

God of the morning, Father of the Soul, we bless You for the light, for it is pleasant to behold the world made beautiful by the King of day, and sweet with the melody of the song of bird, and cheerful with the promise of hope in the swelling buds of spring. We join with Your faithful ones in ascriptions of praise to You for the depth of the riches both of the wisdom and the knowledge of God. Help us to look upon our every faculty of soul, and power of body, as gifts from You, to be used for the advancement of love, truth and beauty, in our own hearts, and in the world. Give us Your own help to bear every burden cheerfully, to stand erect before every responsibility, and if in our efforts to do much good for this day we seem to fail, may we look to Jesus and learn of Him that in a conscience void of offence there is no such thing as failure. Help us to strive with the evil of the world and sin not, that at the close of the day we may look back and say, we have kept ourselves unspotted from the world. Amen.   —L. L. GREENE.

May 9

And why worry about your clothing? Look at the lilies of the field and how they grow. They don't work or make their clothing, yet Solomon in all his glory was not dressed as beautifully as they are. And if God cares so wonderfully for wildflowers that are here today and thrown into the fire tomorrow, he will certainly care for you. Why do you have so little faith?   MATTHEW 6:28-30 (NLT)

> Fairer grows the earth each morning
> To the eyes that watch aright;
> Every dew-drop sparkles warning
> Of a miracle in sight;
> Of some unexpected glory
> Waiting in the old and plain;
> Poet's dream nor traveller's story
> Words such wonders as remain.
>
> —WILLIAM C. GANNETT.

O God, who makes things seen and temporal quiver and flash with Your own informing spirit, so illumine our pathways that the Luz where we meet our duties may become the Bethel where we meet our God. As You clothe the lily with beauty and inspire the bird with song help us to grow into the beauty of holiness, and to know the joy of Your salvation. Whatever our past, open our eyes this day to some better thing which You always have in reserve. Teach us what hinders our attainment and help us burst through the barrier. Make us so conscious of Your indwelling spirit that we may yield to its gracious impellings toward righteousness and peace and joy. Amen.   —THOMAS D. ANDERSON.

May 10

God arms me with strength,
and he makes my way perfect.
He makes me as surefooted as a deer,
enabling me to stand on mountain heights.

PSALM 18:32–33 (NLT)

Listen to the exhortation of the dawn!

Look to this day!
For it is life, the very life of life.
In its brief course lie all the
Varieties and realities of your existence;
The bliss of growth,
The glory of action,
The splendor of beauty:

For yesterday is but a dream,
And tomorrow is only a vision,
But today well-lived makes
Every yesterday a dream of happiness,
And every tomorrow a vision of hope.
Look well, therefore to this day!

Such is the salutation of the dawn.

—FROM THE SANSKRIT.

Dear God, in Your loving kindness, You have brought us to the opening of another day; from darkness to light, from sleep to wakefulness, from rest to labor. We thank You for its opening glory and its coming opportunities; but above all, for the new strength we feel within ourselves to do its work and live its life. As radiant dawn climbs to full-orbed day and glides to setting sun, may we come to this day's close with the consciousness that we have lived a little closer to the great heart of the Eternal in every thought, word and deed, that we have woven into the texture of our lives, and gently as twilight enfolds the fruitful earth, shall "peace that passes understanding" enfold our souls. Amen.   —THOMAS B. PAYNE.

May 11

> Consider it pure joy, my brothers and sisters, whenever you face trials of many kinds, because you know that the testing of your faith produces perseverance. Let perseverance finish its work so that you may be mature and complete, not lacking anything.　　　　　　　　　　　　　JAMES 1:2–4 (NIV)

As the insect from the rock
Takes the color of its wing;
As the boulder from the shock
Of the ocean's rhythmic swing
Makes itself a perfect form,
Learns a calmer front to raise;
As the shell, enameled warm
With the prism's mystic rays,
Praises wind and wave that make
All its chambers fair and strong;

As the mighty poets take
Grief and pain to build their song;
Even so for every soul,
Whatsoe'er its lot may be—
Building, as the heavens roll,
Something large and strong and free—
Things that hurt and things that mar
Shape the man for perfect praise;
Shock and strain and ruin are
Friendlier than the smiling days.

—JOHN WHITE CHADWICK.

Dear Father, as the light of this morning follows the darkness of the night, may we devoutly believe that the light of Your love shall dispel all darkness and bring us into the morning of eternal peace. May we learn each day that our trials and sorrows are but stepping-stones in Your divine economy, to bring us up into the clearer atmosphere of heavenly thought and life. Help us to live closer to Jesus, to understand how even He was made glorious through suffering, and ever learn to conquer in His name. Amen. 　　　　　　　　　　　　—ELMER F. PEMBER.

May 12

God places the lonely in families;
  he sets the prisoners free and gives them joy.
But he makes the rebellious live in a sun-scorched land.

PSALM 68:6 (NLT)

I live for those that love me
For those that know me true,
For the heaven that smiles above me,
And waits my coming, too;

For the cause that lacks assistance,
For the wrongs that need resistance,
For the future in the distance,
For the good that I can do.

—G. L. BANKS.

Father, we bless You for such as love us and those whom we love in the varying forms of affection, thanking You for the sacramental cup of joy in which You give the wine of life to all of Your children, humble or high. We thank You for that love which sets the solitary in families at the beginning, and then reaches wide arms all around, and will not stay its hold till it joins all nations and kindreds and tongues and people into one great family of love. We bless You for the noble men and women whose generous heart has lit the altar fire of philanthropy in many a dark and else benighted place. We thank You for the unbidden faith which springs up in our hearts, impelling us to trust You and love You and keep every commandment of Yours, and that while we know not what a day shall bring forth, we are sure of everlasting life. Amen.

—THEODORE PARKER.

May 13

> The faithful love of the Lord never ends!
>
> His mercies never cease.
>
> Great is his faithfulness;
>
> his mercies begin afresh each morning.
>
> LAMENTATIONS 3:22–23 (NLT)

Gladness of morning—
To hear the lark begin his flight,
And singing, startle the dull Night
From his watch-tower in the skies,
Till the dappled Dawn doth rise;

Then to come in spite of sorrow,
And at my window bid good-morrow
Through the sweetbrier, or the vine,
Or the twisted eglantine.

—JOHN MILTON.

O God, in whose light we see light, who has lifted the shadows of night from our dwellings, complete now in our behalf Your ministry of light, we beseech You, and let the day star arise in our hearts. Make clear You face unto us. Rise with Your morning upon our souls. May the light which envelops us throughout the day be the radiance of Your presence. May our eyes behold only what You reveal and our lives be warmed with the glow of Your love. O, that we may be new-born like the day and live a new life in Your mercies which are new every morning; that our love may rise fresh as the dawn and our obedience be as sure as the path of the law. Let no shadow from the past dim the joy of Your presence. Scatter the darkness of sense and self within us. As the morning reveals, interprets and fulfils the beauties of a world which was wrapped in night, may the mystery of our lives unfold, our latent forces be summoned to service, and our hearts find fulness of joy because we live in You. Amen.

—EVERETT D. BURR.

May 14

> May the favor of the Lord our God rest on us;
>
> establish the work of our hands for us—
>
> yes, establish the work of our hands.
>
> PSALM 90:17 (NLT)

It may be truly said that no man does any work perfectly who does not enjoy his work. Joy in one's work is the consummate tool without which the work may be done indeed, but without its finest perfectness. Men who do their work without enjoying it are like men carving statues with hatchets. A man who does his work with thorough enjoyment of it is like an artist who holds an exquisite tool which is almost as obedient to him as his own hand, and almost works intelligently with him.

—PHILLIPS BROOKS.

O Heavenly Father, we thank You that You have placed us where we are and have given us the work we have to do. We would not seek far and wide for some better place or more honourable task. We pray today for the spirit that shall make us glad in our common toil. We need not fly away to find enjoyment; we have only to feel that in the duties of this day we are in partnership with You—then shall we be happy that You have called us to so divine a fellowship. Make us strong and earnest and brave—that when the evening shadows fall we shall not look regretfully back because we have been unfaithful—but that we may be satisfied and happy in the memory that we have been serving with You. Amen. —ANONYMOUS.

May 15

He has made everything beautiful in its time. He has also set eternity in the human heart; yet no one can fathom what God has done from beginning to end.

ECCLESIASTES 3:11 (NIV)

> I love the flowers that come about with spring,
> And whether they be scarlet, white or blue,
> It mattereth to me not anything,
> For when I see them full of sun and dew,
> My heart doth get so full with its delight,
> I know not blue from red, nor red from white.
>
> —ALICE CARY.

Father Divine, we remember You at the beginning of another day, and the obedience to Your laws of life which You require. About us is Your beautiful world, thrilling with new life. We would that our lives today may be likewise beautiful, restrained from sin against body and spirit. As there is now in the earth, so there is always in human souls a springtide ready to burst forth into beautiful living. In our hearts there is always the stirring energy of a spiritual spring that needs but the warmth of Your heavenly sunshine. Let that warmth now stream into our hearts that our lives today may show forth Your praise. Amen.   —MINOT O. SIMONS.

May 16

> Honesty guides good people;
> dishonesty destroys treacherous people.
>
> PROVERBS 11:3 (NLT)

VIOLET: "Well, but surely at least one ought to be afraid of displeasing God; and one's desire to please Him should be one's first motive."

LECTURER: "He never would be pleased with us, if it were, my dear. When a father sends his son out into the world—suppose as an apprentice—fancy the boy's coming home at night, and saying, 'Father, I could have robbed the till today; but I didn't because I thought you wouldn't like it.' Do you think the father would be particularly pleased?" (Violet is silent.) "He would answer, would he not, if he were wise and good, 'My boy, though you had no father, you must not rob tills.' And nothing is ever done so as really to please our Great Father, unless we would also have done it, though we had had no Father to know of it."

—JOHN RUSKIN.

Father of Life, Your children raise their thoughts in prayer to You at the dawning of each day. Their prayer asserts love, trust and conformity to Your will. May the spirit of prayer abide with us the day through, that we may be dutiful and worthy. The moral law is Your way of life, may we make it our way by intelligent obedience. To know You aright and to find our joy in Your life is to have fullness of being through purity and strength. O Father, may we be as those who broaden and deepen and purify life by word and deed that none may suffer loss through us, but find aid to reach the perfect life in You. Amen.

—WILSON M. BACKUS.

May 17

"Am I only a God nearby," declares the Lord, "and not a God far away?"
"Who can hide in secret places so that I cannot see them?" declares the Lord.
"Do not I fill heaven and earth?" declares the Lord.

JEREMIAH 23:23–24 (NIV)

Through the harsh noises of our day
A low sweet prelude finds its way:
Through clouds of doubt and
    creeds of fear
A light is breaking, calm and clear.

Henceforth my heart shall sigh no more
For olden time and holier shore:
God's love and blessing, then and there
Are now and here and everywhere.
—JOHN GREENLEAF WHITTIER.

Our Father, as we enter upon the duties of this new day, incline our minds and hearts unto You. May we feel, amid its harsh noises, the assurance of Your love and care. If doubt or fear assail us may we turn to You who are the source of life, love and light, and find calm and peace. We would forget the things behind and make the most of the present. We rejoice that today is better than yesterday and that tomorrow will be better than today. You are here now, as You are everywhere always, to bless us with Your love and care. Direct us through the hours of this day and may its close find us better children of Yours. Amen. —JOHN B. REARDON.

May 18

For God is the King of all the earth;
sing to him a psalm of praise.
God reigns over the nations;
God is seated on his holy throne.

PSALM 47:7–8 (NIV)

The sun does not shine for a few trees and flowers, but for the wide world's joy. The lonely pine of the mountain top waves its somber boughs, and cries, "You are my sun!" And the little meadow violet lifts its cup of blue, and whispers with its perfumed breath, "You are my sun!" And the grain in a thousand fields rustles in the wind, and makes answer, "You are my sun!" So God sits, effulgent, in heaven, not for a favored few, but for the universe of life; and there is no creature so poor or so low that he may not look up with child-like confidence, and say, "My Father, You are mine!" —HENRY WARD BEECHER.

O God, the Eternal Source of all life, we rejoice that there are no bounds to Your love. We thank You that You give us all things richly to enjoy. May we learn that Your bounties are for all human beings. Make the hearts of men eager that the ignorant, the lowly, the poor, the wayward, may come into the full estate of knowing that they are children of God. Let them in no way be denied the joy of unfolding the divinity within them. Lead us all into those fields of labor where we can be our best selves and develop our lives by what we do to meet the growing demands of truth and love and goodness. Wherever the morning breaks and the sunshine falls upon human faces, may its cheer make homes happy and true, men and women good, and little children joyous. Amen. —ALVA ROY SCOTT.

May 19

Put on your new nature, and be renewed as you learn to know your Creator and become like him.   COLOSSIANS 3:10 (NLT)

Hear the Master's risen word!
Delving spades have set it free,
Wake! The world has need of thee,
Rise and let thy voice be heard,
Like a fountain disinterred,
Upward springing, singing, sparkling;
Through the doubtful shadows darkling;
Till the clouds of pain and rage

Brooding o'er the toiling age,
As with rifts of light are stirred
By the music of the Word;
Gospel for the heavy-laden,
  answer to the labourer's cry;
"Raise the stone, and thou shalt find Me:
  cleave the wood, and there am I."
                    —HENRY VAN DYKE.

God of light and strength and beauty, for this day we thank You. The morning hours come to us freighted with messages of gladness. You, our Father, are refreshing our spirits, and home seems dearer, love more sacred and the way of duty clearer before our waiting feet. We thank You for life as it is given us, day by day. Help us to fill it with honest, cheerful, fruitful service. May we realize and rejoice in the nobility of labor, and may we learn how it is that a child of Yours, standing in his own place, giving himself to the tasks of the hour, imparts strength and courage to his fellow-worker, and helps the world forward in the path of righteousness and peace. So may Your will be done in and through us. Amen.   —JOHN P. FORBES.

May 20

O the green things growing, the green things growing
The faint sweet smell of the green things growing!
I should like to live, whether I smile or grieve,
Just to watch the happy life of my green things growing.

—DINAH MULOCK CRAIG.

Not all these sweets, these sounds, this vernal blaze,
Is but one joy, express'd a thousand ways;
And honey from the flowers, and song of birds,
Are from the poet's pen, his overflowing words.

—LEIGH HUNT.

O God who is the Creator of life in every form in which it is expressed in the earth, we thank You for the grass and the flowers, the trees and the shrubs, the music of the streams and the melody of the birds. As nature is ever vocal with Your praise, so may our hearts be attuned to deepest joy that we are a part of Your creation and made capable of constant exultation in the beauty and the beneficence of Your purpose therein displayed. In this spirit may we rejoice and be glad in this new day which You have made for us. Amen. —I. J. MEAD.

May 21

Make my joy complete by being like-minded, having the same love, being one in spirit and of one mind. Do nothing out of selfish ambition or vain conceit. Rather, in humility value others above yourselves. PHILIPPIANS 2:2–3 (NIV)

As one familiar with the sonatas and the symphonies of Beethoven, while passing along the street in summer, gets, from out of the open window, a snatch of a song or a piece that is being played, catching a strain here and another there—and says to himself, "Ah, that is Beethoven. I recognize that: it is from such and such a movement of the Pastoral" or whatever it may be—so men in life catch strains of God in the mother's disinterested and self-denying love, in the lover's glow, in the little child's innocent affections. Where did this thing come from? No plant ever brought out such fruit as this? —HENRY WARD BEECHER.

Father of all and giver of every good thing, to You we pray; to You we look for light, for truth, for beauty. In the travail of thought may there come only the highest and best good. Where there is division we ask for unity; where there is confusion we ask for serenity; where there is discord, we ask for harmony. May divergent paths lead to the larger way of widening vision, distinctive service, unstinted love. Hasten the day when Your purpose shall be accomplished in us, and when that which is now imperfect shall become the perfected whole. Grant to us wisdom to pursue noble ends with intelligent zeal, and patient effort, and in a charitable and hopeful spirit. Amen. —C. C. CLARK.

May 22

Then God said, "Let the land produce vegetation: seed-bearing plants and trees on the land that bear fruit with seed in it, according to their various kinds." And it was so. The land produced vegetation: plants bearing seed according to their kinds and trees bearing fruit with seed in it according to their kinds. And God saw that it was good.   GENESIS 1:11–12 (NIV)

It is very interesting to watch a plant grow, it is like taking part in creation. When all outside is cold and white, when the little children of the woodland are gone to their nurseries in the warm earth and the empty nests on the bare trees filled with snow, my window-garden glows and smiles, making summer within while it is winter without. It is wonderful to see flowers bloom in the midst of a snowstorm! I have felt a bud "shyly doff her green hood and blossom with a silken burst of sound," while the icy fingers of the snow beat against the window panes. What secret power, I wonder, caused this blossoming miracle? What mysterious force guided the seedling from the dark earth up to the light, through leaf and stem and bud, to glorious fulfilment in the perfect flower? Who could have dreamed that such beauty lurked in the dark earth, was latent in the tiny seed we planted? Beautiful flower, you have taught me to see a little way into the hidden heart of things. Now I understand that the darkness everywhere may hold possibilities better than even my hopes.

—HELEN KELLER.

Grant us, O God, this day, vitality of brain and heart, to lay hold on the ordinary events and experiences of life, and transmute them into beautiful and permanent values for ourselves and others. May we have courage, love and faithfulness, to conquer adversities and fulfil our duties. And should the winter of discontent and disappointment beat without against our souls, even so may Your Kingdom come. Amen.

—JULIUS P. WEST.

May 23

The saying "One sows and another reaps" is true. I sent you to reap what you have not worked for. Others have done the hard work, and you have reaped the benefits of their labor.

JOHN 4:37–38 (NIV)

Brother—there is no payment
   in the world!
We work and pour our labor at the feet
Of those who are around us and to come.
We live and take our living at the hands
Of those who are around us
   and have been.
No one is paid. No person can have more
Than he can hold.
   And none can do beyond
The power that's in him.

To each child that's born
Belongs as much of all our human good
As he can take and use
   to make him strong.

And from each man,
   debtor to all the world,
Is due the fullest fruit of all his powers,
His whole life's labor,
   proudly rendered up,
Not as return—can moments pay an age?
But as the simple duty of a man.
Can he do less—receiving everything?
   —CHARLOTTE PERKINS GILMAN.

O, Most Bountiful Giver! We thank You this morning for all the conveniences and comforts, the stored knowledge and acquired wisdom, the inspirations and encouragements of our daily life. Truly others have lived as Your children and labored as Your servants, by mind and hand and heart, and we are wondrously permitted to enter into the fruits of their labours. Grant to us this day, O Father, so to strive and so to live that some other life may be cheered and blessed by the spirit and by the fruit of our day's service. May our thoughts and words and deeds somehow express our gratitude for the blessings which we are constantly receiving. Amen.

—WILLIAM H. GOULD.

May 24

What a wonderful thing it is to meet a man or woman whose manners are instantly open and free—opening up a direct road between him or her and yourself!

—EDWARD CARPENTER.

There is a world in us that God keeps to himself, except when He calls some few souls, with special errand for us, to receive a glimpse. It is full of life, and growths, and wonders, that are to be developed and revealed. We ourselves know not what we shall be; but He knows that we shall be like Him.... It is the world of the spiritual microscope. —MRS. A. D. T. WHITNEY.

Our Father and Mother God—we have cried for You as little children cry for parental love to wait upon their wants, and, like babes that cry, we have looked for You in nothing else. We would be now Your sons and daughters of a larger growth, who learn to find You in a more complete and blessed fellowship of service and sacrifice with You, of united thought and will with Yours, of such living as shares in Your perfect and eternal life. Help us so to be and so to live that even in ourselves we may get glimpses of Your infinite good will and faithfulness, and show in our human lives, that God is in His world and all is well. Amen. —GEORGE W. KENT.

May 25

Let us not become weary in doing good, for at the proper time we will reap a harvest if we do not give up.   GALATIANS 6:9 (NIV)

What are we set on earth for?
  Say to toil:
Nor to seek to leave the tending
  of thy vines,
For all the heat of the day, till it declines,
And death's mild curfew shall
  from work assoil.
God did anoint thee with His odorous oil
To wrestle, not to reign; and he assigns
All thy tears over, like pure crystallines,
For younger fellow-workers of the soil
To wear for amulets. So others shall
  Take patience, labor,
    to their heart and hand,
From thy hand, and thy heart,
  and thy brave cheer,
And God's grace fructify
    through thee to all.
The least flower with a brimming cup
  may stand,
And share its dewdrop with another near.
—ELIZABETH BARRETT BROWNING.

Our Father In Heaven, we devoutly thank You for that ceaseless and refreshing tide of blessing that, from the reservoir of Your exhaustless goodness, flows into our hearts and lives. And we further thank You that among the choicest of those blessings, is the one of being, not merely the receptacles of this inflow, but also co-workers with You, and with Your Son, our Saviour, Jesus Christ, in carrying forward to successful issue Your beneficent purposes of grace and salvation. Grant us, we beseech You, day by day, such an infusion of Your Holy Spirit as shall fittingly equip us for the gladsome and effective discharge of the duties of this divine relation, and its exalted privileges. All of which grant for Your mercy's sake. Amen.
—CHARLES P. NASH.

May 26

The deepest secret of life is love. Without love there is no enthusiasm, and without ideals there is no enthusiasm. We freeze our hearts by selfishness, and stifle them by sordidness. We fix our eyes upon the little field circumscribed by our day's activities and ends. With no wide-reaching affection and no uplifting ideal, we make of our life a treadmill and of our duty an unwelcome drudgery. We disclaim the highest endowment of the soul and deny our sonship to God. Narrow faiths and narrow hopes put fetters on the spirit, and small affections keep small the heart.

—PHILIP S. MOXOM.

Our Father, every morning is a fresh witness of Your loving kindness. When we sleep the vigils of Your love are round about us. At the threshold of this new day, may it please You to inspire us with lofty aims, so that we may rise out of our selfish selves into conscious kinship with You. Help us to know the mystery of love, how limitless and all-conquering it is. Animated by its sweet law, may we go out into this great, needy world with hearts to sympathize and words to cheer and hands to minister. Then we shall know the divine sweetness of our Christian faith, the joy of Christlike living; we shall know that love is the fulfilling of the law. Amen.

—Q. H. SHINN.

May 27

Therefore we do not lose heart. Though outwardly we are wasting away, yet inwardly we are being renewed day by day.

2 CORINTHIANS 4:16 (NIV)

Every day is a fresh beginning,
Every morn is the world made new.
You who are weary of sorrow
    and sinning,
Here is a beautiful hope for you,
A hope for me and a hope for you.

Every day is a fresh beginning;
Listen, my soul, to the glad refrain,
And, spite of old sorrow
    and older sinning,
And puzzles forecasted
    and possible pain,
Take heart with the day, and begin again.
—SUSAN COOLIDGE.

O God, who makes all things new, we are glad each day is not only a new day but one unlike any before it. Everything breathes freshness and newness of life; a new heaven is over our heads, a new earth beneath our feet. We know this day will be full of new opportunities for work, new scenes for pleasure, new chances to make better our lives. If yesterday was not all we could wish, if there were failures in duty, or loss of faith in ourselves, and Your great love, may this be filled with larger faith, greater hope, complete love. May we so take heart in this quiet morning hour, that we may be brave and faithful all the day, so that in spite of old sorrows and older sins, the memory of which may now and then shadow our way, we may find ourselves when the evening shall come, nearer heaven in heart and life, and more worthy to be called Your children. Amen. —WILLIAM F. POTTER.

May 28

O friend, never strike sail to a fear! Come into port greatly, or sail with God the seas....
He has not learned the lesson of life who does not every day surmount a fear.

—RALPH WALDO EMERSON.

There is no storm but this
Of your own cowardice
That braves you out;
You are the storm that mocks
Yourself; you are the rocks
Of your own doubt;
Besides this fear of danger there's no
  danger here
And he that here fears danger does
  deserve his fear.

—RICHARD CRASHAW.

You know, O Lord, the weakness of our human nature, and how prone we are not only to shrink from the difficulties and to tremble at the dangers which lie in our way, but to allow imaginary difficulties and dangers to hinder us from living as Your children should. Help us, we pray, to be free from all such fear today. May You be our refuge from whatsoever may threaten us, either without or within. Deliver us from faint-heartedness and enable us to stand fast in the glorious liberty of those who fear nothing but to offend against You and to wrong their own immortal souls. We ask it as disciples of Christ. Amen.

—EDWIN C. SWEETSER.

May 29

When you pass through the waters,
I will be with you;
and when you pass through the rivers,
they will not sweep over you.

ISAIAH 43:2a (NIV)

Whichever way the wind doth blow,
Some heart is glad to have it so;
Then blow it east or blow it west,
The wind that blows, that wind is best.

My little craft sails not alone:
A thousand fleets from every zone
Are out upon a thousand seas;
And what for me were favoring breeze
Might dash another, with the shock
Of doom, upon some hidden rock.

And so I do not dare to pray
For winds to waft me on my way,
But leave it to a Higher Will
To stay or speed me; trusting still
That all is well, and sure that He
Who launched my bark will sail with me
Through storm and calm, and will not fail,
Whatever breezes may prevail,
To land me, every peril past,
Within His sheltering heaven at last.

—CAROLINE ATWATER MASON.

O Lord let us know that we do not sail life's seas alone. You are the God of the storms. You go with us wherever we go. Grant us, our Heavenly Father, that we may not suffer shipwreck of our faith. Grant us that the voyage of our lives may be prosperous, and that at last, whether soon or late we shall find some harbor of rest and peace. Amen.

—GEORGE L. PERIN.

May 30

Blessed is the nation whose God is the LORD,
the people he chose for his inheritance.

PSALM 33:12 (NIV)

Our Memorial Day celebrations will be but a hypocritical play-acting unless they shall remind us of the cause and the country for which our brave soldiers gave their lives. It is not enough for us to recall their names and sing their praises. We must love the country they loved and in our turn be ready to do the hero's part.

—GEORGE L. PERIN.

But what is it to love one's country? Is it to carry a banner in a procession? Is it to shout as we see the flag? Is it to fling bunting from the tops of the buildings, and send off sky-rockets in the evenings? Vastly deeper than that is love of country, deeper than any soldier's uniform, deeper than any pictures of battleships with which we adorn our walls.

—W. H. P. FAUNCE.

God of the Nations, we thank You today for every heroic deed of every heroic soul. We rejoice that in every hour of real emergency there have ever been men who were ready to die for their country. O Lord, may the memory of their sacrifice ever remain to us and to the children of coming generations a sacred heritage. Yet, O Lord, let us not be satisfied to glorify their deeds with a memory. Let us do them the higher honor of consecrating our lives to the service of the country they loved. So shall we, in the honor we render them find the title to our honor. Thus in our land and in our time may Your Kingdom come and Your will be done. Amen.

—GEORGE L. PERIN.

May 31

Yet a time is coming and has now come when the true worshipers will worship the Father in the Spirit and in truth, for they are the kind of worshipers the Father seeks. God is spirit, and his worshipers must worship in the Spirit and in truth.

JOHN 4:23–24 (NIV)

To be glad of life because it gives you the chance to love and to work and to play and to look up at the stars; to be satisfied with your possessions, but not contented with yourself until you have made the best of them; to despise nothing in the world except falsehood and meanness, and to fear nothing except cowardice; to be governed by your admirations rather than your dislikes; to covet nothing that is your neighbor's except his kindness of heart and gentleness of manners; to think seldom of your enemies, often of your friends, and every day of Christ; and to spend as much time as you can, with body and with spirit in God's out-of-doors—these are little guide-posts on the footpath to peace. —HENRY VAN DYKE.

O God of peace and of love. How shall we come to You? How shall we share Your strength and know Your life? Let us commune with Your gracious spirit and so learn Your way. How beautiful the vision which prayer unfolds to us when we worship in spirit and truth! We see the virtues which ennoble and sanctify other lives. Sweet and tender patience appears and in her light ruffled and distorted tempers are subdued and clothed in their right mind. Faith is seen and as irresolution and doubt take their flight, confident trust and cherished conviction appear in magnetic power. So, O Lord, would we read the signs which other lives present. So would we strengthen our own aspirations and make real the vision. So, O Father, would we find Your peace. Amen. —AUGUSTINE N. FOSTER.

June 1

> The King will reply, "Truly I tell you, whatever you did for one of the least of these brothers and sisters of mine, you did for me."   MATTHEW 25:40 (NIV)

A season for simple living with the kindly sun and the blue sky, days of keen delight in little things, of joyous questing after beauty, days for the making of true friends by being a true friend to others, days when we may enlarge our little lives by excursions to strange places, by friendly association, by the companionship of great thoughts, days that may teach us to live nobly, to work joyously, to play harder, to do our labor better. So should each June bring us indeed a golden summer.

—EDWIN OSGOOD GROVER.

Heavenly Father, You give all good things. We thank You for life and hope and cheer. In gratitude we consecrate this day to blessing Your children, and so to serving You who has said, "Inasmuch as you have done it unto these, you have done it unto Me." Teach us the gladness of a life responsive to Your messages through Nature. Grant us the joy of making friends by being friendly with our fellow men. Whatsoever we may do, at work or at play, may it be in the spirit of the Saviour. We begin this day with You. By its ministries may our comrades be helped and our lives together be made nobler, stronger, and well-pleasing in Your sight. Amen.

—MAURICE A. LEVY.

June 2

Enter his gates with thanksgiving and his courts with praise;
give thanks to him and praise his name.
For the Lord is good and his love endures forever;
his faithfulness continues through all generations.

PSALM 100:4–5 (NIV)

Over the shoulders and slopes of the dune,
I saw the white daisies go down to the sea,
A host in the sunshine, an army in June,
The people God sends us to set our hearts free.

The bobolinks rallied them up from the dell,
The orioles whistled them out of the wood,
And all of their singing was "Earth, it is well,"
And all of their dancing was, "Life, Thou art good!"

—BLISS CARMAN.

O You, who are the Father of Light and Love, from whom comes down every good and perfect gift, we thank You for this newborn day, which You send us, for the splendor of Your presence in the sunlit sky above us and the blossoming earth beneath; for springtime flowers that border our paths with loveliness and happy bird song, lifting our hearts to responsive joy and praise. We thank You for life and health, for home and friends, for opportunities and duties, for temptations and trials, yea, for the very sorrows and bereavements which bring us to ourselves in penitence, to others in sympathy, and to You in faith and adoration. Your will be done! Your kingdom come! Amen.   —CHARLES W. WENDTE.

June 3

When I consider your heavens, the work of your fingers,
the moon and the stars, which you have set in place,
what is mankind that you are mindful of them,
    human beings that you care for them?

PSALM 8:3–4 (NLT)

One small life in God's great plan,
How futile it seems as the ages roll,
Do what it may, or strive how it can,
To alter the sweep of the infinite whole!
A single stitch in an endless web,
A drop in the ocean's flow and ebb!

But the pattern is rent
    where the stitch is lost,
Or marred where the tangled threads
    have crossed;
And each life that fails of its true intent
Mars the perfect plan
    that its Maker meant.

—SUSAN COOLIDGE.

O God, the heavenly Father, in whom we live and move, whose life-giving spirit is ever around us like the air we breathe—we lift our thoughts to You in reverence and gladness at the coming of the new day. We are glad for the quiet hours of the night, while the stars shine over us. May we be ready now, with willing and obedient hearts, for the work, the cares, the joys and the friendly converse of the day. We know how small our lives are; may we share the thoughts of Your infinite mind, may Your power and beauty, Your justice and goodness possess us. May our feeble wills be strong to carry the current of the one Good Will that sways the universe. Amen.

—CHARLES F. DOLE.

June 4

Are not two sparrows sold for a penny? Yet not one of them will fall to the ground outside your Father's care. And even the very hairs of your head are all numbered. So don't be afraid; you are worth more than many sparrows.

MATTHEW 10:29–31 (NIV)

I have lived, sir, a long time; and the longer I live, the more convincing proofs I see of this truth, that God governs in the affairs of men.   —BENJAMIN FRANKLIN.

All I have seen teaches me to trust the Creator for all I have not seen. Whatever it be which the great Providence prepares for us, it must be something large and generous; and in the great style of His works. The future must be up to the style of our faculties, of memory, of hope, of imagination, of reason.   —RALPH WALDO EMERSON.

O God, who in Your greatness holds the planets on their way, and in Your providence guides the sparrow's flight, and in Your tenderness marks the sparrow's fall, may we not be blind to Your footprints in the events of every day, but see them guiding our way and feel more and more Your love. Father, we ask not for great things, but we ask You to help us in the little needs and longings that fill our every day, to be the strength of our every endeavor, that in our daily walk, we may feel that the earth is warm with life and joy, that the air is full of strength, that there comes to us from every side some message, sweet and tender, if only we can be patient, trustful, believing that all things work together for good to them who seek to do Your will. Amen.

—JOSHUA YOUNG.

June 5

> For in him we live and move and have our being.
>
> ACTS 17:28a (NIV)

And do not fear to hope.
  Can poet's brain
More than the Father's heart
  rich good invent?
Each time we smell the autumn's
  dying scent,
We know the primrose time
  will come again;
Not more we hope,
  nor less would soothe our pain.
Be bounteous in our faith,
  for not misspent

Is confidence unto the Father lent:
Thy need is sown and rooted for his rain,
His thoughts are as thine own;
  nor are his ways
Other than thine,
  but by their loftier sense
Of beauty infinite and love intense.
Work on! One day,
  beyond all thought of praise
A sunny joy will crown thee with its rays;
Nor other than thy need,
  thy recompense.

—GEORGE MACDONALD.

Our Father, in the gratitude of loved and loving children we thank You for life and all the faith and hope and love Your goodness has awakened in our souls. For the splendors of the world and the greater splendor of the mind radiant with Your love, we bow in rapture and adoration. Overwhelmed at times by the mysteries and vicissitudes of life, we will trust Your will to lead us out of darkness into the light of Your informing spirit of truth and wisdom. Conscious of our weakness and needs, we rejoice that strength and supply are assured to us in the permanence of Your Fatherhood. Lead us more and ever more to realize that in You we live and move and have our being. Amen.

—RICHMOND FISK.

June 6

Ask and it will be given to you;
seek and you will find;
knock and the door will be opened to you.

MATTHEW 7:6–8 (NIV)

When a feller goes a-huntin' for a rose
He shouldn't be a-thinkin' of the thorn;
He must woo it, he must win it—
Where his heart beats he must pin it
An' breathe the breath that's in it
Every morn!

When a feller goes a-huntin' for a rose
He shouldn't see the thorn
   beneath its breast,
But for all its thorny foes.
Red and reckless—one poor rose
Is sweet enough, God knows,
For the best.

—FRANK L. STANTON.

O Lord, our God, so great is our life we may find that for which we look—the good or the bad. Send us into this day with eyes searching for the good. Beholding it may we admire it and admiring it we shall become like it changed into the same image from character to character by the Spirit. May we be more concerned to do right than not to do wrong. Save us from a humility that is weakness and give us largeness of life without pride. May we want nothing so much as opportunity—opportunity to be, to do, to suffer. May we not strive for bigness but for fitness and may our reception of the Christ be our forgiveness and our salvation for His name's sake. Amen.

—T. C. MARTIN.

June 7

> And whatever you do, whether in word or deed, do it all in the name of the Lord Jesus, giving thanks to God the Father through him.
>
> COLOSSIANS 3:17 (NIV)

The beauty of work depends upon the way we meet it—whether we arm ourselves each morning to attack it as an enemy that must be vanquished before night comes, or whether we open our eyes with the sunrise to welcome it as an approaching friend who will keep us delightful company all day, and who will make us feel at evening, that the day was well worth its fatigues. —LUCY LARCOM.

Our Heavenly Father, You give us light for the hours of labor and darkness for the hours of slumber. We toil and then we rest. We sleep and then we arise, to perform the tasks which await us. Convince us, O God, that the life which You have given us to live is more than working that we may rest, and resting that we may work. Persuade us that it is for some great and good end. Help us to understand that even as we live in You so do You fulfill Your eternal purposes in and through us. Teach us that our smallest effort is important to You. So may we dread no duty. So may every moment of every day be precious in our sight. Amen. —ROGER S. FORBES.

June 8

> There are different kinds of gifts, but the same Spirit distributes them. There are different kinds of service, but the same Lord. There are different kinds of working, but in all of them and in everyone it is the same God at work. Now to each one the manifestation of the Spirit is given for the common good.
>
> 1 CORINTHIANS 12:4–7 (NIV)

And those who heard the Singers three
Disputed which the best might be;
For still their music seemed to start
Discordant echoes in each heart.

But the great Master said, "I see
No best in kind, but in degree;
I gave a various gift to each,
To charm, to strengthen, and to teach.

"These are the three great chords of
   might,
And he whose ear is tuned aright,
Will hear no discord in the three,
But the most perfect harmony."
—HENRY W. LONGFELLOW.

O God, our Heavenly Father, we thank You for all Your mercies new every morning, and fresh every evening, but especially we bless You that You call us to Your service and kingdom by Jesus Christ, our Lord, and have vouchsafed to each of us some gracious gift whereby we may accomplish Your holy will concerning us. Grant that we may so improve and use that pearl of price as to enhance greatly the welfare of Your children. Help each to see the good in all, and all to see the good in each, that all may strive together in sinless and sweet accord for the common good and thus for the glory of Your name, and so hasten the happy day when all souls shall be one, as prayed the Saviour of the world. Amen. —ALFRED P. PUTNAM.

June 9

Give praise to the Lord, proclaim his name;
  make known among the nations what he has done.
Sing to him, sing praise to him;
  tell of all his wonderful acts.

1 CHRONICLES 16:8–9 (NIV)

Men talk sometimes as if the passage of a ship through the sea or a bird through the air is a fit symbol of man's passage through this world. I do not think so. A better symbol would be the passage of a plough through the soil leaving a furrow behind. What does the furrow include? All the memory of every beautiful picture and landscape you have ever seen. It includes the memory of every experience, every sweet association, every tie of love, whether of father, mother, wife or children. All these, whether living or dead, speak to you. They have a voice, a language that you will understand.

—GEORGE L. PERIN.

We thank You, O God, for the many influences past and present which have had a share in the moulding of our lives and characters toward a larger usefulness and a more perfect realization of the Christian ideal. We thank You for the mother's love which watched over us through years of helplessness; for the father's love which made provision for our wants, for the human sympathy which has everywhere blessed and strengthened us and made life brighter; for the friends of youth and age who have helped us to better things. Grant, O God, that a memory of these blessings may abide with us so long as life may last, and that as we have been helped by others to walk the way of life we may not forget to extend a helping hand to those who may need our comfort and our sympathy.　　　　—ORIN EDSON CROOKER.

June 10

Now may the God of peace, who through the blood of the eternal covenant brought back from the dead our Lord Jesus, that great Shepherd of the sheep, equip you with everything good for doing his will, and may he work in us what is pleasing to him, through Jesus Christ, to whom be glory for ever and ever. Amen.

HEBREWS 13:20–21 (NLT)

It is not to taste sweet things, but to do noble and true things, and vindicate himself under God's heaven, as a God-made man, that the poorest son of Adam dimly longs. This dim longing for what is noble and true, the still small voice which calls to one imperatively in moments of temptation, is the safeguard which, if hearkened to, not only protects one in severe trials of manliness and womanliness, but also incites to the formation of a fine character, without which all acquisitions, all graces and accomplishments, all talents and all learning, are but as sounding brass and a tinkling cymbal.   —THOMAS CARLYLE.

Almighty God, our heavenly Father, in grateful recognition of Your love and watchful care, we thank You for the repose of the night and the promise of the day. Our desire is to do Your will, and we ask for the guidance and inspiration of Your spirit. Enable us to perform faithfully all the work that You have given us to do. Grant us a sufficiency of Your grace to treat all our fellowmen as children of Yours, and when night comes may we have the blessed assurance that through the experiences of this day we have become a little more like Your own glorious self in love and holiness. We ask it in the name of Jesus, our example, and Saviour. Amen.   —WARREN S. PERKINS.

June 11

Your beauty should not come from outward adornment, such as elaborate hairstyles and the wearing of gold jewelry or fine clothes. Rather, it should be that of your inner self, the unfading beauty of a gentle and quiet spirit, which is of great worth in God's sight.   1 PETER 3:3–4 (NIV)

Now it is June, and the secret is told;
Flashed from the buttercup's glory of gold;
Hummed in the bumblebee's gladness, and sung
New from each bough where a bird's nest is swung;
Breathed from the clover-beds, when the winds pass;
Chirped in small psalms, through the aisles of the grass.

—HENRY JAMES, SR.

Dear Father, in the morning hour of this new day, we thank You for the glorious revelation of Yourself in the open Book of Nature. May we love the beautiful and therein love You, with a true and abiding affection. Grant unto us the understanding that it is only as we have the spirit of the beautiful in our lives that we can appreciate the beautiful without us. So may we value this life, which is from You, as a means of attaining a larger usefulness and for realizing that goodness which is ever heavenly. In simply trying to be nobler, more unselfish, like Christ, we pray, that we may learn how good is life. Amen.   —THOMAS EDWARD POTTERTON.

June 12

You make known to me the path of life;
you will fill me with joy in your presence,
with eternal pleasures at your right hand.

PSALM 16:11 (NIV)

Methinks I love all common things,
The common air, the common flower,
The dear, kind, common thought that springs
From hearts that have no other dower,
No other wealth, no other power,
Save love; and will not that repay
For all else fortune tears away?

—BRYAN WALLER PROCTER.

We thank God for the beauty of the world. We thank God that it is good to be alive. We thank God for the joy that joins us to Your world in gladness, and makes it seem to be the open book of Your graciousness and tenderness and compassion. We thank You also for the ministry of those days that were not bright, but that were full of comfort, even in their darkness, into which God came shrouded, only to reveal Himself more clearly as the light. We thank You for the intervening by the hand of love and tenderness that is human, so that our best nature was called out for love's sake, and all the lower forces of our lives led in the leash of that sweet attraction. We thank God for everything for which our life is better, and pray You will help us to use Your mercies to turn them into strength, not the strength of praise alone, but the strength of service also. Amen. —THOMAS R. SLICER.

June 13

But everything exposed by the light becomes visible—and everything that is illuminated becomes a light. This is why it is said:
"Wake up, sleeper, rise from the dead, and Christ will shine on you."

EPHESIANS 5:13–14 (NIV)

A creed is a rod,
And a crown is of night;
But this thing is God,
To be man with thy might,
To grow straight in the strength of thy spirit,
   and live out thy life as the light.

—ALGERNON CHARLES SWINBURNE.

Life is fuller and sweeter for every fulness and sweetness that we take knowledge of. And to him that has, cannot help being given from everything.

—MRS. A. D. T. WHITNEY.

Infinite Love and Beauty, who stirs in the tiniest seed that breaks its earthly shell to greet the light and warmth of Your beneficence and round its life in blade and flower and ripened fruit—awake in us, we pray, that we may burst the casements of our dead selves and live to bear the fruits of completed lives. Be love alone our creed and service our crown; and in the sweetness and light of these twin ministers draw us on, until having taken full knowledge of the fulness and sweetness of our Lord the Christ, we shall have measured in our spiritual stature, His perfect manliness and strength. Thus shall we have indeed and to us shall be given from everything. Amen.

—ALBERT C. WHITE.

June 14

My flesh and my heart may fail,
but God is the strength of my heart
and my portion forever.

PSALM 73:26 (NIV)

He fails who climbs to power and place
Up the pathway of disgrace.
He fails not who makes truth his cause,
Nor bends to win the crowd's applause.
He fails not, he who stakes his all
Upon the right and dares to fall.
What though the living bless or blame,
For him the long success of fame!

—RICHARD WATSON GILDER.

Our Heavenly Father, help us when we fail to see and know the truth and its blessed influence for good. Help us to combat bravely the evil in the world and to look to You for encouragement and success. Help us, if we fail, to regain our footing and to reach the higher because of the effort which Your love prompts. We gratefully accept the power which Your wisdom gives and thank You for the opportunity to use its strength. Be our guide and we shall fear no failure, nor overestimate the worth of success. So shall we "rejoice in the Lord always"—in failure because of Your help and in success because of Your approval. In the name of Jesus Christ our Lord and Redeemer. Amen.   —WILLIAM E. GIBBS.

June 15

> Cast your cares on the Lord
> and he will sustain you;
> he will never let
> the righteous be shaken.
>
> PSALM 55:22 (NIV)

A singer sang a song of tears,
And the great world heard and wept
For the song of the sorrows of fleeting
  years,
And the hopes which the dead past kept:
And souls in anguish their burdens bore,
And the world was sadder than ever
  before.

A singer sang a song of cheer,
And the great world listened and smiled,
For he sang of the love of a Father dear
And the trust of a little child;
And souls that before had forgotten to
  pray,
Looked up and went singing along the
  way.

—EMMA C. DOWD.

Almighty God, our heavenly Father, our trust is evermore in You, and we would keep that trust as a song within our hearts, which may cheer and bless and strengthen us. When the night is dark and the day is dreary may that song be with us, and when cares oppress and sorrows meet us, may our prayers still rise to You, for You are the God of our lives. Let not the day's discouragements depress us, nor its failures find us weak or helpless, nor its trials leave a stain upon our souls. But because we have Your song of love within our hearts may we march to heavenly music, and ever go upon our way rejoicing. Amen.   —PAUL REVERE FROTHINGHAM.

June 16

Love must be sincere. Hate what is evil; cling to what is good. Be devoted to one another in love. Honor one another above yourselves.

ROMANS 12:9–10 (NIV)

It is only the sincerity of human feeling that abides. As for a thought, we know not, it may be deceptive; but the love, wherewith we have loved it, will surely return to our soul; nor can a single drop of its clearness or strength be abstracted by error. Of that perfect ideal that each of us strives to build up in himself, the sum total of all our thoughts will help only to model the outline; but the elements that go to construct it, and keep it alive, are the purified passion, unselfishness, loyalty, wherein these thoughts have had being. —MAETERLINCK.

O God, our Heavenly Father, help us to take up the cares of this day with an unselfish heart, and in loyalty to what is right and good. Keep us in right relation to those with whom our lot is cast, in sympathy with the unanxious joy of the world and with the deeper life which is its source. We desire to enter into the thought and the love of the most hopeful souls, that, in all the needful pauses of the day, we may find cheer, incentive, and the ampler rest: through Jesus Christ, our Lord. Amen.

—CHARLES H. LEONARD.

June 17

> Do not let your hearts be troubled. You believe in God believe also in me. My Father's house has many rooms; if that were not so, would I have told you that I am going there to prepare a place for you? And if I go and prepare a place for you, I will come back and take you to be with me that you also may be where I am.
>
> JOHN 14:1–3 (NIV)

"Does the road wind up-hill all the way?"
"Yes, to the very end!"
"Will the day's journey take the whole long day?"
"From morn to night, my friend!"
"But is there for the night a resting-place?"
"A roof for all when the dark hours begin."
"May not the darkness hide it from my face?"
"You cannot miss that inn."
"Shall I meet other wayfarers at night?"
"Those who have gone before."
"Then must I knock or call when just in sight?"
"They will not keep you standing at that door."
"Shall I find comfort, travel-sore and weak?"
"Of labor you shall find the sum."
"Will there be beds for me and all who seek?"
"Yea—beds for all who come!"

—CHRISTINA ROSSETTI.

Our Heavenly Father, we thank You for this new day. May it be an open door to faithful service. Open our eyes that we may see all vexations, distresses, and toil as angels in disguise sent to strengthen and fulfill us, to prepare us for larger blessings at our journey's end. As the blue sky of Your loving kindness is broader and more enduring than the clouds that sometimes hide it, so teach us to trust Your unfailing love that overarches and outlasts all weariness and pain. When life and strength fail us here, may we find them transformed and glorious in the city of God hereafter. Be our shield and our reward now and forever. Amen. —JOHN M. WILSON.

June 18

So in Christ Jesus you are all children of God through faith.

GALATIANS 3:26 (NIV)

Those homelier wildflowers, which we call weeds; yellow japanned buttercups and star-disked dandelions, lying in the grass, like sparks that have leaped from the kindling sun of summer; the profuse daisy-like flower which whitens the fields, to the great disgust of liberal shepherds, yet seems fair to loving eyes, with its button-like mound of gold set round with milk-white rays; the tall-stemmed succory, setting its pale blue flowers aflame one after another; the red and white clovers; the broad, flat leaves of the plantain—"the white man's foot," as the Indians called it—those common growths which fling themselves to be crushed under our feet and our wheels, making themselves so cheap in this perpetual martyrdom that we forget, each of them is a ray of the divine beauty.   —OLIVER WENDELL HOLMES.

Our Heavenly Father, however poor and mean and commonplace our lives may seem to be, in our better moments we think of ourselves as Your children. We may have failed sometimes but we shall not utterly fail. In Your sight, nothing is common or worthless. No life shall be cast as rubbish to the void. However commonplace our tasks may seem, let us feel ourselves in partnership with God, and go forth to the duties of the day with high hope and sense of dignity. So shall You make even our little lives of some real service to the world. We pray to You in the spirit of Him, who though the humblest of all, was yet Master of all. Amen.

—GEORGE L. PERIN.

June 19

> When doubts filled my mind,
> your comfort gave me renewed hope and cheer.
>
> PSALM 94:19 (NLT)

There's a real grace of character in forgetting the things which disturb the harmony of life. —HAMILTON W. MABIE.

> Touch your lips with gladness and go singing on your way,
> Smiles will strangely lighten every duty;
> Just a little word of cheer may span a sky of gray
> With hope's own heaven-tinted bow of beauty.
> Wear a pleasant face wherein shall shine a joyful heart,
> As shines the sun, the happy fields adorning;
> To every care-beclouded life some ray of light impart,
> And touch your lips with gladness every morning.
>
> —NIXON WATERMAN.

O You who are from everlasting to everlasting, Our God and Father, we flee to You as the One who is able to save us from all foes within and without. We confess our weakness and our many grievous faults, and beseech You to touch us by Your Spirit, that with penitent and lowly hearts we may seek You as our everlasting Friend and Helper. Be patient yet a while with our shortcomings and frowardness. Suffer us yet a little that Your infinite grace and compassion may arouse us from our spiritual slumber unto the glorious life of obedience and love. In this new day we would be made to feel Your presence and the light and joy and peace, which You promise to all who diligently seek You through Jesus Christ Our Lord. Amen.

—CLARENCE E. RICE.

June 20

In the morning, LORD, you hear my voice;
   in the morning I lay my requests before you
   and wait expectantly.

PSALM 5:3 (NIV)

Now is the high tide of the year,
And whatever of life hath ebbed away
Comes flooding back with a ripply cheer,
Into every bare inlet and creek and bay;
Now the heart is so full that a drop overfills it,
We are happy now because God wills it.

—JAMES RUSSELL LOWELL.

Holy, holy, holy, Lord God Almighty! Early in the morning we approach You. The whole round of creation is burdened with the exuberance of Your life, and everywhere is hallowed ground. We come with unshod feet. The sun, mighty minister of Your great goodness, flooding the world with light and piercing all things with his fiery arrows, calls back to life the sleeping earth, and assures us that we are partakers of Your light and Your love and Your life. O most glorious God! May these Your mercies, fresh every morning, be with us through the day to strengthen us to do Your will, we ask in the name of Him who came that we may have life and have it abundantly. Amen.

—FRANK W. COLLIER.

June 21

Man hath much need of courage;
   and need to brace
His spiritual nerve in solitude;
Self-trusting, self-sustained,
   and self-imbued;
Seeking God in his own heart's
   secret place.
To perfect self, and in that self embrace
The triune essence of truth, beauty,
   and good;
This is fulfillment, this beatitude

Throned high above base fears and
   hopes more base.
What shall it profit us, if, gaining all
The privilege of priest-made paradise,
We lose therewith our self
   which is the soul?
And wherefore should we shrink
   from even the fall,
If haply we should fail with
   steadfast eyes
Fixed only on so bright, so pure a goal?
   —JOHN ADDINGTON SYMONDS.

Heavenly Father, we thank You for the gift of a new day, for the tasks which it brings, and for the strength with which we rise to its requirements. Help us, through all this day, to remember You. You are our strength, our guide, our inspiration. Fill us with the courage born of faith. Let us feel that, seeking to do right, we shall be moved and aided by an unseen Power. In all our experiences this day, help us to speak the truth, to be loyal to friendship, to be steadfast in principle, to fight the good fight and to keep the faith. Bless our endeavors to give heart and hope to other souls; and grant them the presence of Your loving spirit. Amen.   —JOHN CLARENCE LEE.

June 22

Do not be anxious about anything, but in every situation, by prayer and petition, with thanksgiving, present your requests to God. And the peace of God, which transcends all understanding, will guard your hearts and your minds in Christ Jesus.   PHILIPPIANS 4:6–8 (NIV)

Let a man start out at breakneck speed in the morning, pushing and driving and hurrying as if it were a matter of life and death to accomplish a given task before noon, and he will generally end by working himself into a fever of anxiety and harassing care before night, and the man who, under any pretext whatsoever, whether for the sake of wealth or learning or pleasure, has pursued this mad, rushing, whirling method of life for fifteen or twenty years, will find himself thoroughly disqualified for the normal enjoyment of life thenceforward to the end of his days.

—GEORGE L. PERIN.

Most gracious God! You who have sustained us through the night watches, and who now opens to us the day, with its promise of good and opportunity for service, we still depend upon that heavenly faithfulness which never fails. We look to You for the quickening of our best powers. We would be laborers together with You today, not as driven to irksome tasks, but as honored with a welcome privilege. Whether we plant or water may we do it faithfully, and then trust You for the desired increase. May it please You to quiet our anxieties, to lay to rest our unworthy fears, and to assure us of Your over-ruling providence; and thus through all our toiling may we enjoy large measures of the peace that passes understanding. Amen.

—JAMES EDWARD WRIGHT.

June 23

For our light and momentary troubles are achieving for us an eternal glory that far outweighs them all. So we fix our eyes not on what is seen, but on what is unseen, since what is seen is temporary, but what is unseen is eternal.

2 CORINTHIANS 4:17–18 (NIV)

I do not say you can make yourself merry and happy when you are in a physical condition which is contrary to such mental condition, but by practice and effort you can learn to withdraw from it, refusing to allow your judgments and actions to be ruled by it. "What does that matter?" you will learn to say. "It is enough for me to know that the sun does shine, and that this is only a weary fog that is round about me for a moment. I shall come out into the light beyond presently." This is faith—faith in God, who is Light.   —GEORGE MACDONALD.

Our Father, residing in the light incomprehensible and who is seeing and providing all good for Your immortal household, when 'mid investing clouds we shall hail Your presence, transforming weakness into perfect strength and sighs and groans into joy and swelling songs, above all the many rightful subjects of Christian petition, we pray that You will always press us near to You to feel Your loving heartbeats and dwell in the light in which is no darkness at all. We pray not to be spared any of our full part of the burdens needful to this day, but to be given the measure of grace to maintain unfaltering steps. Behold with compassion the errors that befall us as we, too, have compassion for others. Amen.   —JACOB STRAUB.

June 24

Follow God's example, therefore, as dearly loved children and walk in the way of love, just as Christ loved us and gave himself up for us as a fragrant offering and sacrifice to God.   EPHESIANS 5:1–2 (NIV)

We are all perhaps familiar with the story of the little housemaid, who, when she was asked why she thought she had become a Christian, replied, after a little hesitation, "Because I sweep under the mats." A very poor reason at first sight, and only significant from the fact of the master-motive underlying the fact itself. A child's reasoning—but did not quaint old Herbert employ the same fine logic when he sang:

> "Who sweeps a room as for Thy laws.
> Makes that and the action fine!"

—WILLIAM MOODIE.

Dear Lord of Life and Light, at the dawn of another day we rise to thank You for Your watchful care, imparting strength and vitality during the closed hours of the night. Your gift of eternal life is ours by Your creatorship and love, and we would pray that in no way during this coming day shall we dishonor our birthright by evil thought or action. Help us to aspire to hold fast and develop Your holy characteristics, normal to us and made active by our wills. We thank You for the goal revealed to us as our destiny, the spirit displayed by our Master, Jesus Christ, and like Him may we lean on You daily for the strengthening of our faith and the maturing of our plans. Amen.

—CHARLES E. LUND.

June 25

> Come to me, all you who are weary and burdened, and I will give you rest. Take my yoke upon you and learn from me, for I am gentle and humble in heart, and you will find rest for your souls. For my yoke is easy and my burden is light.
>
> MATTHEW 11:28–30 (NIV)

They are tired of what is old,
We will give it voices new;
For the half hath not been told
Of the beautiful and true.
　　—GEORGE MACDONALD.

The common problem, yours, mine,
　everyone's,
Is not to fancy what were fair in life
Provided it could be—but finding first
What may be,
　　than find how to make it fair
Up to our means, a very different thing.
　　　　—ROBERT BROWNING.

O Infinite Heart! Our hearts go out after You, not for past, not for future, not for what was, though dear, not for what may be, though in vision precious—not these the burden of our prayer. Our hearts crave peace, comfort with what is. May we confide in You so utterly that the old pain is eased, the anxious foreboding is dispelled, self-will merged in divine will, self-direction yielding to divine leading. Lo! Our prayer is answered in the making and we are helped. Amen.

—STANFORD MITCHELL.

June 26

A generous person will prosper;
whoever refreshes others will be refreshed.

PROVERBS 11:25 (NIV)

Today is your day and mine, the only day we have, the day in which we play our part. What our part may signify in the great whole, we may not understand, but we are here to play it, and now is our time. This we know, it is a part of action, not of whining. It is a part of love, not cynicism. It is for us to express love in terms of human helpfulness. This we know, for we have learned from sad experience that any other course of life leads toward weakness and misery. —DAVID STARR JORDAN.

Our Father, Author alike of the morning light and Guardian through the darkness and shadow of the night, grant us the right spirit as we go forth to the unknown experiences of this day. We would not look eagerly for our own comfort and happiness, but would find them as Your free gift while we are employed in giving comfort and happiness to others. Illuminate our lives with happy thoughts, cheerful words and blessed hopes, that we may go forth with no purpose but to do Your will, and seeking no reward more glorious, than Your approval whispered into loving and attentive hearts, in Your name. Amen. —LEWIS G. WILSON.

June 27

But thanks be to God, who always leads us as captives in Christ's triumphal procession and uses us to spread the aroma of the knowledge of him everywhere. For we are to God the pleasing aroma of Christ among those who are being saved and those who are perishing. 2 CORINTHIANS 2:14–15 (NIV)

A Persian fable says: "One day
A wanderer found a lump of clay,
So redolent of sweet perfume
Its odors scented all the room.
"What art thou?" was his quick demand;
"Art thou some gem from Samarcand,
Or spikenard in this rude disguise,
Or other costly merchandise?"
"Nay, I am but a lump of clay."

"Then whence this wondrous
    perfume—say?"
"Friend, if the secret I disclose,
I have been dwelling with the rose,"
Sweet parable! and will not those
Who love to dwell with Sharon's Rose,
Distill sweet odors all around,
Though low and mean themselves are
    found?
Dear Lord, abide with us, that we
May draw our perfume fresh from thee.
—ANONYMOUS.

Our Father, which art in heaven—we thank You for the memory of those who lived in Your spirit and labored in Your love. The fragrance of their lives abides with us. We thank You for the prophets of great hopes—for those who have seen the invisible, and have searched patiently for the city of their God. We bless those who by their pure hearts and unselfish lives have revealed unto us our greater selves. Help us to learn of them the way of life. Help us to live in such thoughts and deeds as made them truly great. Keep our hearts so pure today, our vision of the Master life so clear, that our path, before and after us, shall be as the light of day. Amen.

—FREDERICK W. BETTS.

June 28

Sing to the Lord with grateful praise;
    make music to our God on the harp.
He covers the sky with clouds;
    he supplies the earth with rain and makes grass grow on the hills.

PSALM 147:7–8 (NIV)

Tell you what I like the best;
'Long about knee-deep in June,
'Bout the time the strawberries melts
On the vine—some afternoon
Like to jes' git out and rest,
And not work at nothing else.

Orchard's where I'd ruther be—
Needn't fence it in for me!
Jes' the whole sky overhead,
And the whole airth underneath.
                —JAMES WHITCOMB RILEY.

Help us, O You who art the Lord of life, that we may this morning praise You for the beauty of the world and for the joyful privilege of wandering in the green fields and by the sparkling brooks, and of resting tired body and weary limb beneath the sweet orchard shade, gazing with gladdened eyes at the blue canopy above, all forgetful of the toil and din of the far off city. O may our hearts this day be in tune with nature and in harmony with You; and as we contemplate Your works this and every day may our hearts go out in loving and practical sympathy toward those whose lives are spent within the narrow confines of sunless courts. Hear us for the Saviour's sake. Amen.
                —FRANCIS W. BRETT.

June 29

Sing to the Lord, all the earth;
proclaim his salvation day after day.

1 CHRONICLES 16:23 (NIV)

Give us, O give us the man who sings at his work. Be his occupation what it may, he is equal to any of those who follow the same pursuit in silent sullenness. He will do more in the same time—he will do it better—he will persevere longer. One is scarcely sensible of fatigue while he marches to music. The very stars are said to make harmony as they revolve in their spheres. Wondrous is the strength of cheerfulness, although past calculation its power of endurance. Efforts to be permanently useful, must be uniformly joyous—a spirit all sunshine, graceful from very gladness, beautiful because bright. —THOMAS CARLYLE.

Almighty God, we turn to You in adoration and praise as we pause upon the threshold of this new day. Grant, we pray, that a song be in our hearts as we go about the duties of the passing hours. Whatever our experiences, whether of joy or sorrow, may we truly value the truthful spirit. If You call us to bear burdens or to stand upon the mountaintop of exultant achievement may we not forget to sing of You. Yea, O God, we would be ever of the company of trusting souls, for such are near to You. And when earthly days are past and the life of the freed spirit is over, grant that our lives may blend in full accord with the music of love, in sunshine of joy, in the beauty of holiness. We praise You now and ever. Amen.

—STEPHEN H. ROBLIN.

June 30

Let us come before him with thanksgiving and extol him with music and song.

For the Lord is the great God, the great King above all gods.

In his hand are the depths of the earth, and the mountain peaks belong to him.

The sea is his, for he made it, and his hands formed the dry land.

PSALM 95:2–5 (NIV)

Full-leafed in pride of deepest green,
The earth in the sunshine basks serene,
Where linden blossoms crowded cling,
A thousand bees are murmuring.
As showers drift from the freshened land
With a seven-barred bow
  is the rain-cloud spanned.

The wild rose yields her subtlest scents
Where hay cocks pitch their
  fragrant tents.
The longest day's too brief for June,
The night too short for such a moon!
—SARA ANDREW SHAFER.

We thank You, our Father, for the wonderful world in which we live; for the glory of the heavens; for the beauty of the earth; for the bright morning following the star-crowned night; for the song of birds, the hum of bees, the fragrance of flowers, and the laughter of children, for the industry of men and women, for all Your gifts of love. As again the lengthening shadows creep across our pathway, may we redouble our energies that no labor of love may be left undone. So fill us with Your presence, so lead us by Your Spirit this day, that in our homes we may be patient, in our occupations sweet, in our social relations brotherly, in all things Christlike, for Jesus' sake. Amen. —ARTHUR WRIGHT.

July 1

He put a new song in my mouth,
a hymn of praise to our God.
Many will see and fear the Lord
and put their trust in him.

PSALM 40:3 (NIV)

Let me go where'er I will
I hear a sky-born music still:
It sounds from all things old,
It sounds from all things young,
From all that's fair, from all that's foul,
Peals out a cheerful song.

It is not only in the rose,
It is not only in the bird,
Not only where the rainbow glows,

Nor in the song of woman heard,
But in the darkest, meanest things
There alway, alway something sings.

'Tis not in the high stars alone,
Nor in the cups of budding flowers,
Nor in the redbreast's mellow tone,
Nor in the bow that smiles in showers,
But in the mud and scum of things
There alway, alway something sings.

—RALPH WALDO EMERSON.

Dear Father in heaven, we thank You for all the sweet voices of the world, not only for the harmonies of the great masters of song but for the sweet voice of the mother as she sings her song of love, for the bird in the spring time. We thank You for the music in the prattle of children, and the kindly word spoken everywhere. The world is full of music if only we have music in our own hearts. We pray, as we set forth again this morning, for spirits in tune with all that is sweet and good. Wherever we go this day, let the world sing to us and make us glad. Amen. —GEORGE L. PERIN.

July 2

Satisfy us each morning with your unfailing love,
so we may sing for joy to the end of our lives.

PSALM 90:14 (NLT)

A little bird with plumage brown,
Beside my window flutters down,
A moment chirps its little strain,
Then taps upon my windowpane.
And chirps again, and hops along,
To call my notice to its song;
But I work on, nor heed its lay,
Till, in neglect, it flies away.

So birds of peace and hope and love
Come fluttering earthward from above,
To settle on life's windowsills,
And ease our load of earthly ills;
But we, in traffic's rush and din
Too deep engaged to let them in,
With deadened heart and sense plod on,
Nor know our loss till they are gone.

—PAUL LAURENCE DUNBAR.

My voice shall You hear in the morning, O Lord, in the morning will I direct my prayer unto You, and will look up; and looking up, may we not fail to realize that, amid the turmoil of this outward life, You are ever present to give peace and rest in the inner life. Should we fail to recognize that presence we shall lose the comfort which You are ever ready to bestow, and must ourselves bear burdens which You would gladly bear for us or take from us. You know our frame and remember that we are dust. Open our spiritual vision to behold that Divine resources are subject to our daily prayer. In the name of Jesus, the Christ. Amen.   —O. W. SCOTT.

July 3

Blessed are the poor in spirit, for theirs is the kingdom of Heaven.

Blessed are the pure in heart, for they will see God.

Blessed are the peacemakers, for they will be called the children of God.

Blessed are you when people insult you, persecute you and falsely say all kinds of evil against you because of me.   MATTHEW 5: 3, 8, 11 (NIV)

O God, our Heavenly Father, we thank You that You overrule our weakness, failure and sins to the accomplishment of Your divine plan for us. We recall with pleasure our successes in the past year, and if we have failed, You will show us where and when and teach us the way of amendment. We thank You for our Hope and Faith which have come to us from the Bible. Here, on every page and in every biography, have we learned of Christ Jesus, the Way, the Truth and the Life. We thank You that through Him our sins are forgiven, and we have learned to know You, O blessed Father, which knowledge is eternal life. May we walk with Him, moment by moment in a life of loving service to all mankind, during all the remaining days of our life. Amen.

—E. M. WARNER.

July 4

Now the Lord is the Spirit,
and where the Spirit of the Lord is,
there is freedom.

2 CORINTHIANS 3:17 (NIV)

One flag, one land, one heart, one hand,
One nation, evermore!

—OLIVER WENDELL HOLMES.

And for your country, boy, and for that flag, never dream a dream but of serving her, though the service carry you through a thousand hells! No matter what happens to you—no matter who flatters or abuses you—never look at another flag, never let a night pass but you pray God to bless that flag.　　　—EDWARD EVERETT HALE.

Yours, O God, is the kingdom. And blessed is the nation whose God is the Lord. We believe that Your hand has been in the founding and the fortunes of this land. We do homage to it for its ideals, its principles, its glorious company of apostles of truth, its noble army of martyrs for liberty and humanity; we love and cherish it as our home and our shrine; but we hallow it, we stand in awe of it, as the scene of Your special activity, the instrument of Your holy purposes. May its vision not pass; may the clouds that hang over it be dispersed by the clear shining of the sun of righteousness and peace; may the dream of freedom with fraternity be realized here, even here, upon these shores, that Your saving health may be known among all nations. Amen.

—C. ELLWOOD NASH.

July 5

> If you, then, though you are evil, know how to give good gifts to your children, how much more will your Father in heaven give good gifts to those who ask him!
>
> MATTHEW 7:11 (NIV)

Far up the crag, 'twixt sea and sky,
Where winds tempestuous, blowing by,
Leave giant boulders swept and bare;
Where forked lightnings fitful flare,
And petrels sound their stormy cry.

A dainty bluebell, sweet and shy,
Lifted its head complacently,

As guarded by the tenderest care,
Far up the crag.

And now, whenever fear draws nigh,
In thought I stand 'twixt sea and sky,
And, as of old in my despair,
I bless the Power that set it there—
That tiny thing with courage high,
Far up the crag!

—FLORENCE E. COATES.

Eternal Presence, may we now speak to You? Or, consciously within Your presence, should our lips be still? Are You the Infinite Mercy, and shall we say, be merciful? Shall we persuade the love that cannot once withhold itself? We would not ask, were prayer to change established law. But, we will open here our hearts, and so receive the blessedness that seeks us and has sought us—sought us as the sunlight sought us early—seeks us as the raindrops seek us in the storm. Not more can You withhold the goodness from us. We wait receptively, unbarring all our rust-hinged doors to welcome the true favors that now find us. In sweet trust, asking or unasking, we abide ever in You. Amen.

—PERRY MARSHALL.

July 6

Never be lacking in zeal, but keep your spiritual fervor, serving the Lord.

ROMANS 12:11 (NIV)

God is a kind Father. He sets us all in the places where he wishes us to be employed, and that employment is truly "our Father's business." He chooses work for every creature which will be delightful to them, if they do it simply and humbly. He gives us always strength enough and sense enough for what He wants us to do; if we either tire ourselves or puzzle ourselves, it is our own fault. And we may always be sure, whatever we are doing, that we cannot be pleasing Him if we are not happy ourselves.

—JOHN RUSKIN.

Father Divine, Your are indeed kind. Yours are the ways of kindness, of wisdom, and of love—the ways of pleasantness and the paths of peace. In simple and humble spirit as becomes Your children, may we walk with You accomplishing the work to which You call us. Our work is Your work, our business the Father's business; the business of justice, mercy and truth. When loyal and true, we are what we are, and do what we do by Your grace. So help us to honor You in all the duties of life—"Not slothful in business—fervent in spirit"—pleasing You and therefore happy ourselves. Amen.

—ISAAC P. CODDINGTON.

July 7

Therefore, as we have opportunity, let us do good to all people, especially to those who belong to the family of believers.　GALATIANS 6:10 (NIV)

Threefold is the form of Space:
Length, with ever restless motion,
Seeks eternity's wide ocean;
Breadth with boundless sway extends;
Depth to unknown realms descends.

All as types to thee are given;
Thou must onward strive for heaven,
Never still or weary be,
Wouldst thou perfect glory see;

Far must thy researches go
Wouldst thou learn the world to know;
Thou must tempt the dark abyss
Wouldst thou prove what Being is.

Naught but firmness gains the prize—
Naught but fulness makes us wise—
Buried deep, truth ever lies!
　　　　—PROVERBS OF CONFUCIUS.

Our Heavenly Father, help us this day to make good our privilege to feel and think of You as we do. Help us this day to make ourselves part of our brotherhood, and our brotherhood part of You. We know not what the day has in store for us, but we pray to You to help us have in store for it our better heart, our better hands. Send Your holy spirit into our life to calm and to strengthen; that we may be steadfast and true; that we may give and be forgiven. Bless all Your children this day, and may our labor end as it began, in You, with You, for You. Amen.　　　—LOUIS H. BUCKSHORN.

July 8

> "For I know the plans I have for you," declares the Lord, "plans to prosper you and not to harm you, plans to give you hope and a future."
>
> JEREMIAH 29:11 (NIV)

O Impatient Ones! Do the leaves say nothing to you as they murmur today? They are not fashioned this spring, but months ago; and the summer just begun will fashion others for another year. At the bottom of every leaf-stem is a cradle, and in it is an infant germ; and the winds will rock it, and the birds will sing to it all summer long, and next season it will unfold. So God is working for you and carrying forward to the perfect development all the processes of our lives.   —HENRY WARD BEECHER.

O Eternal Father, giver of all spiritual grace, we thank You for Your presence in our hearts. May we realize that You have the best possible plan for every human life. Help us to be patient and joyful in the consciousness that You are carrying forward Your blessed work in us. Your love, O Lord, is equal to Your wisdom, and You will always do what is best for us. May Your holy will be our delight, so that we may each trust in You at all times and cheerfully say, Your will, O Lord, not mine, be done. You who cares for the birds and the lilies are ever mindful of us, Your children. Deliver us from worry and may Your peace guard our hearts and minds in Christ Jesus. Amen.
—GEORGE H. CHENEY.

July 9

> You honor me by anointing my head with oil.
>   My cup overflows with blessings.
> Surely your goodness and unfailing love will pursue me all the days of my life,
>   and I will live in the house of the Lord forever.
>
> PSALM 23:5b-6 (NLT)

Let us hope that one day all mankind will be happy and wise; and though this day never should dawn to have hoped for it cannot be wrong. And in any event, it is helpful to speak of happiness to those who are sad, that thus at least they may learn what it is that happiness means. They are ever inclined to regard it as something beyond them, extraordinary, out of their reach. But if all who may count themselves happy were to tell, very simply, what it was that brought happiness to them, the others would see that between sorrow and joy the difference is but as between a gladsome, enlightened acceptance of life and a hostile gloomy submission; between a large and harmonious conception of life, and one that is stubborn and narrow.

—MAETERLINCK.

O Lord, we thank You for the special providence which is over everything which You have created, and wherein You reside with all Your infinite perfections. We thank You that You care for us all, that in our day of joy we know it is You who fills our cup, by giving us the faculties which make it run over at the brim. We thank You that You are with us in our days of hardship and of calamity, that when our own heart cries out against us, You are greater than our heart, and, understanding all things, bless us in secret ways; and when we are cast down and go stooping and feeble, with hungering eyes and a failing heart, that You still are with us, and lead us from strength to strength and bless us continually. Amen.   —THEODORE PARKER.

July 10

So if the Son sets you free,
you will be free indeed.

JOHN 8:36 (NIV)

Were any of us really disappointed or melancholy in a hayfield? Did we ever lie fairly back on a haycock and look up into the blue sky, and listen to the merry sounds, the whetting of scythes and the laughing prattle of women and children, and think evil thoughts of the world or our brethren? Not we! Or, if we have so done we ought to be ashamed of ourselves, and deserve never again to be out of town during hay-harvest.

—THOMAS HUGHES.

Dear Heavenly Father, we devoutly thank You for the beautiful open face of Nature shining upon us; for the splendor of the fields where the birds wing their merry flight; for the breath of the flowers and the grass beneath the scythe, like the odor of incense; and most of all, for the merry shouts of women and children and men in the meadow, in the heyday of happiness, as they fill their souls with the freedom of the children of God, and live in the open where no evil breath can come. Grant that we may live spiritually forever in the fragrant hayfields of life, where the birds sing and the children shout, and where no covering or roof can ever shut out the sunshine of life's eternal bliss. Amen.

—ROBERT S. KELLERMAN.

July 11

Trust in the Lord with all your heart
and lean not on your own understanding;
6 in all your ways submit to him,
and he will make your paths straight.

PROVERBS 3:5–6 (NIV)

A story is told of a king who went into his garden one morning and found everything withering and dying. He asked an oak that stood near the gate what the trouble was. He found that it was sick of life and determined to die, because it was not tall and beautiful like the pine. The pine was out of heart because it could not bear grapes like the vine; the vine was going to throw its life away, because it could not stand erect and have as fine fruit as the pomegranate; and so on throughout the garden. Coming to the heartsease, the king found its bright face uplifted, as full of cheerfulness as ever. Said the king, "Well, heartsease, I am glad to find one brave little flower in this general discouragement and dying. You don't seem one bit disheartened."

"No, your majesty. I know I am of small account; but I concluded you wanted a heartsease when you planted me. If you had wanted an oak, or a pine, or a vine, or a pomegranate, you would have set one out. So I am bound to be the best heartsease that ever I can."　　　　　　　　　　　　　　　　　　—WILLIAM MOODIE.

Like the wise King of old, I pray, gracious Lord, give me wisdom. May Your Pillar of Light guide my footsteps so that I go not astray in the wilderness of sin and selfish ambition. Help me to acquire a pure heart and a contented spirit. Amidst all the vicissitudes of fortune, let faith induce me to say, "Whatever God does is well." Amen.

—M. M. EICHLER.

July 12

Show me your ways, Lord, teach me your paths.
Guide me in your truth and teach me,
    for you are God my Savior,
    and my hope is in you all day long.

PSALM 25:4–5 (NIV)

What shall I do to be just?
What shall I do for the gain
Of the world—for its sadness?
Teach me, O seers that I trust!
Chart me the difficult main
Leading out of my sorrow and madness,
Preach me the purging of pain.

Shall I wrench from my finger the ring
To cast to the tramp at my door?
Shall I tear off each luminous thing
To drop in the palm of the poor?
What shall I do to be just?
Teach me, O Ye in the light,
Whom the poor and the rich alike trust;
My heart is aflame to be right.

—HAMLIN A. GARLAND.

Infinite Spirit, You see us just as we are. In Your sight there can be no make-believe; we need not seek to offer You as a penance for our sins some cheap alms to the poor, for Your favor cannot be bought. We pray simply that we may be just—that we may be true. If we have wronged anyone, help us to right the wrong. If we have been false to ourselves or false to our neighbors, O Lord, make us true—we seek no easy admission to a far-off heaven, we seek Your presence here and now, today, by the only pathway open, the pathway of righteousness and truth. That we may enter this pathway, grant us we pray the illumination of Your Holy Spirit. Amen.   —GEORGE L. PERIN.

July 13

> Be very careful, then, how you live—not as unwise but as wise, making the most of every opportunity, because the days are evil. EPHESIANS 5:15-16 (NIV)

The law of worthy life is fundamentally the law of strife. It is only through labor, painful effort, by grim energy and resolute courage, that we move on to better things.
—THEODORE ROOSEVELT.

If we would please God we must watch every stroke and touch upon the canvas of our lives; we may not think we can lay it on with a trowel and yet succeed. We ought to live as miniature painters work, for they watch every line and tint.
—SPURGEON.

As we begin this new day, O our Father, may such energy and vigor, such strength and courage, such faith and hope be ours that the problems and tasks awaiting us may be boldly and gladly met as challenges to our powers. May that abundant life be in us which shall make our difficulties a tonic, and the struggle to achieve high aims a joy. May we be resourceful, equal to life, adequate to every situation, able to stand this universe—men who can. May we count it a privilege to live, to have a vision of life's possibilities, and to have the fellowship of so many good men and women by the way. Amen. —GEORGE R. DODSON.

July 14

> Jabez cried out to the God of Israel, "Oh, that you would bless me and enlarge my territory! Let your hand be with me, and keep me from harm so that I will be free from pain." And God granted his request.   1 CHRONICLES 4:10 (NIV)

With place, with gold, with power—
  oh, ask me not
With these my little hour of life to blot.
A little hour indeed! and I would fain
Its moments spend in what is
  worth its pain.
What traveler would faint through
  troublous lands
To gather only what must
  leave his hands
The moment that he takes
  his homeward ship?

Earth's goods and gauds give
  every man the slip;
But wealth of thought and
  richer wealth of love,
Must pass for coin in any world above.
The good to others done
  while here I strive
Is all at last that shall my dying shrive;
And, setting sail,
  my slight self-conquest's store
Is all my freight if I shall come to shore.
          —ANONYMOUS.

O Father, God! The span of our influence is both near and far; may it also be direct and strong. You have planted mighty virtue and unquenchable love in our hearts. Love knows the secret of imparting virtue's value to all the wretchedness in life. So, we beseech You, direct our hearts to altitudes of holiness and set our feet in the highways of helpfulness. May the charm of gentleness be in every service today, and may the tone of tenderness carry love's message over all barriers to the hearts that need. Thus would we keep our confidence with You and bind ourselves more profitably to our fellows. So shall Your great name be honored among men. Amen.

          —J. O. RANDALL.

July 15

That is what the Scriptures mean when they say, "No eye has seen, no ear has heard, and no mind has imagined what God has prepared for those who love him." But it was to us that God revealed these things by his Spirit. For his Spirit searches out everything and shows us God's deep secrets.

1 CORINTHIANS 2:9–10 (NLT)

What seems to grow fairer to me as life goes by, is the love and peace and tenderness of it. Not its wit and cleverness and grandeur of knowledge, but just the laughter of little children, and the friendship of friends, and the cozy talk of the fireside, and the sight of flowers and the sound of music.　　　　　—J.R.GREEN.

Now that You give us the light of a new day, grant that it carry with it the brightness of hope and courage for whatsoever the day may offer. Always behind the clouds is the shining that never fails; always beyond the labor which irks us is the joy of attainment. Open our eyes that we may see the best which shall be in the day; its love of friends, its sights of beauty, its music, its wisdom such as no day before could possess, its voices of the Spirit awaiting the listening ear, its tears of compassion and sympathy. Give us our daily bread such as shall feed the heart and enrich the mind and grant us forgiveness when we are blind to the common treasures of this Your world. Amen.　　　　　—GEORGE A. THAYER.

July 16

In the same way, let your light shine before others, that they may see your good deeds and glorify your Father in heaven.   MATTHEW 5:16 (NIV)

Methought that in a solemn church
   I stood.
Its marble acres,
   worn with knees and feet,
Lay spread from door to door,
   from street to street.
Midway the form hung high
   upon the rood
Of Him who gave His life to be our good;
Beyond, priests flitted, bowed,
   and murmured meet
Among the candles shining still
   and sweet.

Men came and went,
   and worshipped as they could;
And still their dust a woman
   with her broom,
Bowed to her work,
   kept sweeping to the door.
Then saw I slow through
   all the pillared gloom
Across the church a silent figure come.
"Daughter," it said,
   "Thou sweepest well my floor!"
"It is the Lord!" I cried,
   and saw no more.

—GEORGE MACDONALD.

Our Father, who is ever with us, help us this day so to reveal You through our common tasks, our relations with one another, in our homes and at our work, that men may know and love You better. This is Your most beautiful world. May we not mar its glory by our selfishness, but by the gentleness and sweetness of our lives make it more beautiful. May we this day not add to another's burden of care or pain. But may we by our words and deeds sweeten and brighten and strengthen the lives of those whom we meet. For Your goodness and mercy to us, for the opportunity of service, for love and sympathy, we thank You and pray that our devotion to Your truth may reveal the thankfulness of our hearts. Amen.   —ARTHUR L. WHEATHERLY.

July 17

And surely I am with you always, to the very end of the age.

MATTHEW 28:20 (NIV)

For I, a man, with men am linked,
And not a brute with brutes; no gain
That I experience must remain
Unshared; but should my best endeavor
To share it, fail—subsisteth ever
God's care above, and I exult
That God, by God's own ways occult,
May—doth, I will believe—bring back
All wanderers to a single track.

—ROBERT BROWNING.

Father of all souls in all worlds, our best friend forever, in Your good keeping we cannot wander beyond Your loving care. We thank You for life, for the fair world we live in, enriched by Your countless benefits, for the glad tidings of Your fatherly love that never fails, for the brotherhood that binds together all Your children, and for the immortal hope that beckons us up and on. By faithful living may we make life divine, and by brotherly service show You our gratitude and love. May the gospel of Jesus prevail in all hearts, speedily bring all wanderers home, draw our souls heavenward, and prepare us for higher and larger realms of service, where we shall forever live to Your glory. Amen.

—RUSH R. SHIPPEN.

July 18

And God is able to bless you abundantly, so that in all things at all times, having all that you need, you will abound in every good work.

2 CORINTHIANS 9:8 (NIV)

That man has a liberal education who has been so trained in youth that his body is the ready servant of his will, and does with ease and pleasure the work that it is capable of; whose intellect is a clear logic engine, ready to spin the gossamer as well as forge the anchors of the mind—one full of life and fire but whose passions are trained to come to heel by a rigorous will; the servant of a tender conscience; who has learned to love beauty, to hate vileness and to respect others as himself; such a one is in harmony with nature; they will get on together. —THOMAS HENRY HUXLEY.

Our Father, we would face this day in conscious companionship with You. Give us to know Your will, to do Your work. Help us to interpret aright Your constant revelation of love in nature and in the experiences of life. Give us strength so to will and so to act that we may make this day rich in the joy that comes from helpful living. May divine impulse find quick expression in righteous deed. In Your unresting effort to make this world Your own may we join with glad hearts. Rejoicing in Your love, strong in the consciousness of Your presence, may we go to our day's work with unwavering purpose to do Your will. Amen. —LATHAN A. CRANDALL.

July 19

A lily grows mysteriously, pushing up its solid weight of stem and leaf in the teeth of gravity. Shaped into beauty by secret and invisible fingers, the flower develops we know not how. But we do not wonder at it. Every day the thing is done; it is Nature, it is God. We are spiritual enough at least to understand that. But when the soul rises slowly above the world, pushing up its delicate virtues in the teeth of sin, shaping itself mysteriously into the image of Christ, we deny that the power is not of man. A strong will, we say, a high ideal, the reward of virtue, Christian influence—these will account for it. Spiritual character is merely the product of anxious work, self-command, and self-denial. We allow, that is to say, a miracle to the lily, but none to the man. The lily may grow; the man must fret and toil and spin.

—HENRY DRUMMOND.

This morning, our God, we need You! Give us Yourself afresh in the holy inspiration of heart warmth and burning love, that today we may have power from above while we walk and toil with things and folks of earth. May we be the vase to hold the blossoming beauty of Your unfolding. So may that beauty which You give unfold in acts which we are led to perform, and the holiness of this day set fast character drawn from You. Thus may we all who are Your children gladden the earth with unfolding beauty and kindness and shut out the things that are earthly. Amen.

—E. E. SMALL.

July 20

Therefore everyone who hears these words of mine and puts them into practice is like a wise man who built his house on the rock. The rain came down, the streams rose, and the winds blew and beat against that house; yet it did not fall, because it had its foundation on the rock. MATTHEW 7:24–25 (NIV)

The more simply you live, the more secure is your future; you are less at the mercy of surprises and reverses. An illness or a period of idleness does not suffice to dispossess you; a change of position, even considerable, does not put you to confusion. Having simple needs, you find it less painful to accustom yourself to the hazards of fortune. You remain a man, though you lose your office or your income, because the foundation on which your life rests is not your table, your cellar, your horses, your goods and chattels, or your money. In adversity you will not act like a nursling deprived of its bottle and rattle. Stronger, better armed for the struggle, presenting like those with shaven heads, less advantage to the hands of your enemy, you will also be of more profit to your neighbor. —CHARLES WAGNER.

O God who is ever the same, with the growing light of a new day, we would again take Your name upon our lips; and again invite the dear consciousness of Your presence. We do not know what this day may yield us. It may bring disaster; perhaps cherished hopes must be surrendered; plans may miscarry, clouds may gather, and storms may rage, but we will not be unmanned. We will not surrender our hold on You. May we thus be enabled to meet disaster with courage, and unlooked for joy with the poise of humility. Guard our goings-out and our comings-in, and lead us into the beauteous paths of ripe content. Amen. —JAMES HARRY HOLDEN.

July 21

Love is patient, love is kind. It does not envy, it does not boast, it is not proud. It does not dishonor others, it is not self-seeking, it is not easily angered, it keeps no record of wrongs. Love does not delight in evil but rejoices with the truth. It always protects, always trusts, always hopes, always perseveres.

1 CORINTHIANS 13:4–7 (NIV)

Love wore a suit of hodden gray
And toiled within the fields all day.

Love wielded pick and carried pack
And bent to heavy loads the back.

Though meagre fed and sorely lashed,
The only wage Love ever asked,

A child's wan face to kiss at night,
A woman's smile by candle light.

—MARGARET SANGSTER.

Our Father in Heaven, we thank You for love. How rich a gift it has been to us, and how exhaustless. It has been the source of all other gifts. We thank You for the brightness and gladness with which love invests the sunny day, and more for the patience and hope which it inspires when the sky is overcast and the way grows weary. In joy or sorrow we can ask nothing better than that it be our constant guest. We thank You for home life which offers us every hour its opportunity to give and to receive love. May it be to us the symbol of Your great household which Your love pervades. And as we thus think of it may our home life grow to us more holy and divine and Your love for all Your children more personal and tender until Your kingdom come and Your will be done on earth as it is in heaven. Amen.

—VINCENT E. TOMLINSON.

July 22

Whoever does not love does not know God,
because God is love.

1 JOHN 4:8 (NIV)

The entire object of true education is to make people not merely do the right things, but enjoy the right things—not merely industrious, but to love industry—not merely learned, but to love knowledge—not merely pure, but to love purity—not merely just, but to hunger and thirst after justice. —JOHN RUSKIN.

O Father, fill us with Your love today, with love for You, and love for the morning light and all Your glory. Fill us with love for the work that You give us to do, with love for the truth that You reveal to us and with love for the ideals of purity and righteousness that You set before us. May we have love for all Your children. Make us realize that they are all our brothers and sisters. Make us strive to have Your will done in their lives. Make us eager to have them know You. Amen.

—CHARLES B. BLISS.

July 23

Dear children, let us not love with words or speech
but with actions and in truth.

1 JOHN 3:18 (NIV)

If you were toiling up a weary hill,
Bearing a load beyond your strength
  to bear.
Straining each nerve untiringly and still
Stumbling and losing foothold
  here and there
And each one passing by
  would do so much
As give one upward lift and go his way,
Would not the slight reiterated touch
Of help and kindness lighten all the day?

If you were breasting a keen wind
  which tossed
And buffeted and chilled you
  as you strove,
Till baffled and bewildered quite, you lost
The power to see the way,
  and aim and move,
And one, if only for a moment's space,
Gave you a shelter from the bitter blast,
Would you not find it easier to face
The storm again when the brief rest
  was past?

—SUSAN COOLIDGE.

Our Father, as we thank You for the friendly service and sympathy that bless and strengthen our daily lives, we pray that our gratitude may move us to give a like service and sympathy as freely as we receive. In the day to whose beginning You have brought us, let our hearts and hands be ready to meet the needs of those with whom we come in touch. So influence our wayward wills that we shall not walk in selfish ways, nor forget the ties that bind us to one another, and to You. Keep us conscious of our birthright as Your children, that our acts and aims may be filial and fraternal and loyal to Jesus Christ Our Lord. Amen. —COSTELLO WESTON.

July 24

May integrity and uprightness protect me,
because my hope, Lord, is in you.

PSALM 25:21 (NIV)

It matters little where I was born,
Whether my parents were rich or poor,
Whether they shrank from the cold world's scorn
Or walked in the pride of wealth secure;
But whether I live an honest man,
And hold my integrity firm in my clutch,
I tell you brother, plain as I am,
It matters much.

—FROM THE SWEDISH.

Dear Father in Heaven, good Giver of all,
For birth in a land fair and free,
For parents with pluck,
    if not the best luck,
Who toiled and who suffered for me.
Who never knew fear,
    though the scorners were near,
Whom circumstance filled not
    with pride,
I thank Thee! These gifts,
    more than all on the lists,
Have mattered with me, and abide.

While striving and struggling
    my manhood to build,
To live like Thine own perfect Son,
I find on Earth's face not just
    one single place
Where such work so well can be done
As in the fair land which from
    Thy gracious hand
Comes to me a home to enjoy,
Where man, who should grow,
    may all liberty know
In seeking the soul's high employ. Amen.

—FREDERICK C. PRIEST.

July 25

Don't object that your duties are so insignificant; they are to be reckoned of infinite significance, and alone important to you. Were it but the more perfect regulation of your apartments, the sorting away of your clothes and trinkets, the arranging of your papers—"Whatsoever your hand finds to do, do it with all your might," and all your worth and constancy. Much more, if your duties are of evidently higher, wider scope; if you have brothers, sisters, a father, a mother, weigh earnestly what claim does lie upon you on behalf of each, and consider it as the one thing needful, to pay them more and more honestly and nobly what you owe. What matter how miserable one is if one can do that? That is the sure and steady disconnection and extinction of whatsoever miseries one has in this world. —THOMAS CARLYLE.

Creator of things, Father of Spirits, standing at the dawn of a new day we seek Your blessing. We know not what awaits us, You know, grant us guidance! Help us to see all our duties in the light of Your countenance. You have made the little and the large, help us to see our duties in their relation to Your plans. Whatsoever we do, help us to do all to Your glory. Help us to sweep our floors as to Your laws, right our rooms as a part of Your universe, care for our clothes as gifts from You. Help us to see You in the souls You have sent into the world, to treat them as thinking-thoughts of Yours, expressions of Your life. May we owe no man anything but to love, may the sun never set on an unpaid bill. For Your name's sake. Amen. —O. P. GIFFORD.

July 26

This is the day the LORD has made.
We will rejoice and be glad in it.

PSALM 118:24 (NLT)

Write it on your heart that every day is the best day in the year. No man has learned anything rightly until he knows that every day is doomsday. Today is a king in disguise. Today always looks mean to the thoughtless, in the face of a uniform experience that all good and great and happy actions are made up precisely of these blank todays. Let us not be so deceived, let us unmask the king as he passes.

—RALPH WALDO EMERSON.

Our Father, we thank You for this morning that ushers in the only day of which we have promise. Whether it proves to be a day of sunshine or of clouds—of joy or of sorrow—may we live it with thankfulness, with perfect confidence that You will always give us that which is for our own good. Help us to spend this day in doing well what our hands find to do; may our souls breathe the spirit of love and helpfulness to all, and may we have abundantly the influence of Your divine spirit to keep us pure. Amen.

—LUTHER F. MCKINNEY.

July 27

I like the man who faces what he must
With heart triumphant and
   a step of cheer;
Who fights the daily battle without fear;
Sees his hopes fail,
   yet keeps unfaltering trust
That God is God;
   that somehow, true and just,
His plans work out for mortals;
   not a tear
Is shed when fortune,
   which the world holds dear,

Falls from his grasp;
   better, with love, a crust
Than living in dishonor; envies not,
Nor loses faith in man; but does his best,
Nor even murmurs at his humbler lot;
But with a smile and words of hope,
   gives zest
To every toiler; he alone is great
Who by a life heroic conquers fate.

—SARAH KNOWLES BOLTON.

Gracious Father, last night we laid ourselves down in peace to sleep, but it was You who made us to dwell in safety, and when we awoke this morning we found ourselves still with You. Your loving favor was keeping faithful watch and ward while we slumbered. We thank You for Your kindly care of our lives during the darkness and danger of the night. Confident of Your continued presence and armed with Your unfailing strength, we would go forth to meet the duties and delights of the new day. God with us, we will overcome every temptation, endure every trial, bear every burden, and improve every opportunity of character-building and service-rendering, in the trustful and courageous spirit of Jesus Christ our Lord. Amen.

—RALPH E. CONNER.

July 28

Whether you turn to the right or to the left,
your ears will hear a voice behind you,
saying, "This is the way; walk in it."

ISAIAH 30:21 (NIV)

How large a part of our Godward life is travelled, not by clear landmarks seen far off in the promised land, but as travellers climb a mountain peak, by putting footstep after footstep, slowly and patiently, into the prints which someone going before us, with keener sight, with stronger nerves, tied to us by the cord of saintly sympathy, has planted deep into the pathless snow of the bleak distance that stretches up between humanity and God.... So we ascend by one another. We live by one another's blessings. —PHILLIPS BROOKS.

Our Father, we thank You for the light of a new day. May a new spirit and new courage come to our hearts. We thank You for all those who by patient toil and self-forgetting effort have made life as sweet and precious to us as it is. If we can no longer hear the voices nor see the faces of those we love or have reason to revere, may we be able to see their footprints and to take the way they trod, though that way seem steep and hard. May we be assured that the upward way leads to the expanding view and brings us to the splendor of the setting sun or of the still more glorious dawn. Amen.

—HILARY BYGRAVE.

July 29

We have different gifts, according to the grace given to each of us. If your gift is prophesying, then prophesy in accordance with your faith; if it is serving, then serve; if it is teaching, then teach; if it is to encourage, then give encouragement; if it is giving, then give generously; if it is to lead, do it diligently; if it is to show mercy, do it cheerfully.
ROMANS 12:6–8 (NIV)

A prince went into the vineyard to examine it. He came to a peach tree, and said, "What are you doing for me?"

The tree said, "In the spring I give my blossoms and fill the air with fragrance, and on my boughs hangs the fruit which men will gather and carry into the palace for you."

"Well done!" said the prince. To the chestnut he said, "What are you doing?"

"I am making nests for the birds, and shelter cattle with my leaves and spreading branches."

And the prince said, "Well done!" Then he went down to the meadow and asked the grass what it was doing.

"We are giving our lives for others, for your sheep and cattle that they may be nourished."

And the prince said, "Well done!"

Last of all he asked the tiny daisy what it was doing, and the daisy said, "Nothing, nothing. I cannot make a nesting-place for the birds, and I cannot give shelter for the cattle, and I cannot send fruit into the palace, and I cannot even give food for the sheep and cows—they do not want me in the meadow. All I can do is to be the best little daisy I can be."

And the prince bent down and kissed the daisy, and said, "There is none better than you."

—ANONYMOUS.

Help us, O Father, not to wait for the great opportunities which may never come. Help us to do with faithfulness the duties which lie close at hand. In our homes this day and wherever we may be—at school or on the street or at our work—fill our hearts with the spirit of Christ and let that spirit speak in every word which passes our lips and shine from our faces and work with our hands. Amen.
—WALTER A. TUTTLE.

July 30

But our citizenship is in heaven. And we eagerly await a Savior from there, the Lord Jesus Christ, who, by the power that enables him to bring everything under his control, will transform our lowly bodies so that they will be like his glorious body.   PHILIPPIANS 3:20–21 (NIV)

I will be glad all day for this cool draught
And the clear drops I dash upon my brow;
For the fresh glint of sunlight on the tree
And the bird singing on the bough.

I will be glad for that stored
   strength of life
Which lasts the day because
   the spirit wills;

For the live air that wings
   from far and breathes
The vigor of the everlasting hills.

What scope of toil,
   what loss or what reward,
I do not know. It is enough that now
I pledge the day's good cheer
   with this cool draught
And the drops dashed upon my brow.
         —CHARLES P. CLEAVES.

Our Father, we are nursed in Your arms, we are rested in the heart of Jesus, so that we know no more the emptiness of earth and the poverty of time, for our citizenship is in heaven, already do we walk the streets of gold. Out of the highest rapture may we come to do earth's plainest work, earth's hardest toil, with patient hearts and willing hands, knowing that death can be but for a moment, that all things are meant, in the sovereignty of God to give themselves up to the rule of life. Thus may Your children be loyal citizens, patient workers, honest merchantmen, wise parents. Be with all men who trust You; melt the mountains before their coming, and open the gates of difficulty 'ere they reach them, and give them to feel that the greatness of Your mercy is the proof of its divinity. Amen.   —JOSEPH PARKER.

July 31

For I am convinced that neither death nor life, neither angels nor demons, neither the present nor the future, nor any powers, neither height nor depth, nor anything else in all creation, will be able to separate us from the love of God that is in Christ Jesus our Lord.   ROMANS 8:38-39 (NIV)

These verses seem to me to express completely the remedial power of God's love. In this rough and tumble world of ours, of hard conditions, of disasters many, of untold misery, there are temptations enough for men to lose faith in God's love. It is well now and then to have an outburst of faith like this with the assurance that nothing can ever separate any child of God from the divine compassion and the divine care.
—GEORGE L. PERIN.

Our Heavenly Father, it is good for us to believe that through all storms and all darkness and all sickness and all infirmity, even through death itself, Your love abides. As we enter upon this day, we know not whither we shall go, but we thank You for the assurance that we may not go away from You. You follow us with Your care and wrap us around with Your love, as with a garment. In all that we do today may we know that You see us, and if our way be steep, may we be sure that You love us. Amen.
—GEORGE L. PERIN.

August 1

The commandments, "You shall not commit adultery," "You shall not murder," "You shall not steal," "You shall not covet," and whatever other command there may be, are summed up in this one command: "Love your neighbor as yourself."

ROMANS 13:9 (NIV)

Begin the morning by saying to yourself, I shall meet this day with the busybody, the ungrateful, the arrogant, deceitful, envious, unsocial. All these things happen to them by reason of their ignorance of what is good and evil. But I who have seen the nature of the good that it is beautiful, and of the bad that it is ugly, can neither be injured by any of them—for no one can fix on me what is ugly—nor can I be angry with my neighbor, nor hate him. We are made for cooperation; to act against one another, that is contrary to nature; and it is acting against one another to be vexed and turn away.

—MARCUS AURELIUS.

Eternal Spirit of Love, teach us the power of love. Help us to learn that love is supreme, and hence envies not, nor vaunts itself, nor seeks its own, but suffers long and is kind. We, who in Jesus of Nazareth have seen the glory of Your likeness and experienced the sweetness of Your love, desire like Him to reveal You in our lives, to be loving and gentle, sincere and generous, to cooperate with friend and stranger in all that is good, to live so that they can work with us for the advancement of everything righteous. Fill us, therefore, with Your spirit, and send us forth today in Your service. Amen.

—WILLIAM W. GUTH.

August 2

The God who made the world and everything in it is the Lord of heaven and earth and does not live in temples built by human hands. And he is not served by human hands, as if he needed anything. Rather, he himself gives everyone life and breath and everything else. ACTS 17:24–25 (NIV)

"God!" let the torrents,
   like a shout of nations,
Answer! and let the ice-plain echo,
   "God!"
"God!" sing, ye meadow streams,
   with gladsome voice
Ye pine groves, with your soft
   and soul-like sounds!
And they, too have a voice,
   yon piles of snow,
And in their perilous fall shall thunder,
   "God!"

Ye living flowers that skirt
   the eternal frost!
Ye wild goats sporting round
   the eagle's nest!
Ye eagles, playmates of
   the mountain storm!
Ye lightnings, the dread arrows of
   the clouds!
Ye signs and wonders of the elements!
Utter forth "God!" and fill the hills
   with praise!
     —SAMUEL TAYLOR COLERIDGE.

Heavenly Father, how long have Your servants thirsted after You—O spring of everlasting life! In this land of our home the meditations of ages surround us, and through the treasured thoughts of the wise in many generations we are lifted into a light beyond the solitary soul. Countless are Your witnesses, Eternal God! The stars without number are but a little part of them; and the prayers and aspirings of every heart of man can never cease to speak of You. Humbled and blind amid Your manifold glories, may we find rest in the simplicity of Christ, and be among the pure in heart who alone can see You. Amen. —JAMES MARTINEAU.

August 3

Wait for the Lord; be strong and take heart and wait for the Lord.

PSALM 27:14 (NIV)

O God, my master God,
   look down and see
If I am making what Thou wouldst of me.
Fain might I lift my hands up in the air
From the defiant passion of my prayer;
Yet here they grope on this
   cold altar stone,
Graving the words I think
   I should make known.
Mine eyes are Thine.
   Yea, let me not forget,
Lest with unstaunched tears
   I leave them wet,
Dimming their faithful power,
   till they not see
Some small, plain task that might be
   done for Thee.

My feet, that ache for paths
   of flowery bloom,
Halt steadfast in the straitness
   of this room.
Though they may never be
   on errands sent,
Here shall they stay,
   and wait Thy full content.
And my poor heart,
   that doth so crave for peace,
Shall beat until Thou bid
   its beating cease.
So, Thou dear master God,
   look down and see
Whether I do Thy bidding heedfully.

—ALICE BROWN.

O God, our Heavenly Father, from whom comes to us again this gift of life, may we be able to use as You would have us the fresh revelation and energy of each morning hour. May we be helped to see more clearly that task with all its blessings, which You place within our reach today. Freshen our souls anew with the coming sunlight and quicken our will that we may perceive and fulfill our present duty gladly, eagerly, successfully, however humble in the spirit of those who remember that if done for Your sake and beneath Your laws even servile labors shine. Amen.

—HOBART CLARK.

August 4

For you make me glad by your deeds, Lord;
I sing for joy at what your hands have done.

PSALM 92:4 (NIV)

We thank You for all that You have made, and that You have called it Good! We thank You! We enter into Your work, and go about Your business.

—EDWARD EVERETT HALE.

O, it is great, and there is no other greatness. To make some work of God's creation a little fruitfuller, better, more worthy of God; to make some human hearts a little wiser, manfuller, happier—more blessed, less accursed—it is a work for God.

—THOMAS CARLYLE.

Heavenly Father, we would begin the day with noble purpose; may we scorn all meanness, and lift up our heads unto the Lord as men who have a great expectation. Our hope is in a living God; You will not allow our life to wander into darkness; if for a small moment we are forsaken, we shall be gathered with ineffable and everlasting mercies. In the confidence of Your presence, in the assurance of Your sustaining grace, we look steadfastly to heaven, and then we look hopefully to earth, and we know that, having begun the day with prayer and praise and pious expectancy, its hours shall all be gladdened and its even-tide shall be a benediction. Guide us with Your eyes; sustain us by Your mighty power; keep us this day without sin. Amen.

—JOSEPH PARKER.

August 5

And we all, who with unveiled faces contemplate the Lord's glory, are being transformed into his image with ever-increasing glory, which comes from the Lord, who is the Spirit.   2 CORINTHIANS 3:18 (NIV)

The scenery around your house may be monotonous, without a mountain or sea or lake or hill; but an upward look at the clear sky will put you in instant communication with infinite beauty and majesty. No spot on earth is common or barren over which the skies bend in solemn silence. No human life need be barren or common which is connected by the great network of moral law with any other being.

—J. H. CARLISLE.

Our God and Father, the author of beauty, the rewarder of all them that seek You, we, Your children, come to You at the opening of this new day. May we have hearts so pure that we shall see You; minds so open that we shall talk with You; and lives so true that we shall reveal You. Let toil become to us as a sacrament. Reveal to us the beauty of life as well as of holiness and help us to live with upturned faces, so that we may catch the glory of Your presence, and reflect it to all around us. May we walk with You, thinking Your thoughts, having Your visions of beauty and of life. When life's evening shall come gather us in Your arms of love to be with You in the home which You have prepared for us and have beautified with earth's fairest treasures through Jesus Christ, Our Lord. Amen.   —JOHN GALBRAITH.

August 6

How good is man's life, the mere living! How fit to employ
All the heart and the soul and the senses forever in joy!

—ROBERT BROWNING.

I am glad to think
I am not bound to make the world go right;
But only to discover and to do,
With cheerful heart, the work that God appoints.
I will trust in Him,
That He can hold His own; and I will take
His will, above the work He sendeth me, to be my chiefest good.

—JEAN INGELOW.

Our Heavenly Father, all Your works prove Your goodness; the world You give us is good; the powers with which You endow us are adapted to deeds of goodness. We know full well that we do evil as well as good. Some of our days close in sadness.... At the beginning of this day we pledge ourselves to try harder than ever to do something good, to make somebody happy, to keep our minds filled with pure thoughts, to set our ambitions on worthy objects; and we pray that You who are "the Power not ourselves that makes for righteousness" shall work with us that through our effort and Your help the day shall end in joy and peace. Amen.   —LEE S. McCOLLESTER.

August 7

I will sing to the Lord all my life;
I will sing praise to my God as long as I live.

PSALM 104:33 (NIV)

Our lives are songs; God writes the words,
And we set them to music at pleasure;
And the song grows glad, or sweet, or sad,
As we choose to fashion the measure.
We must write the music, whatever the song,
Whatever its rhyme or metre;
And if it is sad, we can make it glad,
Or, if sweet, we can make it sweeter.

—ELLA WHEELER WILCOX.

We thank You, O God, that You have made us responsive to all the beauty and gladness about us, and that we may make our lives one grand, sweet song. We know there is much that may spoil the song. But we thank You, that if we follow the great Leader, we can change all discordant notes into harmony. Help us through Him to tune our lives into accord with Yours. Especially may we live in peace with each other. Make us strong to return good for evil, to meet irritability with patience, unkindness with gentleness and harsh words with quiet speech. So may our lives "be filled with music, and the cares that infest the day, shall fold their tents like the Arabs, and as silently steal away." Amen.   —JAMES M. PAYSON.

_____

_____

_____

_____

_____

_____

_____

August 8

Back of the canvas that throbs the painter is hinted and hidden,
Into the statue that breathes the soul of the sculptor is bidden,
Under the joy that is felt lie the infinite issues of feeling;
Crowning the glory revealed is the glory that crowns the revealing.
Great are the symbols of being, but that which is symbolled is greater;
Vast the create and beheld, but vaster the inward creator.

—RICHARD REALF.

O Lord, who has created us surely for good and not evil, for You are good and do good, will go with us through all the day. Help us to keep in mind Your presence, that we may walk before You and be perfect, that we may walk with You and be pleasing to You, that we may walk after You, humbly, reverently. May we prize the glories that come with the hours, not suffering them to make us conceited or self-centered, or unduly independent, but utilize them as means to make us more fully a part of You. Give us this day complete victory over each temptation as it arrives, and may we feel when night falls that we have acquitted ourselves well in the campaign, and done what we could to make, not only ourselves, but the world around us, better. Amen.

—JAMES MUDGE.

August 9

For God, who said, "Let light shine out of darkness," made his light shine in our hearts to give us the light of the knowledge of God's glory displayed in the face of Christ. 2 CORINTHIANS 4:6 (NIV)

> Each night is followed by its day,
> Each storm by fairer weather,
> While all the works of nature sing
> Their songs of joy together.
> Then learn, O heart, their songs of hope!
> Cease, soul, thy thankless sorrow;
> For though the clouds be dark today,
> The sun will shine tomorrow.

—T. EDGAR JONES.

Father of light! Who causes light to shine out of darkness and makes day to follow the night; we thank You for Your loving care that has brought us from the slumber and rest of night to behold the light of a new day. May we rejoice in it, and cheerfully enter upon its duties and experiences. May the grace of Your presence make our sunshine, that we may walk in the light of heaven, breathe its atmosphere and engage in its service; doing Your will in the service of one another and in the service of love, truth and goodness. May the light of faith, hope, and love shining within us, dispel all darkness and sorrow from our lives, that light which shines so lustrously from the life of Jesus Christ our Lord. Amen. —ROBERT T. POLK.

August 10

For none of us lives for ourselves alone,
and none of us dies for ourselves alone.

ROMANS 14:7 (NIV)

Never say, "It is nobody's business but my own what I do with my life." It is not true. Your life is put into your hands as a trust, for many others besides yourself. If you use it well, it will make many others happy; if you abuse it, you will harm many others besides yourself. —JAMES M. PULLMAN.

Almighty Father, whom, though we have not seen, we love, we know not what this day may bring forth but we know that it shall be for good as our trust is in You. We look up and adore You, and we believe and love and obey. Throughout all the hours of this day may we be "diligent in business, fervent in spirit, serving the Lord." We believe in the victory of good over evil, of light over darkness; help us to bear our part courageously in the battle. Be merciful to us and make us merciful to one another. May we be numbered with those who are pure in heart, and see God in the humblest service to the humblest people. We beseech You to answer according to Your love not only these prayers which we utter with our lips but also the silent prayers of our heart. Amen. —HAROLD PATTISON.

August 11

In everything I did, I showed you that by this kind of hard work we must help the weak, remembering the words the Lord Jesus himself said: "It is more blessed to give than to receive." ACTS 20:35 (NIV)

Prince Florimel and Prince Carimel were twin brothers, the sons of a king, and no one could tell which of the two ought to succeed to the throne, for they were both exactly the same age. So one day they went to a wise magician and asked him which of them ought to be king after their father's death.

"He who is most worthy," said the magician.

"But how shall we find out who is most worthy?"

"He who possesses the magic flower that grows in the enchanted forest shall be found most worthy," he answered.

So the two brothers travelled through the enchanted forest until they found the magic flower; but it grew in such a dangerous place that Carimel would not attempt to reach it. Florimel, however, clambered down the rocks and plucked the flower; and when he had got it, what do you think he did with it? Why, he gave it to his brother, for the name of that magic flower was Unselfishness.

—WILLIAM MOODIE.

Our Father, with thankful hearts for all Your goodness to us in the past—we seek Your Holy Spirit's guidance for the day before us. Help us to live not for self alone, but for the good of all with whom we mingle. May the needy, suffering, and struggling ones all about us gather strength because of our devotion to You. So inspire us to forget ourselves, that we may the better remember our Master, and the privileges and duties of a life's service to Your children. Infinite One, thus help us, this day, and in all the days to come, to live to Your glory! Amen. —LEWIS P. BATES.

August 12

For I was hungry and you gave me something to eat, I was thirsty and you gave me something to drink, I was a stranger and you invited me in, I needed clothes and you clothed me, I was sick and you looked after me, I was in prison and you came to visit me.   MATTHEW 25:35–36 (NIV)

To do something for someone else; to love the unlovely; to give a hand to the unattractive; to speak to the uncongenial; to make friends with the poor and folks of lowly degree; to find a niche in the church of the Lord, and to do something out of sheer love for Him; to determine in His house to have His mind; to plan to win at least one for the Master; to aim to redeem past time that is lost; to will to let one's light shine; to cut off practices that are sinful and costly; to add the beauty of holiness—this is to make one's life a thing of beauty and this is to grow in grace, for growing in grace is simply copying the beautiful life of the altogether lovely One.

—EDWARD F. REIMER.

Infinite Father, we rejoice that it is possible for us to be workers together with You by giving our sympathy, love, and help to Your needy children. As You have honored us by appointing us to such a gracious ministry, may we seek to honor You in return by trying to do Your blessed will. In all lowly and gentle ways, may we do what we can to bind up the broken-hearted, to relieve the distressed, to strengthen the weak. Let none who suffer look to us in vain for some manifestation of the Christ-like Spirit. May we so meet and treat the sad, the lonely, the tempted, that they shall take knowledge of us that we have been with Jesus. So may His heavenly teaching bear sweet fruit in our conduct and characters, and so may the Kingdom which He came to establish grow apace in the world. In His name. Amen.

—WILLARD C. SELLECK.

August 13

Dear friends, let us continue to love one another, for love comes from God. Anyone who loves is a child of God and knows God. 1 JOHN 4:7 (NLT)

Let me feel that I am to be a lover. I am to see to it that the world is better for me, and to find my reward in the act. Love would put a new face on this weary old world in which we dwell as pagans and enemies too long; and it would warm the heart to see how fast the vain diplomacy of statesmen, the impotence of armies and navies and lines of defense, would be superseded by this unarmed child. This great, overgrown, dead Christendom of ours still keeps alive at least the name of a lover of mankind. But one day all men will be lovers: and every calamity will be dissolved in the universal sunshine. —RALPH WALDO EMERSON.

What manner of love You have bestowed upon us, dear Lord, that we should be called Your children! As You have loved us, so teach us each to love the world. This day someone will go forth to business on land or sea burdened with heavy cares: some father disheartened and discouraged will take up the trials of yesterday wondering what the end will be—some mother dismayed with her lot will cry "How long?" Help us, O Lord to minister to them in word or look, in prayer or gift. As the sun shall this day bring light and life to this old earth causing it to yield its highest purpose, so grant that Your love may give through us a new inspiration to all mankind. Hasten the time when all shall love You as You have loved the world. Then will each love the other. Then will the sword and the spear be molten into the plowshare and the pruning hook, and the desert shall bud and blossom as the rose. Amen. —EDWIN ALONZO BLAKE.

August 14

Create in me a pure heart, O God,
and renew a steadfast spirit within me.

PSALM 51:10 (NIV)

Thou art, O God, the life and light
Of all this wondrous world we see;
Its glow by day, its smile by night,
Are but reflections caught from thee.
Where'er we turn, thy glories shine,
And all things fair and bright are thine.

—THOMAS MOORE.

Almighty God, our Heavenly Father, who has safely brought us to the beginning of this day, defend us in the same with Your mighty power. Grant that this day we fall into no sin. Create in us a clean heart and renew a right spirit within us. Open our eyes that this day may be a fresh disclosure of You, the Unseen Presence; endow us with Your strength that, in joy and pain, it may lead us into Your house not made with hands, eternal in the heavens. Enable us so to use the things of the world that while they abide we may not lose Your presence, and when they pass we may not stand alone. So shall the spirit of Christ inflame us. Amen.

—FREDERICK W. PERKINS.

August 15

We are hard pressed on every side, but not crushed; perplexed, but not in despair; persecuted, but not abandoned; struck down, but not destroyed.

2 CORINTHIANS 4:8-9 (NIV)

It ain't no use to grumble and complain,
It's just as cheap and easy to rejoice;
When God sorts out the weather and sends rain,
Why, rain's my choice.

—JAMES WHITCOMB RILEY.

When you get into a tight place, and everything goes against you, till it seems as if you could not hold on a minute longer, never give up then, for that's just the place and time that the tide will turn. —HARRIET BEECHER STOWE.

Father, we pray that in every emergency of our lives we may be faithful to the duty which the day demands, and with reverent spirits acquit us like men, doing what should be done, bearing what must be borne, and so growing greater from our toil and our sufferings, till we transfigure ourselves into noble images of humanity, which are blameless within and beautiful without, and acceptable to Your spirit. So may Your kingdom come and Your will be done on earth as it is in heaven; for Yours is the kingdom and the power and the glory, the dominion and honor forever and ever. Amen.

—THEODORE PARKER.

August 16

A cheerful heart brings a smile to your face;
a sad heart makes it hard to get through the day.

PROVERBS 15:13 (MSG)

It was only a glad "Good Morning"
As she passed along the way;
But it spread the morning's glory
Over the livelong day.
　　　　—CARLOTTA PERRY.

Smile upon the troubled pilgrims
Whom you pass and meet;
Frowns are thorns, and smiles are
　　blossoms,
Oft to weary feet.
Do not make the way seem harder
By a sullen face;
Smile a little, smile a little,
Brighten up the place.
　　　　—ELLA WHEELER WILCOX.

Father, in this morning hour, we would look into Your face and feel the sweetness of that transforming influence which is forever baptizing Your world with light and gladness, adding beauty to beauty and glory to glory. Baptize us anew, with this all-pervading spirit and send us out into this day's work to meet its varied experiences with trusting hearts and smiling faces. May we each send forth a brightening, gladdening influence to cheer and strengthen and uplift every weary, troubled pilgrim whom we meet on this day's journey. So may it be ours to enter into closer and diviner fellowship with Your, our Father, whose greatest joy is to impart joy and blessing to Your waiting children. Amen.　　　　—ANNETTE J. SHAW.

August 17

The grass withers and the flowers fall,
but the word of our God endures forever.

ISAIAH 40:8 (NIV)

There are nettles everywhere,
But smooth green grasses are more common still;
The blue of heaven is larger than the cloud.

—ELIZABETH BARRETT BROWNING.

Flower in the crannied wall,
I pluck you out of the crannies—
Hold you here, root and all, in my hand,

Little flower—but if I could understand
What you are, root and all, and all in all,
I should know what God and man is.

—ALFRED TENNYSON.

O God, who has gemmed the heavens with round, revolving worlds, the earth with beauty and the coronet of our minds with royal faculties, we do not know what "the little flower is, root and all, and all in all" and yet, dear Lord, through the clear and the convincing revelation of Your dear Son; through the divine image which You have implanted within us; through the mighty and the persuasive witness from experience, we do feel and believe that You are the great creator, preserver and benefactor; that You have called us to do a noble, a specific work; that we ought not to neglect the gift that is in us; to this end You will help us to be pure, brave, faithful and strong, that we may fight the good fight, and win the crown of righteousness. Amen.

—ALBERT HAMMATT.

August 18

Therefore encourage one another and build each other up, just as in fact you are doing.

1 THESSALONIANS 5:11 (NIV)

O ye, so far above me on the Height,
I cannot hear your voices as ye stand
Facing the vast, invisible to me.
But I can see your gestures of delight,
And something guess of that wide,
  glorious sea,
The glimmering isles of that
  enchanted land,
The winds which from that
  ocean freshly blow.
And so your Vision lifts me
  toward the Height,
Although ye have forgot me far below.

But you, my brother, you, my near of kin,
Who some few steps above me
  on the steep
Look smiling back to cheer me ever on,
Who lend a hand as I the chasm leap,
And stay your haste that I
  the crag may win,
Thinking it scorn for Strength
  to climb alone;
You with your morning song
  when sings the lark,
You, with unflagging purpose
  at high noon,
And quiet-hearted trust when
  comes the dark—
To you I owe it that I climb at all.

—MARY FRANCES WRIGHT.

Spirit of the Infinite Life! We praise You that our visions of the Divinest rise far beyond the borders of our known and familiar fields, that the resources of our unwearied life are in those mysterious regions that we have not explored. And yet we rejoice that the shadows of these holy visions fall across our common ways, reporting thus from the Infinite and the unknown the possibilities of greater fortunes yet to be. In this life of Yours may we dwell, seeing You in the life about us and evermore seeking to lead the life toward those high places that are always waiting the coming of those who aspire toward You. Amen.

—E. L. REXFORD.

August 19

This righteousness is given through faith in Jesus Christ to all who believe. There is no difference between Jew and Gentile, for all have sinned and fall short of the glory of God, and all are justified freely by his grace through the redemption that came by Christ Jesus. ROMANS 3:22-24 (NIV)

The flowers got into a debate one morning as to which of them was the flower of God and the rose said: "I am the flower of God, for I am the fairest and the most perfect in beauty and variety of form and delicacy of fragrance of all the flowers."

And the crocus said: "No, you are not the flower of God. Why, I was blooming long before you bloomed. I am the primitive flower; I am the first one."

And the lily of the valley said modestly: "I am small, but I am white; perhaps I am the flower of God."

And the trailing arbutus said: "Before any of you came forth I was blooming under the leaves and under the snow. Am I not the flower of God?"

And all the flowers cried out: "No, you are no flower at all; you are a come-outer."

And then God's wind, blowing on the garden, brought this message to them: "Little flowers, do you not know that every flower that answers God's spring call, and comes out of the cold, dark earth, and lifts its head above the sod and blooms forth, catching the sunlight from God and flinging it back to men, taking the sweet south wind from God and giving it back to others in sweet and blessed fragrance— do you not know they are all God's flowers?" —LYMAN ABBOTT.

Our Heavenly Father, in Your sight, there are no nations, there is no north and no south, no east and no west; there is no black and no white; Jew and Gentile, bond and free—all are Yours. O, Lord, give us so much breadth of sympathy that we shall be able to understand at least dimly the universality of Your love. Amen.

—GEORGE L. PERIN.

August 20

I can do all things through him who strengthens me.

PHILIPPIANS 4:13 (ESV)

Sound, sound the clarion, fill the fife!
To all the sensual world proclaim
One crowded hour of glorious life
Is worth an age without a name.

—WALTER SCOTT.

Do not pray for easy lives. Pray to be stronger men. Do not pray for tasks equal to your powers. Pray for powers equal to your tasks. Then the doing of your work shall be no miracle. But you shall be a miracle. Every day you shall wonder at yourself, at the richness of life which has come to you by the grace of God.

—PHILLIPS BROOKS.

Our Heavenly Father, we thank You for the rest of the night and the joy and beauty of the morning. This day we accept as a loving tribute of Your Love to Your children. May we not mar it by unhallowed thoughts, unkind, hasty and regretful speech and shameful and evil deeds. May ours be the illumination which comes from moral and spiritual conquest. May we feel the ties that bind us tenderly to You and to one another; and work for that large human brotherhood, which holds in its strong embrace even the most distant and isolated member of the human family. May we go forth to our work with a deep and abiding faith in the power of good over evil and willing to do our share in the building up of Your kingdom of love and righteousness, peace and good will here upon earth. Amen. —HENDRIK VOSSEMA.

August 21

God-loyal people don't stay down long;
Soon they're up on their feet,
 while the wicked end up flat on their faces.

PROVERBS 24:16 (MSG)

We learn wisdom from failure much more than from success, often discover what will do by finding out what will not do, and probably he who never made a mistake never made a discovery. Horne Tooke used to say of his studies in intellectual philosophy that he had become all the better acquainted with the country through having had the good luck sometimes to lose his way.   —SAMUEL SMILES.

Our Father, in the strength of our nightly rest and daily bread we go forth to whatever needs us or awaits us. Nothing from You is too difficult for us to attempt; nothing too grievous for us to bear. Teach us how priceless is Your gift of life, how close we are to the fountain of strength, how sure of success is every effort to bring good to pass. Reverently and believingly would we hearken to You in our inmost souls. Let not our failures dishearten us, or the delay of results cause chill of doubt or fear. May our presence have strength and peace for others, and our lives proclaim that You live and are good to all. In the name of Christ we lift our prayer. Amen.

—SAMUEL C. BEANE.

August 22

Now this I know: The LORD gives victory to his anointed.
He answers him from his heavenly sanctuary
  with the victorious power of his right hand.
Some trust in chariots and some in horses,
  but we trust in the name of the LORD our God.

PSALM 20:6-7 (NIV)

At Bannockburn Lord Randolph Murray was being sorely pressed by a large body of cavalry. Sir James Douglas got leave from Bruce to go to his aid, but just as he came up he found the English in disorder, and many horses galloping away with empty saddles. "Halt!" he cried to his men; "These brave men have already repulsed the enemy; let us not diminish their glory by seeking to share it."

—WILLIAM MOODIE.

O God of Hosts! On many a field of battle will Your soldiers fight this day. Help them to be brave and true. Give them a glorious victory. Help us who watch to give them full credit for their valor. May we not diminish by seeking to share their glory. May we not render their deeds commonplace by insisting that "It is so easy, so natural, for them to be good," implying that their struggle has not been hard or that their victories had not been what ours have proven to be. Help us, O Lord, with valor to fight our own battles and run our own race and with gratitude to be glad in others' victories. Amen.

—J. FRANK CHASE.

August 23

This is how we know what love is: Jesus Christ laid down his life for us.
And we ought to lay down our lives for our brothers and sisters.

1 JOHN 3:16 (NIV)

The bee that sips her sweets
    from flowers fair,
Flying on careless wing now here,
    now there,
With azure skies above,
    green sward below,
And soft south wind to bear her
    to and fro,
Might seem the soul
    of self-devoted ease,
Her life a draught of nectar without lees.
Not so! Her prime is full
    of strenuous deed

That shames our own in generous meed
Of work for other's good.
    Long summer days
She builds her golden house,
    with guerdons stays
Her Queen, uprears her young,
    and stores her food—
Then sudden shuns her wealth,
    her home, her brood,
And seeks new haven
    on an unknown sea,
Leaving her life-work to posterity.

—HENRY HOYT MOORE.

Gracious Father in heaven, and all about me, Your gentleness does ever tend to make life greater and richer. Your providence is so wholesomely good, I would fain be completely at home in it. You are very gracious. Help me to be as gracious in my way as You are in Your wonderful way. When I acknowledge that You are good and wise, there comes a joyous freedom to my spirit that makes life a sweet pleasure. I desire ever to work in the fullness of this faith without grudging, without suspecting, an open, glad and fruitful service. Oh, help me then to love my fellows more, and You sincerely! Amen.

—ELIHU GRANT.

August 24

Do to others as you would have them do to you.

LUKE 6:31 (NIV)

Drudgery is the gray angel of success.... Look at the leaders in the professions, the solid men in business, the master-workmen who begin as poor boys and end by building a town to house their factory-hands, they are drudges of the single aim.... "One thing I do."

Mr. Maydole, the hammer-maker of Central New York, was an artist:

"Yes," he said, "I have made hammers for twenty-eight years."

"Well, then you ought to be able to make a pretty good hammer by this time."

"No, sir," was the answer, "I never made a pretty good hammer—I make the best hammer made in the United States." —WILLIAM C. GANNETT.

O Lord, we remember our daily duties before You, the hard toil which You give us in our manifold and various avocations, and we pray that there may be in us such a confidence in our nature, such earnest obedience to You, we reverencing all Your qualities and keeping Your commands, that we shall serve You every day, making our life one great act of holiness to You. May our continuous industry be so squared by the golden rule that it shall nicely fit with the interests of all with whom we have to do, and so by our handicraft all mankind shall be blessed. Amen.

—THEODORE PARKER.

August 25

Make it your goal to live a quiet life, minding your own business and working with your hands, just as we instructed you before. Then people who are not believers will respect the way you live, and you will not need to depend on others.

1 THESSALONIANS 4:11-12 (NLT)

His larger life ye cannot miss
In gladly, nobly using this.

—BAYARD TAYLOR.

There are saints enough if we only know how to find them—sainthoods of the fireside and of the marketplace. They wear no glory round their heads; they do their duties in the strength of God; they have their martyrdoms and win their palms, and though they get into no calendars, they leave a benediction and a force behind them on the earth when they go up to heaven.   —PHILLIPS BROOKS.

Our Father, in whose life are our lives, help us to use all things nobly and so find joy in You. We thank You for faithful souls who in humblest station have reflected Your life and have worked for blessing. In Your strength they have sought to build Your kingdom, and though they have had no glory of men they yet have wrought for You and have won place in Your heart. Because they have aided the world and others have entered into their labors their good work shall remain and its quiet influence shall be a benediction. Though they have lived obscure lives and have filled obscure places they have been precious in Your sight and are numbered with Your saints. May we, like them, eternally serve You. Amen.   —GEORGE H. YOUNG.

August 26

For you were once darkness, but now you are light in the Lord.
Live as children of light.   EPHESIANS 5:8 (NIV)

We can't choose happiness either for ourselves or for another; we can't tell where that will lie. We can only choose whether we will indulge ourselves in the present moment, or whether we will renounce that for the sake of obeying the divine voice within us—for the sake of being true to all the motives that sanctify our lives. I know this belief is hard; it has slipped away from me again and again; but I have felt that if I let it go forever, I should have no light through the darkness of this life.

—GEORGE ELIOT.

O God, You know the hours in which we desire You. You know that You have made us to love truth and to walk in the light and when we are unjust, unkind, unloving, then we are not true to ourselves—then we forget that we are living souls and that You are our Father. Let us not draw nigh to You with our lips while our hearts are far from You, but, knowing how dependent and frail we are, may we feel that it is a good and helpful thing to draw nigh unto You by faith and prayer—and to take thought of that Infinite Love which holds us all in its arms of strength and mercy. Lift up our minds today, warm our affections, and deepen within us the feeling of reverence, of gratitude, and guide all the longings of our hearts aright. Amen.

—JOSHUA YOUNG.

August 27

What agreement is there between the temple of God and idols? For we are the temple of the living God. As God has said:

"I will live with them and walk among them,
and I will be their God, and they will be my people."

2 CORINTHIANS 6:16 (NIV)

Life may be given in many ways,
And loyalty to truth be sealed
As bravely in the closet as the field,
So bountiful is fate;
But then to stand beside her,
When craven churls deride her,
To front a lie in arms and not to yield,
This shows, methinks, God's plan
And measure of a stalwart man,
Limbed like the old heroic breeds,
Who stands self-poised
　on manhood's solid earth,
Not forced to frame excuses
　for his birth,
Fed from within
　with all the strength he needs.
—JAMES RUSSELL LOWELL.

Heavenly Father, in this new day may we recognize a new opportunity for seeking Your purpose in us; to become stronger children of Yours, and worthier followers of Your Son. Whatever be our trial give us courage to stand without compromise, for that which we believe to be true; give us grace to rise superior to praise or blame, timidity or self-interest; to be loyal to the best in us, and be ever ready to protest against wrong and injustice. Help us to know ourselves as temples of Yours; to know that the essential principal in us is not dust, but God; to rise to that dignity of sonship that compels one to choose the right and say: "Here I stand, I cannot do otherwise." In His name. Amen. —HERBERT H. GRAVES.

August 28

May the words of my mouth
and the meditation of my heart
be pleasing to you,
O Lord, my rock and my redeemer.

PSALM 19:14 (NLT)

All we have willed or hoped or dreamed of good shall exist;
Not its semblance, but itself; no beauty, nor good, nor power
Whose voice has gone forth, but each survives for the melodist,
When eternity affirms the conception of an hour.
The high that proved too high, the heroic for earth too hard,
The passion that left the ground to lose itself in the sky,
Are music sent up to God by the lover and the bard;
Enough that he heard it once: we shall hear it by and by.

—ROBERT BROWNING.

O God, our heavenly Father! We come before You at this morning hour, thanking You for Your loving care, that has protected us through the night, and for the blessed sleep, that has brought refreshment to our bodies and minds. We are grateful, O Father, for this new day, rich in hope and promise and opportunity, and we pray that, as its hours pass, we may be kept very near to You, that the "words of our mouth and the meditations of our heart, may be acceptable in Your sight," that when the day is done, and we come to You at its close, we need in no wise to be ashamed. Amen.

—NELLIE MANN OPDALE.

August 29

With God, one day is as good as a thousand years, a thousand years as a day. God isn't late with his promise as some measure lateness. He is restraining himself on account of you, holding back the End because he doesn't want anyone lost. He's giving everyone space and time to change.   2 PETER 3:8-9 (MSG)

How often does the chopper
  of some stone,
While toiling at his task
  of heave and shock,
Find in the heart-space of a severed rock
The impress of some fern
  that once had grown,
Full of aspiring life and color-tone,
Deep in the forest
  where the shadows flock,

Till, caught within the adamantine block,
It lay for ages hidden and unknown!
So many a beauteous thought
  blooms in the mind
But unexpressed, droops down
  into the soul
And lies unuttered in the silence there
Until some opener of the soul shall find
The fern-like fossilled dream,
  complete and whole,
And marvel at its beauty past compare.
      —ALFRED L. DONALDSON.

O mighty Potter, to whose steadfast eyes
A thousand years lie open as one day,
Thy patient hand set firm on
  life's great wheel
This heavy, shapeless clay.
Rough and imperfect,
  yet it owns Thy touch;

Spare not, nor stay,
  the pressure of Thine hand;
Make known Thy power;
  and soon, or late, let love
Perfect what love hath planned!
Amen.
      —L. H. HAMMOND.

August 30

The earth is the Lord's, and everything in it,
the world, and all who live in it.

PSALM 24:1 (NIV)

The dark green summer,
   with its massive hues,
Fades into Autumn's tincture manifold;
A gorgeous garniture of fire and gold
The high slope of the ferny hill indues.
The mists of morn
   in slumbering layers diffuse
O'er glimmering rock,
   smooth lake, and spiked array
Of hedgerow thorns a unity of gray.

All things appear their tangible form
   to lose
In ghostly vastness. But anon the gloom
Melts, as the sun puts off his muddy veil.
And now the birds
   their twittering songs resume,
All summer silent in the leafy dale.
In spring they piped of love
   on every tree,
But now they sing the song of memory.

—HARTLEY COLERIDGE.

Ever blessed Father, in whose pleasant world we are glad to awake again, looking forward to a happy and useful day, we seek Your loving guidance through these hours. May we look abroad with gratitude and love upon this beautiful earth, doubly beautiful in the waning summer time, when a new splendor comes across the hills, and You reveal Yourself, as of old, in the burning bush. Grant that we may look through nature up to nature's God. Grant that the mists of doubt and uncertainty which often hide You from us may be dispersed in the sunlight of a happy faith, and that the heart, so often sad and silent, may once more lift its cheerful song to You. Amen.

—ALFRED GOODING.

August 31

Praise be to the God and Father of our Lord Jesus Christ, the Father of compassion and the God of all comfort, who comforts us in all our troubles, so that we can comfort those in any trouble with the comfort we ourselves receive from God.

2 CORINTHIANS 1:3-4 (NIV)

No rare creative inspirations throng
My quiet spirit, silent, sad and lone;
No Sapphic flame hath
   on its altar shone;
No music to my nature doth belong.
Thou art the sunlight,
   I am Memnon's stone,
Thou art the zephyr, I give back its song;
The harp Aeolian can do no wrong
To the soft airs which wake
   an answering tone:

Upon my soul,
   Oh, then breathe tenderly;
Subdue the discord,
   still the jarring strain;
So may the harp-strings yield
   but melody.
If notes discordant give
   thy keen ear pain,
Set the fine chords again to harmony;
Let but sweet echoes of thyself remain.

—ADA FOSTER MURRAY.

O You who are the source of all that is and the giver of all that makes life blessed, we thank You that Your providence abides through every change and that You do cheer the loneliest lot with the comfort of Your presence. You have been with us in times past and now on this last day of the summer months, we would thank You for the blessings of the closing season and ask for the continuance of Your unfailing care and the enrichment of our souls with the gifts of Your Spirit. Bring us into harmony with all that is pure and good, and enable us to walk in the light of Your favor and in the paths of Your commandments. Amen.

—CHARLES H. VAIL.

September 1

'Neath harvest moon the stricken
   summer lies
Still smiling bravely in her brightest
   bloom,
Her heart yet holds no hint of gloom,
No trace of sadness in her sunlit eyes.
We love thee, Summer,
   child of Paradise—
A myriad host announce
   thy coming doom
Chanting the requiem of
   thy wintry tomb,

While lovingly look down
   the tender skies;
A holy hush is in the hazy air
As in thy radiant beauty thou dost sleep!
Nature, arrayed in rainbow colors fair,
Is strong of heart her vigil long to keep:
We know the secret thou dost
   seek to tell—
Thou art immortal, Summer,
   fare thee well.

—ANNA A. GORDON.

Heavenly Father, behind all changes You lurk in eternal constancy. Never lingering, each good of life gives place to the better You have in store, and in glory and gladness resigns to that which comes after. From the good that is, may we learn to pass cheerfully to the better that is to be—from the cool morning and sunny noon to the purple gloaming and the star-lit night, from the tender spring and glowing summer to the golden autumn and snow-pure winter, from the sweet life that now is to that fullness of realization whose sweeter splendors eye hath not seen nor the heart of man conceived. We place our hands in Yours and would walk with You in holiest trust and serenest peace. Amen.

—THOMAS W. ILLMAN.

September 2

And this hope will not lead to disappointment. For we know how dearly God loves us, because he has given us the Holy Spirit to fill our hearts with his love.

ROMANS 5:5 (NLT)

"I will be happy all the day
Let come what may."
'Twas early morning
   when the word was said,
And like a journey 'cross a weary plain
There stretched the hours,
   but I was comforted
As heart and voice sung
   o'er the sweet refrain,
"I will be happy all the day
Let come what may."

"I will make hope and only hope
My horoscope."
The sombre, brooding clouds
   of discontent
Oppress one's spirit
   like a throbbing pain;
One frets and moans
   in one's environment,
But with a look ahead I sing again,
"I will make hope and only hope
My horoscope."

—FREDERICK A. BISBEE.

Yea, Lord, we thank You that we may hope and be happy all the day for Omnipotence is our Father and our changeless Friend, and we have naught to fear. We are glad of life and thank You for all that makes it heroic or beautiful or sweet. We rejoice in our home, in our dear ones, and in the precious human loves that reflect the love divine. Pardon our sins, we pray, and work out Your purposes in us. May we work and hope on and be glad in You filling this day so full of useful employ that when the night shall come, we shall lie down to sleep Your loving children like tired but happy children, and so find rest and refreshment for another day with men and You. Amen.

—CARL F. HENRY.

September 3

There's a dance of leaves in that aspen bower,
There's a titter of winds in that beechen tree,
There's a smile on the fruit, and a smile on the flower,
And a laugh from the brook that runs to the sea.

—WILLIAM CULLEN BRYANT.

O sweet September! Thy first breezes bring
The dry leaf's rustle and the squirrel's laughter,
The cool, fresh air, whence health and vigor spring
And promise of exceeding joy hereafter.

—GEORGE ARNOLD.

O Lord, we thank You for the spring, which brought her handsome promise, for the gorgeous preparation which the summer made in his manly strength, and we bless You for the months of autumn, whose sober beauty now is cast on every hill and every tree. We thank You for the harvests which the toil and the thought of man have gathered already from the surface of the ground, or dug from its bosom. We bless You for the other harvests still growing beneath the earth, or hanging abundant beauties in the autumnal sun from many a tree, all over our blessed Northern land. Amen.

—THEODORE PARKER.

September 4

Give, and it will be given to you. A good measure, pressed down, shaken together and running over, will be poured into your lap. For with the measure you use, it will be measured to you.　　　　　　　　　　　　　　　　LUKE 6:38 (NIV)

Do right, and God's recompense to you will be the power to do more right. Give, and God's reward to you will be the spirit of giving more: blessed spirit, for it is the Spirit of God Himself, whose Life is the blessedness of giving. Love, and God will pay you with the capacity of more love; for love is Heaven, love is God within you.

—FREDERICK W. ROBERTSON.

O Lord, we thank You for Your manifold gifts to the children of men. You give life and all the sustenance of life. You give our fair and beautiful world. You give us the power of hope and faith and thought. From Your own giving may we learn that it is more blessed to give than to receive. Teach us, O Lord, to give more freely and more gladly, and may we learn how our own life and joy and growth are involved in the spirit in which we give and serve. In all our giving and all our serving may we keep before us the vision of the Master who gave Himself that we might live. Amen.

—GEORGE L. PERIN.

September 5

For he chose us in him before the creation of the world to be holy and blameless in his sight. In love he predestined us for adoption to sonship through Jesus Christ, in accordance with his pleasure and will.   EPHESIANS 1:4-5 (NIV)

Our birth is but a sleep and a forgetting:
The soul that rises with us, our life's star,
Hath had elsewhere its setting,
And cometh from afar.
Not in entire forgetfulness,
And not in utter nakedness,
But trailing clouds of glory, do we come
From God who is our home:
Heaven lies about us in our infancy,
At length the man perceives it die away
And fade into the light of common day.
                                    —WILLIAM WORDSWORTH.

O Eternal God, who is without beginning of days or end of years, from whom comes all our life; pardon, we beseech You, the sins of Your children, wherein we have darkened Your own image within us. Let not our light die away amid the common toil and daily care, but so glorify our life with Your spirit, that we may gladly present both souls and bodies to Your service an acceptable sacrifice, and, learning to love You above all things, may be approved in Your sight as true disciples of Your Son Jesus Christ. Amen.   —WILLIAM E. GASKIN.

September 6

I praise you, for I am fearfully and wonderfully made.
Wonderful are your works;
　my soul knows it very well.

PSALM 139:14 (ESV)

A haze on the far horizon,
The infinite tender sky,
The ripe, rich tint of the corn-fields,
And the wild geese sailing high,

And all over upland and lowland
The charm of the goldenrod—
Some of us call it Autumn,
And others call it God.

—WILLIAM H. CARRUTH.

Once more, O God, You part the curtains of night to bless us with a new day. In its dawning You reveal Yourself to us anew. Fresh beauties break upon our vision; new evidences of Your goodness appear; new joys rise in our hearts. We thank You for the harvest of corn that feeds our bodies and the harvest of beauty that feeds our souls; for the blue of the distant hills and the wide stretch of meadow and prairie; for golden flower and flying bird; for the nearness of Your presence in the brooding haze; for the thoughts unutterable that rise within us. In thankfulness may we go forth to our daily tasks and live in consciousness of Your eternal presence and love. Amen.

—RODNEY F. JOHONNOT.

September 7

I come under your windows, some fine morning, and play you one of my adagio movements, and some of you say—This is good, play us so always. But, dear friends, if I did not change the stop sometimes, the machine would wear out in one part and rust in another. How easily this or that tune flows!—you say—there must be no end of such melodies in him. I will open the poor machine for you one moment, and you shall look. Every note marks where a spur of steel has been driven in. It is easy to grind out the song, but to plant these bristling points which make it was the painful task of time. —OLIVER WENDELL HOLMES.

We thank You, Father, for Your love which, like the morning light, fails not to greet us at each opening day. While its radiant beams light up the pathway from our hearts to Yours, we come, with eager steps, for morning worship and for praise. Take, we pray, the hand outstretched out to You and lead us safely through another day. Grant us the strength to do our very best and leave results with You. We do not ask for ease, but victory; not for the praise of men, but for the blessing of our God upon our heaven-appointed task. Grant us the joy supreme of knowing, when the sun has set, that we have left undone no duty to our God or fellowman. Amen.

—J. W. ANNAS.

September 8

Yours, Lord, is the greatness and the power
and the glory and the majesty and the splendor,
for everything in heaven and earth is yours.
Yours, Lord, is the kingdom;
you are exalted as head over all.

1 CHRONICLES 29:11 (NIV)

Admit into thy silent breast
The notes of but one bird
And instantly thy soul will join
In jubilant accord.

The perfume of a single flow'r
Inhale like breath of God,

And in the garden of thy heart
A thousand buds will nod.

Toward one star in heaven's expanse
Direct thy spirit's fight,
And thou wilt have in the wide world,
My child, enough delight.

—JOHANNA AMBROSIUS.

Our Father In Heaven, as You turn the earth once more toward the light to give us another day may we not forget that all things come from You. You give us this beautiful earth, adorned with a thousand varied beauties, crowded with opportunities and possibilities, for our home. Day and night, sunshine and the rain, labor and trial, joy and victory, all are from Your hand. Whatever the circumstances of our life, whatever our labor and place, help us to remember that life is a school in which to learn, an arena where we may fight and win. May we gain wisdom and strength to win the victory which is life eternal, and in finding that may we find peace and be content in You. Amen. —FREDERICK A. TAYLOR.

September 9

Give me the gospel of the fields
  and woods—
The sermons written in
  the book of books;
The sweet communion of the things
  of earth
Fresh with the warm baptism of the sun.
Give me the offertory of bud and bloom,

The perfect caroling of happy birds.
Give me the creed of one of
  God's fair days
Wrought in the beauty of its loveliness;
And then, the benediction of the stars,
His eloquent ministers of the night.

—JAMES RAVENSCROFT.

Heavenly Father, we praise You for the breaking day, the singing birds, the dew in the meadows, the fragrance of the flowers, ascending like old-time incense from Jewish altar, the sun gilding the hilltops, the veiled stars, the gliding river, mirroring in its depths, sedge and tree and overhanging sky. You have ordained that we nestle in the bosom of nature and feel the touch of God. Pour strength into our beings from bird and flower, and Your spirit which moves in them, that our youth may be renewed like the eagle's. So shall the memories of earth enrich our heaven. We praise and supplicate in the name of Jesus. Amen.

—L. A. FREEMAN.

September 10

Is anyone among you in trouble? Let them pray.
Is anyone happy? Let them sing songs of praise.

JAMES 5:13 (NIV)

Just whistle a bit if the day be dark
And the sky be overcast:
If mute be the voice of the piping lark,
Why, pipe your own small blast.

And it's wonderful how o'er the gray sky-track,
The truant warbler comes stealing back.
But why need he come? For your soul's at rest,
And the song in the heart—ah, that is best.

—PAUL LAURENCE DUNBAR.

Our Heavenly Father, we thank You for the assurance that all things work together for good to them that love You. Help us to live this day in joyous faith in that promise. May we realize that behind all clouds the sun still shines, and that the Father's wisdom never errs, and his love never fails. Give us courage for this day's conflicts, grace for its trials, and strength for its duties. Guide our feet in the way of Your commandments and fill our souls with the joy of Your presence. May our lives no less than our lips praise You. Amen.   —CHARLES F. RICE.

September 11

For each true deed is worship; it is prayer,
And carries its own answer unaware.
Yes, they whose feet upon
   good errands run
Are friends of God,
   with Michael of the sun;
Yes, each accomplished service of the day
Paves for the feet of God a lordlier way.

The souls that love and labor
   through all wrong,
They clasp His hand and
   make the Circle strong;
They lay the deep foundation
   stone by stone,
And build into Eternity God's throne!

—EDWIN MARKHAM.

Our Heavenly Father, we, Your children, turn to You in gratitude and hope for this new day of opportunity. May our high calling in Christ Jesus loom large before our eyes. Deliver us, we humbly beseech You, from making ourselves and our concerns chief in thought and effort. May we find our lives in saving those whose sky is dark, whose burdens are heavy, and whose faith is perishing. With zest, as do the angels, when we hear Your Spirit's voice, may we turn and obey. To let these hours of service prove to us, not only that You are, but that You are the rewarder of them that diligently seek You. Through Jesus Christ, our Lord. Amen.

—DEWITT S. CLARK.

September 12

But now, this is what the Lord says—
he who created you, Jacob, he who formed you, Israel:
"Do not fear, for I have redeemed you;
I have summoned you by name; you are mine."

ISAIAH 43:1 (NIV)

Good name, in man or woman, dear my lord,
Is the immediate jewel of their souls.
Who steals my purse, steals trash; 'tis something, nothing;
'Twas mine, 'tis his, and has been slave to thousands;
But he that filches from me my good name,
Robs me of that which not enriches him,
And makes me poor indeed.

—SHAKESPEARE.

God of all righteousness and charity, breathe upon me the spirit of thine own charity and righteousness, that I may deal worthily with the good name of every human being with whom I have to do. Help me, that I may bring no injury to the fair fame of any. May the law of kindness be in my lips, and the spirit of helpful justice in my heart. Inspire me to come, whenever I ought, to the rescue of the slandered, that I may deliver them into the liberty of human fellowship. And not to me alone, O God, but to all men, teach this divine lesson of fair judgment and sweet help, that they may live together as children in thy gracious family. Amen.

—WILLIAM N. CLARKE.

September 13

I searched for love in heart of city's hum;
I searched for love
  upon the shining sand
Of ocean beach;
  and then on towering cliffs I sung
A pleading song that love
  unto my heart might come;
But love came not.

I searched for love no more,
  but labored sore
To ease those hearts whom
  sorrow'd touched before,
Faint hope that in sweet work
  I'd surely find
Some compensation for a fate unkind—
When, lo! Love came.

—BESSIE L. RUSSELL.

For love and life and light
  and breath and ease,
For work, success and hope,
  for power to please,
For conscience clear,
  for faith without alloy,
For common share in
  common human joy,
I thank Thee, gracious God!

For loneliness and shadow,
  sickness, care,
For failure, doubt, remorse,
  death, and despair,
For sleepless nights,
  for aching heart and brain,
For common share in
  common human pain,
I thank Thee, gracious God! Amen.

—MARGARET WENTWORTH.

September 14

Taste and see that the Lord is good.
Oh, the joys of those who take refuge in him!

PSALM 34:8 (NLT)

In fallow fields the goldenrod
And purple asters beck and nod.
The milkweed launches fairy boats;
In tangled silver the cobweb floats.
Pervasive odors of ripening vine,
Fill the air like a luscious wine.

The gentian blooms
  on the browning waste;
With coral chains is the alder laced.
The blackbirds gather, and wheel and fly,
The swallows twitter a low "Goodbye!"
—SARA ANDREW SHAFER.

Father in Heaven, we love You, we cannot help it. Your blessings around us on every side tell us of Your love. Our love leaps involuntarily from our hearts responsive to these numberless delights. We thank You for the rich harvests that burden the fields, for the acres of beauty that reach over hill and through meadow, for the stars that make cheerful the night. Help us to bless You when the storms come to disappoint and destroy. May we realize that the tempest comes from the Good Father, that He has sent it, a great blessing in disguise. Great Father, help us to know and feel that everything coming from You is good. So may Your Kingdom come to Your children of earth. Amen. —CHARLES EDWARD DAVIS.

September 15

Once, out of all the anguish and the sorrow of my heart,
I wrote a song, and put my pent-up passion in its art.
And the great world never heeded this soulful human groan,
For it bore a burden infinitely heavy of its own.

Once, out of all the happiness and joy within my breast,
I made a little song and blithely sent it on its quest.
And the great world, with its infinitely many joys, divine,
Still had room and instant welcome for this little song of mine.

—WILLIAM F. DIX.

O God, I thank You that You have numbered me with the children of the day. O Immanuel, make Your Presence to be a sun within me this day. May I dispel clouds or reveal the rainbows ever half-hidden in robes of mists. May I melt snows and bring springtime freshets of joy. May I shed light that shall turn groans into songs. May I shine on till I shall stand before the Great White Throne that is encompassed with an unbroken rainbow, and take up the angelic music among that starry host of souls who have found the true "music of the spheres," and are: "Forever singing as they shine, 'The hand that made us is divine.'" Amen.   —ELLIOTT F. STUDLEY.

September 16

> [Jacob] had a dream in which he saw a stairway resting on the earth, with its top reaching to heaven, and the angels of God were ascending and descending on it. ... When Jacob awoke from his sleep, he thought, "Surely the Lord is in this place, and I was not aware of it." GENESIS 28:12,16 (NIV)

All is best, though we oft doubt
What the unsearchable dispose
Of highest wisdom brings about,
And ever best found in the close.

Oft He seems to hide His face,
But unexpectedly returns,
And to his faithful champion hath in place
Bore witness gloriously.

—JOHN MILTON.

Our Father, we have ever dwelt in You, though sometimes we have forgotten it. While our eyes slept, it may be that to our spirit's sight a ladder was set up on the earth and the top of it reached to heaven, and on it Your angels were ascending and descending to help us. Now again, O Father, comes to us from Your hand of love the food and the tasks of a new day. Help us then to put away the error from which we fled or should have fled yesterday. This morning let us set up the stone of our Bethel that through the day we may be reminded in all we do, that You are in this place with us. Whether we see You or not, let us take courage and make this a day nearer to You. Fill us with Jesus' own large sympathies for others, with Jesus' purpose to seek and to serve the right, and especially grant us Jesus' complete trust in Your perfect goodness. In His name, we ask it. Amen. —MERRILL C. WARD.

September 17

As far as earth is from the sky,
So Love is high.
Where Alpine lakes their vigils keep
Is Love more deep.

In Nature there no boundaries are
That tell how far Love goes;

Love's measure, as each countless star,
God knows.

One only thing we know:
  Love comes to stay;
Though God's to give, it is not even His
To take away.

—MARIAN ALDEN.

O God, our Heavenly Father, we recognize our dependence upon You for the bounties of Your never-failing Providence, and as we enter upon this new day to which You have safely brought us, we ask for Your help that we may receive it as a gift from You and may consecrate ourselves more perfectly in the least things as well as in the greatest, to Your service. Help us to be faithful to all the duties and responsibilities of our lot. Deliver us from all useless discontent, all idle doubts and foolish fears. In all our dealings may we be simple and sincere. Strengthen us to do at every moment that which we feel to be right and good in Your sight, and through loyal obedience to Your will may we rise into a clearer vision of the things that belong to Your heavenly kingdom. Amen. —WILLIAM H. FISH.

September 18

My son, do not despise the Lord's discipline,
and do not resent his rebuke,
because the Lord disciplines those he loves,
as a father the son he delights in

PROVERBS 3:11-12 (NIV)

Some people are always grumbling because roses have thorns. I am thankful that thorns have roses.

—ALPHONSE KARR.

There are those who want to get away from all their past; who if they could, would fain begin all over again. Their life seems one long failure. But you must learn, you must let God teach you, that the only way to get rid of your past is to get a future out of it. —PHILLIPS BROOKS.

Our Heavenly Father, remembering You fills life with all that is most beautiful and bright. Our deepest sorrows, our most bitter experiences come when we forget You. No life can be a failure which strives to do Your will. Sorrow may come to us, but just as an artist may darken a flower, in painting, before retouching it to make its color all the brighter, so we know that You, who give color to the flowers, may for a season permit sorrow to darken our lives; but You are only in the midst of Your work. At Your retouch, life becomes the more beautiful. Help us to pray, not simply, "Lord, remember me," for it is not possible for You to forget Your children; we pray "assist us to be always mindful of You." Amen. —E. McP. AMEE.

September 19

Praise be to the God and Father of our Lord Jesus Christ! In his great mercy, he has given us new birth into a living hope through the resurrection of Jesus Christ from the dead, and into an inheritance that can never perish, spoil or fade. This inheritance is kept in heaven for you.   1 PETER 1: 3-4 (NIV)

The sooner we read, mark, learn, and inwardly digest a little Eastern apothegm of Howard Hinton's the better: Two balls were together in a box, a gold and a gilt ball. The gilt ball was carefully done up in tissue paper, and securely wedged into one corner; but the gold ball was loose, and went rolling about with every movement of the box.

"Oh, please, do take care of yourself!" said the gilt ball, peeping out apprehensively from the folds of the tissue paper.

"Why, where's the harm?" answered the gold ball, as it took a fresh lurch to an opposite corner.

"Oh, how can you?" cried the other; "You'll rub it off."

"Rub what off?" asked the gold ball....

The gold won't rub off.... Only the gingerbread gilt.

—ELLICE HOPKINS.

Heavenly Father, we hear the loving call of this new day and on the wings of the morning we would speed to the work and worship of the beautiful hours You have given us. We thank You that You have made us for the hurry of the marketplace as well as for the quiet of the home. May our own lives be brightened by contact with our fellowmen. May the pure gold of the Spirit of Christ be ours in purity of personal thought, in the benediction of words of strength and sweetness and in the varied service we may render our neighbors in the name of Jesus our Lord and Saviour. Amen.

—JAMES F. ALLEN.

September 20

I sought the Lord, and he answered me;
he delivered me from all my fears.

PSALM 34:4 (NIV)

O heart of mine, we shouldn't worry so!
What we've missed of calm
   we couldn't have, you know!
What we've met of stormy pain,
And of sorrow's driving rain,
We can better meet again,
If it blow!

For we know,
   not every morrow can be sad;
So, forgetting all the sorrow
We have had,
Let us fold away our fears,
And put by our childish tears,
And through all the coming years,
Just be glad.

—JAMES WHITCOMB RILEY.

Heavenly Father, Your very name fills our hearts with confidence and peace. For we know that out of Your Fatherly goodness all earthly providences are bestowed and administered for our good. So, for our unwilling submission, when You have led us into hard and thorny pathways, we ask Your generous forgiveness; and for our ingratitude when pleasure and prosperity have attended us, we entreat Your tender patience. As You have commanded us to rejoice in Your salvation, may our hearts be filled with gladness today; and, as You have counselled us that when we lack wisdom, we may ask of You, we beseech You to bestow upon us now and evermore the wisdom of cheerfulness and joy. In the name of Jesus, Amen.   —EDMUND L. SMILEY.

September 21

Never walk away from someone who deserves help;
  your hand is God's hand for that person.
Don't tell your neighbor "Maybe some other time" or "Try me tomorrow"
  when the money's right there in your pocket.

PROVERBS 3:27-28 (MSG)

We all shrink, like cowards, from new duties, new responsibilities. We do not venture to go out of the beaten track of our daily life. Close to us, on each side of the road, are those whom we might help or save with one good action, one kind word. But we are afraid. We say: "I am not prepared; I am not ready; I have not time; I am not qualified; find some better person; send some one else." Perhaps we have only one talent, and, therefore, instead of using it, we hide it, and when the Master comes we shall meet him with the old answer: "I was afraid, and went and hid your talent in the earth. Lo! There you have what is yours." —JAMES FREEMAN CLARKE.

From the base sin of selfishness, O Lord, deliver us. Teach us by Your life of ministry and sacrifice for others that the more fully and willingly we lose ourselves in service for our fellowmen, the more surely we shall find ourselves in You. As we go forth this day in paths that You have prepared for us, help us to so forget ourselves in acts of kindness and words of comfort that each one whom our lives may touch, may become thereby a happier, purer, stronger soul. Take care of these lives of ours, while, with You, in busy streets and crowded shops where greed is grasping and sin is lurking, we shall try to care for souls of others, who need the help that we might give. Then, at the eventide today or on the morrow, it will be our joy like Yours to find ourselves again in hearts made happy, in lives inspired, in souls redeemed. Amen.

—GEORGE B. DEAN.

September 22

In fact, this is love for God: to keep his commands. And his commands are not burdensome, for everyone born of God overcomes the world. This is the victory that has overcome the world, even our faith. 1 JOHN 5:3-4 (NIV)

Before God's footstool to confess
A poor soul knelt and bowed his head,
"I failed!" he wailed. The Master said,
"Thou didst thy best—that is success!"
—ANONYMOUS.

Straight from the Mighty Bow, this truth is driven:
"They fail, and they alone, who have not striven."
Fly far, O shaft of light, all doubt redeeming,
Rouse men from dull despair and idle dreaming.
High Heaven's Evangel be, gospel God-given;
They fail, and they alone, who have not striven.
—CLARENCE URMY.

We thank You, O God, for the light that reveals to us the divine estimate of life, that lifts the veil of mystery from struggle and sacrifice and enables us to interpret their meaning as elements of successful living. We praise You for the truth that assures us that we are in this world to win, to overcome, to be more than conquerors. We pray that we may be too busy to dream and too brave to doubt. Strengthen us for life's conflict, help us to carry our burdens cheerfully, fight courageously, strive lawfully, that we may be worthy to be counted among those who shall receive the crown of righteousness and hear at last the "Well done" of the Master. Amen.
—GEORGE S. SCRIVENER.

September 23

Be diligent and faithful, patient and hopeful, one and all of you; and may we all know, at all times, that verily the Eternal rules above us, and that nothing finally wrong has happened or can happen. —THOMAS CARLYLE.

If you entered the workshop of a blacksmith, you would not dare to find fault with his bellows, anvils and hammers. If you had not the skill of a workman, but the consideration of a man, what would you say? "It is not without cause the bellows are placed there; the artificer knew, though I do not know, the reason." You would not dare to find fault with the blacksmith in his shop, and do you dare to find fault with God in His world? —ST. BERNARD.

We thank You, O loving Father, that we are not alone in the universe with longing for the higher life. There are a thousand revelations of You in our fellowmen. And when we cannot find You, for blindness, in nature or in ourselves, we can see You revealed in the heroic lives that surround us. In the abstract You are hard to find; in the lives of men You are always visible. We thank You that there is a contagion of rightness and that love is a vital seed that fills the world with its kind. We are fearful of love sometimes, fearing to waste it on a loveless world. Help us to see that every atom we give becomes an ocean to ourselves. Amen. —ALBERT C. GRIER.

September 24

For in one place the Scriptures say, "What are mere mortals that you should think about them, or a son of man that you should care for him? Yet for a little while you made them a little lower than the angels and crowned them with glory and honor. You gave them authority over all things."　　　　HEBREWS 2:6-8 (NLT)

To be at all—what is better than that?
I think if there were nothing more developed,
　the clam in its callous shell in the sand were august enough
I am not in any callous shell;
I am cased with supple conductors, all over
They take every object by the hand, and lead it within me;
They are thousands, each one with his entry to himself;
They are always watching with their little eyes, from my head to my feet;
One no more than a point lets in and out of me such bliss and magnitude,
I think I could lift the girder of the house away if it lay between me
　and whatever I wanted.　　　　—WALT WHITMAN.

Our Heavenly Father, we thank You for all the delicate beauty as well as for the rugged strength of these bodies in which You have set us to live. But more wonderful than the habitation of the soul is the soul itself. You have made us a little lower than the angels, You have crowned us with glory and honor, and we join reverently in the words of the great poet-prophet who said of man—"In action how like an angel, in apprehension how like a God!" O Lord, we thank You for this great thought of our own life. Yet let us not be vain nor proud. We pray rather that we may be inspired to live so earnestly and so nobly that we shall prove our title now to all that we have dreamed as our natural birthright. So shall we feel ourselves today sons and daughters of God. Amen.　　　　—GEORGE L. PERIN.

September 25

I do believe the common man's task is the hardest. The hero has the hero's aspiration that lifts him to his labor. All great duties are easier than the little ones, though they cost far more blood and agony. —PHILLIPS BROOKS.

Thus man is made equal to every event. He can face danger for the right. A poor, tender, painful body, he can run into flame or bullets or pestilence, with duty for his guide.... I am not afraid of accident as long as I am in my place.... Every man's task is his life-preserver. The conviction that his work is dear to God and cannot be spared, defends him. —RALPH WALDO EMERSON.

O You who are the giver of every good and perfect gift, help us better to understand the measure of Your giving; that we count not those blessings only which make life smooth and easy and of tame comfort but the things that make life resolute and hearty, and that put to test the vigor of our souls, that give us chance to prove our high nobility and unfaltering courage; the things that build for the soul's fine substance of eternal worth—these are Your blessings, too, for which we thank You. Give us entrance into Your eternal living through strong activity and zest of life; that manhood have its eager challenge and womanhood its glowing opportunity to assert themselves as winning joy through bafflement and Your strong peace that does not pass away, through steadfast consecration to high service. Amen.

—GEORGE H. BADGER.

September 26

Live wisely among those who are not believers, and make the most of every opportunity. Let your conversation be gracious and attractive so that you will have the right response for everyone. COLOSSIANS 4:5-6 (NLT)

If I can put one touch of a rosy sunset into the life of any man, or woman I shall feel that I have worked with God. He is in no haste; and if I do what I may in earnest I need not worry if I do no great work. Let God make His sunsets; I will mottle my little cloud. To help the growth of a thought that struggles toward the light, to brush with gentle hand the earth stain from the white of one snowdrop—such be my ambition. —GEORGE MACDONALD.

Help us, our Father, to know that we have here at hand all that we need to make this day what it ought to be; that we need not look afar, but in the duty of this present moment, in the opportunity to learn, to serve and thus to grow, which the morning offers, is all that is necessary to make this day sound and serviceable; in such a day we shall find enduring joy and from it You, the Giver of all days, will derive satisfaction, since it will do its full share in fulfilling Your purpose. And may we see that if we make our todays what they should be You will take care of the tomorrows. Amen. —HERBERT E. BENTON.

September 27

Yet true godliness with contentment is itself great wealth. After all, we brought nothing with us when we came into the world, and we can't take anything with us when we leave it.   1 TIMOTHY 6:6-7 (NIV)

My neighbor hath a little field,
Small store of wine its presses yield,
And truly but a slender hoard
Its harvest brings for barn or board.
Yet tho' a hundred fields are mine,
Fertile with olive, corn and wine;
Tho' Autumn piles my garners high,
Still for that little field I sigh.
For ah! methinks no otherwhere

Is any field so good and fair.
Small tho' it be, 'tis better far
Than all my fruitful vineyards are,
Amid whose plenty sad I pine—
"Ah, would the little field were mine!"
Large knowledge void of peace and rest,
And wealth with pining care possest—
These by my fertile lands are meant.
That little field is called Content.

—ROBERTSON TROWBRIDGE.

Heavenly Father, as prayed Your servant of old, so we this morning repeat "Give us neither poverty nor riches." Help us this day, in whatsoever state we are, therewith to be content. May no complaining word proceed out of our mouths. Above all may no murmuring thought lodge within us. So shall we rest in peace with You, and God, even our God, shall bless us. Yet, O Lord, forbid that we should remain satisfied with any portion, which our best effort, with Your assistance, can improve. Then shall we grow in grace and more and more approach the stature of true men and women, in Christ Jesus. Amen.   —M. EMORY WRIGHT.

September 28

Why, my soul, are you downcast?
Why so disturbed within me?
Put your hope in God,
for I will yet praise him, my Savior and my God.

PSALM 42:11 (NIV)

Forenoon and afternoon and night—Forenoon
And afternoon and night—Forenoon, and—what?
The empty song repeats itself. No more?
Yea, that is life. Make this forenoon sublime,
This afternoon a psalm, this night a prayer,
And time is conquered, and thy crown is won.

—EDWARD ROWLAND SILL.

Help me, O Lord, if I shall see
Times when I walk from hope apart,
Till all my days but seem to be
The troubled weekdays of the heart.

Help me to find, in seasons past,
The hours that have been good or fair,
And bid remembrance hold them fast,
To keep me wholly from despair.

Help me to look behind, before,
To make my past and future form
A bow of promise, meeting o'er
The darkness of my day of storm.
Amen.

—PHOEBE CARY.

September 29

> There the angel of the Lord appeared to him in flames of fire from within a bush. Moses saw that though the bush was on fire it did not burn up. So Moses thought, "I will go over and see this strange sight—why the bush does not burn up." When the Lord saw that he had gone over to look, God called to him from within the bush, "Moses! Moses!" And Moses said, "Here I am."   EXODUS 3:2-4 (NIV)

The iris-pillar suggested the burning bush on Horeb. In Moses' time, nature, in the regard of science, was a mere bush, a single shrub. Now it has grown, through the researches of the intellect, to a tree. The universe is a mighty tree; and the great truth for us to connect with the majestic science of these days, and to keep vivid by a religious imagination, is, that from the roots of its mystery to the silver-leaved boughs of the firmament, it is continually filled with God, and yet unconsumed.

—T. STARR KING.

Almighty God, our Heavenly Father, who in all ages has been revealing Yourself to men as a God of righteousness and love, we approach Your throne of grace this morning confessing our unworthiness and pleading for Your forgiving love. While humbling ourselves before You because of the consciousness of our unworthiness, we yet approach You, our Father, with filial trust and confidence, yea, with gladness of heart and holy boldness in the all-prevailing name of Jesus Christ our Lord. We bless You for Your watchful care over us amid all the dangers, temptations and difficulties of the past. Truly You have been with us, and although Your people have often been surrounded by fire, the bush has not been consumed. In the future as in the past, be our God and Guide and finally bring us into Your everlasting Kingdom, through Jesus Christ our Lord. Amen.   —A. K. MACLENNAN.

September 30

Search me, O God, and know my heart;
test me and know my anxious thoughts.
Point out anything in me that offends you,
and lead me along the path of everlasting life.

PSALM 139:23-24 (NLT)

Would you like to hear what sort of questions the schoolboys had to answer eighteen centuries ago? Very well; you shall. A rabbi, who lived nearly twenty years before Christ was born, set his pupils thinking by asking them, "What is the best thing for a man to possess?"

One of them replied, "A kind nature;" another, "A good companion;" another, "A good neighbor." But one of them, named Eleazer, said, "A good heart."

"I like your answer best, Eleazer," said the master, "for it includes all the rest."

—FRANCIS AUGUSTUS COX.

Our Father in heaven, we are happy to believe that You wish us to have the best. You teach us that the best possession we can have is a good heart, for out of the heart are the issues of life. You are the searcher of hearts—if our hearts are hard You can give us hearts of flesh, if they are sinful You can create clean hearts within us. Even if they are desperately wicked You can make them new. Grant us, therefore, Your Holy Spirit we humbly beseech You, that our hearts may be pure and good. Thus may we ever possess the best possible treasure, and thus may we perfectly love You and worthily magnify Your holy name. Through Jesus Christ our Lord. Amen.

—WILLARD T. PERRIN.

October 1

But the fruit of the Spirit is love, joy, peace, forbearance, kindness, goodness, faithfulness, gentleness and self-control. Against such things there is no law.

GALATIANS 5:22-23 (NIV)

Month of fruits and falling leaves,
Under thy opalescent skies
The vagrant summer idly lies,
While coming Autumn deftly weaves
Rare tints for tall ungarnered sheaves
Of goldenrod, kissing the eyes
Of purple asters as she dyes
The vine that swings beneath the eaves.

And all the bending hedgerows seem
A Joseph's coat of colors. Hues
That shame the rainbow's royal arch
Set all the harvest fields a-gleam
With beauty, fresh with fragrant dews
To crown the season's onward march.
　　　　　—GEORGE W. SHIPMAN.

Author and Giver of every good and perfect gift whose infinite presence and power underlie all growth and life and activity, who reveals Yourself in the varied forms of beauty which come so rapidly in the revolving year, in the green grass and blossoming roses and lilies and refreshing, fast-succeeding fruits, we thank You that You are now crowning the year with Your goodness and inviting us to gather in from tree, garden, field, forest, mine, what will feed, clothe, protect us during the wintry season given us, free from arduous labors, to find enjoyment in books, music and social intercourse. These blessings remind us to present to You the fruits of the spirit, love, joy, peace, long suffering, kindness, goodness, faithfulness, meekness, temperance. Amen.
　　　　　—CALVIN S. LOCKE.

October 2

The Lord is close to the brokenhearted
and saves those who are crushed in spirit.

PSALM 34:18 (NIV)

One answered,
  on the day when Christ went by,
"Lord, I am rich; pause not for such as I.
My work, my home, my strength,
  my frugal store,
The sun and rain—
  what need have I of more?
Go to the sinful who have need of Thee,
Go to the poor, but tarry not for me.
What is there Thou should'st do
  for such as I?"
And He went by.

Long years thereafter, by a palace door,
The footstep of the Master
  paused once more
From whence the old voice
  answered piteously—
"Lord, I am poor,
  my house unfit for Thee;
Nor peace nor pleasures
  bless my princely board,
Nor love nor health;
  what could I give Thee, Lord?
Lord, I am poor, unworthy,
  stained with sin—"
Yet He went in.

—MABEL EARLE.

We who are poor in spirit, turn to You who are the giver of every good and perfect gift, to hold out our empty hands and pray that You will make us rich. During the past days and years we have been out in Your world striving for more things and then more things and yet more things, forgetful of the fact that a man's life consists not in the abundance of the things which he possesses. Now, realizing the poverty of our real lives, we ask You to bestow upon us those eternal riches which pertain to the human soul and possessing which we shall have treasure in heaven where moth and rust do not corrupt nor thieves break through and steal. So shall we be rich indeed. Amen.

—FRANK OLIVER HALL.

October 3

Be strong in the Lord and in his mighty power.

EPHESIANS 6:10 (NIV)

Be strong!
We are not here to play, to dream, to drift.
We have hard work to do,
    and loads to lift.
Shun not the struggle; face it.
    'Tis God's gift.

Be strong!
Say not the days are evil—
    who's to blame?
And fold the hands and acquiesce—
    O shame!

Stand up, speak out, and bravely,
    in God's name.

Be strong!
It matters not how deep intrenched
    the wrong,
How hard the battle goes,
    the day how long,
Faint not, fight on!
    Tomorrow comes the song.
      —MALTBIE DAVENPORT BABCOCK.

Our Father, we thank You for this new morning. Truly the light is sweet and a pleasant thing it is for the eyes to behold the same. Lift upon us the light of Your countenance and bid us go in peace. So shall we begin the day aright. With gentle skill You do deal with us. You are not careless with us or hasty or impatient. Help us to be strong in You. May we be able to cast out of our lives everything that would grieve You and harm us. With a loving spirit may we serve You this day. May we be rooted and grounded in love. However hard the battle may go, give us courage and confidence to believe that through Christ, strengthening us, we can do all things required of us. Lord, increase our faith. Amen.

      —J. E. HAWKINS.

October 4

Jesus replied, "Anyone who loves me will obey my teaching. My Father will love them, and we will come to them and make our home with them."

JOHN 14:23 (NIV)

Nobody proves God's being. But, suddenly, one sees God is here. One speaks and God answers. Thereafter all is sure. —EDWARD EVERETT HALE.

There is nothing that so persuades us of the great realities of moral and spiritual being as the man in whom God is manifest, the type of our human nature at its best, and the endorsement of the sublime faith that God in humanity is the supreme revelation of Himself! —HORATIO STEBBINS.

Blessed Father, as the morning light has triumphed in its struggle to overcome darkness, so You gently but irresistibly call us from slumber to the glories and duties of the new day. May we be strong in the sweet assurance that the unfolding hours are full of blessing because You are caring for us. Help us to do Your will by enabling us to minister to those around us. May the words of our mouth and the industry of our hands reveal Your guiding love. Enable us to order our ways by the habit of trust that we have learned through Your constancy. We ask You to disappoint our fears, steady our hearts, and show us the way of obedience, peace and service so that we may realize the good through the day and rejoice in it, as disciples of Christ. Amen. —JAMES D. CORBY.

October 5

Thou knowest not what argument   All are needed by each one;
Thy life to thy neighbor's creed hath lent;   Nothing is good or fair alone.

—RALPH WALDO EMERSON.

Men will not be content to live every man for himself, nor to die every man for himself. In work, in art, in study, in trade—in all life, indeed, the children of God, called by a Saviour's voice, will wish to live in the common cause. They will live for the common wealth—this is the modern phrase. They will bear each other's burdens—this is the phrase of Paul. They will live in the life of love. And it will prove true as it was promised, that all things are added to the community which thus seeks the Kingdom of God and His Righteousness.   —EDWARD EVERETT HALE.

Eternal God, who does still create the light, and make the morning and the evening of our days, by Your light we look to You. In Your light we worship You. Gird us with strength to work with You to bring Your Kingdom in. May we lose and find ourselves again in the larger whole of life by ministering to others' needs; by bearing others' burdens; by sharing their joys and tears and the common fruits of toil, thus making our life and faith in You become their own. Let Your work appear unto Your servants, and establish the work of our hands upon us; yea, the work of our hands establish; and let Your beauty and Your glory be upon us forever and ever. Amen.

—C. E. HOLMES.

October 6

Jesus took the five loaves and two fish, looked up toward heaven, and blessed them. Then, breaking the loaves into pieces, he kept giving the bread and fish to the disciples so they could distribute it to the people. They all ate as much as they wanted, and afterward, the disciples picked up twelve baskets of leftovers!

LUKE 9:16-17 (NIV)

Master, to do great work for Thee,
   my hand
Is far too weak!
   Thou givest what may suit,
Some little chips to cut with care minute,
Or tint, or grave, or polish. Others stand
Before their quarried marble,
   fair and grand,
And make a life-work of the grand design
Which Thou hast traced;
   or, many-skilled, combine
To build vast temples,
   gloriously planned.

Yet take the tiny stones
   which I have wrought
Just one by one,
   as they were given by Thee,
Not knowing what came next
   in Thy wise thought.
Let each stone by Thy master-hand
   of grace
Form the mosaic as Thou wilt for me
And in Thy temple-pavement
   give it place.
—FRANCES RIDLEY HAVERGAL.

Father, we are shortsighted and weak, and hence cannot do our best work without Your aid. We rejoice in the privileges and opportunities of this day. You have counted us worthy to work for You. You can use our loaves and fishes, but require us to bring thus our little, all for Your blessing. We are inspired with hope to make our consecration to You. Make this a day of glorious service. Guide us in our thoughts and work. Glorify Yourself in our life. And wherever the close of this day may find us may it be with the feeling that we have done our best by Your blessing and help. Amen.

—J. W. FULTON.

October 7

Jesus Christ is the same yesterday and today and forever.

HEBREWS 13:8 (NIV)

"Whatever the weather may be,"
  says he—
"Whatever the weather may be,
It's the songs ye sing,
  an' the smiles ye wear,
That's a-making the sun
  shine everywhere;
An' the world of gloom is a world of glee,

Wid the bird in the bush,
  an' the bud in the tree
An' the fruit on the stim o' the bough,"
  says he,
"Whatever the weather may be,"
  says he—
"Whatever the weather may be!"

—JAMES WHITCOMB RILEY.

O Father of Lights, with whom can be no variation, neither shadow that is cast by turning, help us today to trust You so that our joy may be unclouded. Your love is unchanging in its radiance and warmth. Therefore, let it glow in me and through me light someone who may be in darkness. O strong Son of God, who is the same, yesterday, today, yea, and forever, enable us, we beseech You, to be brave and cheery as though You are in the darkest hours as in the brightest. Teach us that the storm and trial is just our opportunity to shine. Cleanse us of all disobedience and darkness. Be our constant Comforter. Let others see that it is Christ within us. Amen.

—THOMAS W. SMITH.

October 8

For those who are led by the Spirit of God are the children of God.

ROMANS 8:14 (NIV)

Look up to God, and say, "Make use of me for the future as You will. I am of the same mind; I am equal with You. I refuse nothing which seems good to You. Lead me whither You will. Clothe me in whatever dress You will. Is it Your will that I should be in a public or private condition; dwell here, or be banished; be poor or rich? Under all these circumstances I will make Your defense to men. I will show what the nature of everything is." —EPICTETUS.

Merciful Father, we begin this day, knowing not what the end may be, with thoughts of You and Your loving kindness. May this be to us a day of joy, a day upon which we can look back and say we have been blessed by You. We pray for that spirit that enabled others to labor in the cause of love and righteousness, and while we may not be able to accomplish all the good we have set our hearts upon, may the thought that our lives and our labors have not been in vain, inspire us and others with courage to continue the work of helping and blessing our fellowmen. Amen.

—DONALD FRASER.

October 9

He will not let you stumble;
   the one who watches over you will not slumber.
Indeed, he who watches over Israel
   never slumbers or sleeps.

PSALM 121:3-4 (NLT)

Men deny the Divine Existence with as little feeling as most assert it. Even in our true systems we go on collecting mere words, playmarks and medals, as the misers do coins; and not till late do we transmute the words into feelings, the coins into enjoyments. A man may for twenty years believe the immortality of the soul; in the one-and-twentieth, in some great moment, he for the first time discovers with amazement the rich meaning of this belief, and the warmth of this well.

—RICHTER.

O You who slumbers not, nor sleeps, in the dawn of this new day we look trustingly to You. While the night has been enfolding us, Your loving care has held us in the everlasting arms. May this day be for us a fresh consecration. May we be ennobled in You. May we share Your life in things small or great. However humble our lives— however emptied our experience of that which wins the plaudits of men, may we manifest You. By us may Your Kingdom come and Your will be done. Amen.

—GEORGE H. YOUNG.

October 10

For, "Who can know the LORD's thoughts?
Who knows enough to teach him?"
But we understand these things, for we have the mind of Christ.

1 CORINTHIANS 2:16 (NLT)

Thou wilt not hold in scorn
   the child who dares
Look up to Thee, the Father—
   dares to ask
More than Thy wisdom answers.
   From Thy hand
The worlds were cast;
   yet every leaflet claims
From that same hand
   its little shining sphere
Of starlit dew; thine image, the great sun,
Girt with his mantle
   of tempestuous flame,
Glares in mid-heaven;
   but to his noontide blaze
The slender violet lifts its lidless eye,
And from his splendor steals
   its fairest hue,
Its sweetest perfume
   from the scorching fire.

—OLIVER WENDELL HOLMES.

Great Spirit of life and power, we do not shrink in terror before You, but come to You in trust and love. Though we cannot fathom the mystery of Your life nor measure the might of Your power, yet we have learned to call You Father; and even as the violet lifts its face to the noonday sun to find the secret of its life, so we lift our faces to You, to find the secret of our lives. You answer us with tenderness. You speak to us in love. Fresh from sleep, we put our hands in Yours to be led forth to the duties of the day. May we go forth with that confidence and hope, which are born of trust in You, our Father. Amen.

—GEORGE L. PERIN.

October 11

Remain in me, as I also remain in you. No branch can bear fruit by itself; it must remain in the vine. Neither can you bear fruit unless you remain in me. I am the vine; you are the branches. If you remain in me and I in you, you will bear much fruit; apart from me you can do nothing. JOHN 15:4-5 (NIV)

Now believe me, God hides some ideal in every human soul. Some time in our life we feel a trembling, fearful longing to do some good thing. Life finds its noblest spring of excellence in this hidden impulse to do our best. There is a time when we are not content to be such merchants or doctors or lawyers as we see on the dead level or below it. The woman longs to glorify her womanhood as sister, wife or mother. Here is God—God standing silently at the door all day long—God whispering to the soul that to be pure and true is to succeed in life and that whatever we get short of that will burn up like stubble, though the whole world try to save it.

—ROBERT COLLYER.

God of all power and might, come into our lives with Your might and Your power. Awaken us from that slumber of death-in-life which easily and sweetly steals through the door, and, like some new Delilah, binds the strong will within. Come, come as the fresh morning sun, to drive away the mist of our sloth and indecision. Come, enter; and bring with You the upstirring power and the wide radiance of the life divine. Come, enter, and abide! When You are absent, though life be easy, it does not satisfy us; but when You are present, though life be hard, it does also content us. O God of all power and might, come into our lives with Your might and Your power. Amen.

—MELVIN BRANDOW.

October 12

> What good is it, my brothers and sisters, if someone claims to have faith but has no deeds? Can such faith save them?　　　　　　　　JAMES 2:14 (NIV)

If you really want to help your fellowmen, you must not merely have in you what would do them good if they should take it from you, but you must be such a man that they can take it from you. The snow must melt upon the mountain and come down in a spring torrent, before its richness can make the valley rich. And yet in every age there are cold, hard, unsympathetic wise men standing up aloof, like snowbanks on the hilltops, conscious of the locked-up fertility in them and wondering that their wisdom does not save the world.　　　　　　　　—PHILLIPS BROOKS.

O God, who has kept us safely during the unconsciousness of our slumbering hours and brought us refreshed to this morning light, prepare us for the duties of this day by filling us with the assurance that we are Yours, and that You love us. Help us to be more like You, to love You more and serve You better. May we manifest our love to You by our willingness to be of service to our fellowmen. Make us warm-hearted and true, helpful and kind, reflecting Your love and doing Your will. We are glad to live in this beautiful world. And we pray that we may be faithful co-laborers with Jesus Christ, in bringing light, love and joy to all lives. Amen.　　　—EUGENE M. GRANT.

October 13

A few more smiles of silent sympathy, a few more tender words, a little more restraint in temper, may make all the difference between happiness and half-happiness to those I live with. —STOPFORD A. BROOKE.

Others shall sing the song,
Others shall right the wrong,
Finish what I begin,
And all I fail to win,

What matter, I or they,
Mine or another's day,
So the right word be said,
And life the sweeter made?

—JOHN GREENLEAF WHITTIER.

Father, so little of the world in which we live is Your world, so much our world, the petty, dwarfed world of our own small vision, that we lose heart and fail to do our share. Help us to see that, as in the densest swamps the sweetest flowers grow, so, even in our darkest hours, we still may be sweet at heart, saying the word, doing the deed, giving the sympathy, that will make the world sing and blossom. If there are times when pain and darkness obscure our vision of You, help us to look on to the sunset of our day, when the black pall is transfigured at the touch of Your glory— when sorrow and failure transcended by gentleness are our beauty and salvation. Amen. —JOHN M. DAVIDSON.

October 14

Be joyful in hope, patient in affliction, faithful in prayer.

ROMANS 12:12 (NIV)

There is not a man in the world who is not saved by hope every day of his life. Rob one of hope and you have robbed him of his power. Nothing may so quickly unnerve a man and render him helpless as to take hope out of his heart. What is poverty? What is sickness? What is disaster? What are daily burdens? What signifies the desertion of friends, what of death itself so long as a man can hope? The man who hopes will brush every difficulty out of the way. He will put aside every suggestion of failure. Take hope out of a man's heart and you have taken all. Put hope into a man's heart and you have given all. —GEORGE L. PERIN.

We thank You, O God, for the light of another morning, for the privilege of entering upon another day. We shall meet with those who do not understand life nor the world in which we live. It is to them only a place to bear burdens, to toil, to endure. Give us, O Father, understanding minds and hearts. Teach us to know that life is a great opportunity, that Your plans for each one are very broad, that the world is full of open doors; and inspired by this knowledge may no despondent soul cross our path without being helped and made to feel that every life through the love of God and the guidance of God may be made sublime. Amen. —ALEXANDER DIGHT.

October 15

> And my God will meet all your needs according to the riches of his glory in Christ Jesus.
>
> PHILIPPIANS 4:19 (NIV)

Ho! For the bending sheaves,
Ho! For the crimson leaves
Flaming in splendor!
Season of ripened gold,

Plenty in crib and fold,
Skies with a depth untold
Liquid and tender.

—JAMES RUSSELL LOWELL.

Source Infinite and Eternal of Light and Life; Creator of being flowing on forever; Minister far and wide of unspeakable bounty; through whose power rise the riches of Nature; from whose abundance descend all gifts to man; Soul of our souls and safeguard of the world; to whom all Intelligence looks through every dawn; and by whose support the heart of man is stayed; let there be to our steps paths of brightness; to our lives laws of justice, kindness, and trust, that we may abound in doing good and by grace, mercy, and truth duly shown, may obtain grateful remembrance evermore. Amen.

—EDWARD C. TOWNE.

October 16

Consider how the wild flowers grow. They do not labor or spin. Yet I tell you, not even Solomon in all his splendor was dressed like one of these. If that is how God clothes the grass of the field, which is here today, and tomorrow is thrown into the fire, how much more will he clothe you—you of little faith!

LUKE 12:27-28 (NIV)

There is something in the autumn
   that is native to my blood
Touch of manner, hint of mood;
And my heart is like a rhyme,
With the yellow and the purple
   and the crimson keeping time.

The scarlet of the maples
   can shake me like a cry
Of bugles going by.
And my lonely spirit thrills
To see the frosty asters like a smoke
   upon the hills.

—RICHARD HOVEY.

O Father, my heart is lonely till I feel Your spirit near, and then the glory of the season brings a message to my soul. Help me now to see Your master hand in the great beauty of the world. May my soul that feels the glad riot of color know that he who gives such beauty and bounty has for me far richer blessings in the great fields of the future. May this day, begun with Nature's rhythm be set with the music of holy purpose and noble service. And may the music sound not alone for me, but for others that we together may march forward in the spirit of Him who loved the lilies of the field and the fowls of the air. Amen.

—CHARLES E. VARNEY.

October 17

Thousands of years ago a leaf fell on the soft clay, and seemed to be lost. But last summer a geologist in his ramblings broke off a piece of rock with his hammer, and there lay the image of the leaf, with every line and every vein and all the delicate tracery preserved in the stone through those centuries. So the words we speak and the things we do today may seem to be lost, but in the great final revealing the smallest of them will appear. —JAMES RUSSELL MILLER.

Our Father we thank You for the light of this new day. Tenderly You have withdrawn the curtain of the night and shown us the beauties and glories of Nature, reminding us of Your own blessed verdict in the dawn of creation, "Behold, they are very good." Good indeed is it to live in such a world, and we thank You for our being. We ask this morning, dear Lord, not for the perishing things of earth, but for continued power and disposition to enjoy You and Your works, for a faith that never wavers and a hope that never grows dim, for such a portion of this world's goods as the wise may enjoy without harm and the righteous hold without wrong. Amen.

—JAMES SALLAWAY.

October 18

Give thanks to the Lord, for he is good;
his love endures forever.

1 CHRONICLES 16:34 (NIV)

Nay, I wrong you, little flower,
Reading mournful mood of mine
In your looks, that give no sign
Of a spirit dark and cheerless:
You possess the heavenly power
That rejoices in the hour,

Glad, contented, free and fearless,—
Lifts a sunny face to heaven
When a sunny day is given;
Makes a summer of its own,
Blooming late and all alone.

—HENRY VAN DYKE.

We thank You, O Father, that, to those who obey the command of Jesus to consider them, the flowers become prophets of God and preachers of righteousness. We thank You for the worship which they render to You, so pure, so brave, so glad, and so acceptable. They may not hinder You and You work Your perfect will in them; O give us the wisdom and the grace to make You welcome to our hearts until in us also You shall work Your perfect will. So may we find our true use and felicity, and render unto You the praise that is Your due. And this we ask through Jesus Christ, our Lord. Amen.

—CHARLES R. TENNEY.

October 19

Season of mists and mellow fruitfulness!
Close bosom friend of the maturing sun;
Conspiring with Him how to load
   and bless
With fruit the vines that round the
   thatch-eaves run;
To bend with apples the moss'd
   cottage trees,
And fill all fruit with ripeness
   to the core;
To swell the gourd,
   and plump the hazel-shells
With a sweet kernel;
   to set to budding more
And still more later flowers for the bees,
Until they think warm days will never
   cease,
For summer has o'er brimmed their
   clammy cells.

—JOHN KEATS.

Our dear Heavenly Father, You have ever been wooing us by a thousand influences and voices to Yourself and our souls are ever restless till they rest in Your love. The voices of nature everywhere speak to us of Your goodness and Your power and all verdure and blossom and fruitage is but the answer of the inanimate world to Your call of life. Shall we do less than these, O God, when upon us You have stamped Your own image and made our being the house beautiful for Your indwelling! We are Your disciples indeed if we bear much fruit and have love one for the other. Mold us, fashion us, mature us, dear Lord, till the angels, watching at the gates and on the towers, say we look like You. And this we ask in Jesus' name. Amen.

—GEORGE M. SMILEY.

October 20

Even the sparrow has found a home, and the swallow a nest for herself,
   where she may have her young—
   a place near your altar, Lord Almighty, my King and my God.
Blessed are those who dwell in your house; they are ever praising you.

PSALM 84:3-4 (NIV)

I pluck an acorn from the greensward, and hold it to my ear and this is what it says to me: "By and by the birds will come and nest in me. By and by I will furnish shade for the cattle. By and by I will provide warmth for the home in the pleasant fire. By and by I will be shelter from the storm to those who have gone under the roof. By and by I will be the strong ribs of the great vessel, and the tempest will beat against me in vain, while I carry men across the Atlantic."

"O foolish little acorn, will you be all this?" I ask.

And the acorn answers, "Yes, God and I."

—LYMAN ABBOTT.

Almighty God, we believe that You are present and controlling in all the operations of Nature. Not a sparrow falls to the ground without Your notice. All life is of Your giving. Plants, animals, and worlds alike are governed by Your laws. We realize in some measure Your Omnipotence. We should fear to draw near to You if You had not revealed Yourself to us in Jesus Christ as a God of love. You, O God, are love. We believe that You will give to all Your children eternal life. As from the acorn comes the oak, clothed in royal beauty, seemingly life from death, so from what seems death shall our immortal spirits rise to dwell forever with You. We adore You, O God. We love You for Your goodness and Your love shown to us. Be gracious unto us and bless us for our Saviour's sake. Amen.

—CYRUS NORTHROP.

October 21

> "Am I a God who is only close at hand?" says the Lord.
>   "No, I am far away at the same time.
> Can anyone hide from me in a secret place?
>   Am I not everywhere in all the heavens and earth?" says the Lord.
>
> JEREMIAH 23:23-24 (NLT)

I suppose every day of earth, with its hundred thousand deaths and something more of births—with its loves and hates, its triumphs and defeats, its pangs and blisses, has more of humanity in it than all the books that were ever written, put together. I believe the flowers growing at this moment send up more fragrance to heaven than was ever exhaled from all the essences ever distilled.

—OLIVER WENDELL HOLMES.

Our Heavenly Father, You are in all nature and in all human history. If we really know our world and our fellowmen and ourselves, we shall know You. As we enter upon the work of this new day, we pray that we may feel Your presence with us. You are never far away from us; we cannot get away from our world, and we cannot fly from ourselves. You are with Your world and You are with Your children. We ask not so much for Your presence, as for the consciousness of Your presence. May we learn to know You in the world about us and in the secret places of our own hearts. Then shall all life be fragrant and beautiful and this day somewhat divine. Amen.

—GEORGE L. PERIN.

October 22

Therefore, as God's chosen people, holy and dearly loved, clothe yourselves with compassion, kindness, humility, gentleness and patience.

COLOSSIANS 3:12 (NIV)

The best thing to take people out of their own worries, is to go to work and find out how other folk's worries are getting on. —MRS. A. D. T. WHITNEY.

Socrates thought that if all our misfortunes were laid in one common heap, whence every one must take an equal portion, most persons would be content to take their own and depart. —PLUTARCH.

Our Father in Heaven, the light of this new day is the light of Your countenance, therefore we rejoice. In Your sunshine our souls find strength for the burdens You give, and even through Your shadows we reach the peace which passes understanding. Yet You are comfort to us that we may comfort the troubled and the distressed with the comfort wherewith we ourselves are comforted. Set our feet in the paths of service. Make us, we pray, glad ministers of Your mercy, and in binding up the wounds of others may we have balm for our own. By this day, may we grow in patience and power, and in the knowledge of Your love. Amen. —LEON O. WILLIAMS.

October 23

Life has a thousand pages—
  love and scorn,
Hope and adventure, poverty and sin,
Despair and glory, loneliness forlorn,
Age, sorrow, exile, all are writ therein—
And on each page, however stern or sad,
Are words which gleam
  upon the crabbed scroll,
Revealing words,
  that make our spirits glad,
And well are worth the study of the soul.
We may not lightly shrink from any leaf,
For on it may be writ the word we need.
God turns the page—
  whatever joy or grief
He opens for us, let us wisely read.

—PRISCILLA LEONARD.

Fill our souls with Your light, O God, that we may ever hope. Give us the poise of endless progress. Make our souls free and joyous as the bird's wing. Give us the courage of our convictions in all places, under all conditions. Make us brave. Take away all forms of fear, whether of man, of nature, or of You, and make us feel that each is our mighty friend, but You supreme over all, faithful each moment to our being, in ten thousand sweet, true, tender, life-giving, life-sustaining ministries. Teach us to look for You everywhere, and to see Your order, and Your beauty, facing all things Heavenward. May our ideals be perfect holiness, perfect strength, perfect love, perfect service. Make our faith great in the higher estate, where our faculties, only dawning here, shall rise in a glorious morning of the soul. Amen.   —A. N. ALCOTT.

October 24

And do not forget to do good and to share with others,
for with such sacrifices God is pleased.

HEBREWS 13:16 (NIV)

Suppose a kindly word of mine
Could lift the clouds and bring sunshine;
Am I my brother's keeper?

Suppose the weary worker toils,
For scanty pittance delves and moils;
Am I my brother's keeper?

Suppose in penury and fear
My neighbor see the wolf draw near;
Am I my brother's keeper?

Perhaps—who knows?—perhaps I'm not!
Self-centered soul! Hast thou forgot
The marvel of our common lot,
The mystic tie that binds us all
Who dwell on this terrestrial ball,
Stupendous hope of time and song,
The bourne for which the ages long?
How hard our hearts must seem to Thee,
Exhaustless Fount of Charity!
 —HENRY NEHEMIAH DODGE.

We thank You, our Father, for the light of a new day and for its opportunities of service for You and Your great Cause. We rejoice that You not only set duty clearly before us, but also grant power to perform it. May we realize not only that we are "our brother's keeper," and that our lives are helpful or harmful every day, but may we be increasingly grateful that we may every day by Your grace be fellow-helpers and workers together with God. Amen. —WILLIAM FULL.

October 25

You crown the year with your bounty,
and your carts overflow with abundance.

PSALM 65:11 (NIV)

It is of no use to dispute about the Indian Summer. I never found two people who could agree as to the time when it ought to be here, or upon a month and day when it should be decidedly too late to look for it. It keeps coming. For my part, I think we get it now and then, little by little, as "the Kingdom" comes. That every soft, warm, mellow, hazy, golden day, like each fair, fragrant life, is a part and outcrop of it; though weeks of gale and frost, or ages of cruel worldliness and miserable sin may lie between.   —MRS. A. D. T. WHITNEY.

Vouchsafe Your blessing, O Heavenly Father, upon this morning service of thanksgiving and prayer. We thank You that each year You send seedtime and harvest, to us Your children. For the beauty and bounty of the Autumn, for all Your material gifts, for friends and home, and for our precious Christian faith, we are deeply grateful to You. Give us the attentive mind, the receptive heart, that we may see Your providence and love in every event of life. Banish fear and doubt from our minds. Guard us from all temptations. May the Spirit of Christ abide in our hearts, and enable us to glorify You in all our works and lives. In its power and glory may Your Kingdom come, and remain upon the earth forever. Amen.   —ELBERT W. WHITNEY.

October 26

There is no one like the God of Israel.

He rides across the heavens to help you, across the skies in majestic splendor.

The eternal God is your refuge, and his everlasting arms are under you.

DEUTERONOMY 33:26-27b (NLT)

Pleasant smiles, gentle tones, cheery greetings, tempers sweet under a headache or a business care or the children's noise; the ready bubbling over of thoughtfulness for one another, and the habits of smiling, greeting, forbearing, thinking in these ways; it is these above all else which makes one's home "a building of God; a house not made with hands," these that we hear in the song of "Home, Sweet Home."

—WILLIAM C. GANNETT.

Almighty Father, the light of another day breaks in upon our lives, to reveal to us unfinished tasks and unsought duties. The sorrows and joys of the coming day are hidden from our sight, enswathed in the folded hours of toil. But You know all our heedless ways and tempers that chafe from impatience; You see the measure of our needs and consider our desires. Give unto us the consciousness of Your everlasting arms about us. And then when the shadows lengthen and the twilight hushes the hum of toil, our spirits shall know no weariness and bear no stain. Give ear unto this our morning prayer, O You Light of Light. Amen.

—FRANCIS TREADWAY CLAYTON.

October 27

As for me and my household, we will serve the Lord.

JOSHUA 24:15b (NIV)

How can people help loving things, when they are full of life magnetism, that even a finger touch gets the thrill of? It is not the sunshine, or any other tangible why, that accounts for the pleasantness of old house corners. It is the pureness and the pleasantness that have clustered there; the very walls have drunk these in.

—MRS. A. D. T. WHITNEY.

Our Heavenly Father, will You keep our home life bright and sweet? Guard our lips from harsh words, our lives from shame. If quarrels arise, help us to be the first to forgive and forget. In the hour of temptation may we say no, because of a father's splendid honor, and a mother's pure face! In the time of trial or seeming defeat may we be brave and of good cheer! Teach us that home is made dear, not by its furnishings, but by the memories and inspirations of the hours we spent under its roof with those who loved us and were always tender and true! Bind us together in the bonds of love and peace, and keep us always united and a happy family. Amen.

—HENRY R. ROSE.

October 28

Remember this: Whoever sows sparingly will also reap sparingly, and whoever sows generously will also reap generously.

2 CORINTHIANS 9:6 (NIV)

There are loyal hearts,
  there are spirits brave,
There are souls that are pure and true;
Then give to the world the best you have,
And the best shall come back to you.

Give love, and love to your heart will flow,
A strength in your utmost need;

Have faith, and a score of hearts will show
Their faith in your word and deed.

For life is the mirror of king and slave,
'Tis just what you are and do;
Then give to the world the best you have,
And the best will come back to you.

—MADELINE S. BRIDGES.

Almighty Father, we come to You for a Father's blessing, that this day we may go about Your work and enter into Your business, alive in Your spirit and strong in Your strength. We ask this for ourselves, each of us, that we may be knit to each other as brothers with brothers, to bear each other's burdens. We ask it most of all for home, that in homelife there always may be joy and peace and love, each seeking another's good, brothers and sisters with sisters and brothers, fathers and mothers with their children, that home may be the place of Your holy spirit and the home of joy. Today we would come and go as Your messengers, in our own lives welcoming the Father, who is with us seeking Your strength and asking for Your good will. Bless us today with Your blessing. Amen. —EDWARD EVERETT HALE.

October 29

> I keep my eyes always on the Lord.
> With him at my right hand, I will not be shaken.
>
> PSALM 16:8 (NIV)

We are never more discontented with others than when we are discontented with ourselves. The consciousness of wrongdoing makes us irritable, and our heart in its cunning quarrels with what is outside it, in order that it may deafen the clamor within.

In the conduct of life, habits count for more than maxims, because habit is a living maxim, become flesh and instinct. To reform one's maxims is nothing; it is but to change the title of the book. To learn new habits is everything, for it is to reach the substance of life. Life is but a tissue of habits.

—HENRI-FRÉDÉRIC AMIEL.

Our Heavenly Father, we pray that our daily life may take on that dignity and calmness and tranquillity which are the possession of those who truly and inwardly trust and confide in the eternal Goodness, who believe that our days are ordered by a Higher Power, and that through all there runs a thread—a chain of Infinite Love, binding us all to You and to one common universal good and blessedness. In this faith, keep us, O Holy Father, and, filled with love to You and to our neighbor, may we pursue our way and do our work, anxious only to have You in all our thoughts. In Your name, Amen.

—JOSHUA YOUNG.

October 30

Now to the King eternal, immortal, invisible, the only God,
be honor and glory forever and ever. Amen.

1 TIMOTHY 1:17 (NIV)

Thus pass away the generations of men! Thus perish the records of the glory of nations! Yet, when every emanation of the human mind has faded, when in the storms of time the monuments of man's creative art are scattered to the dust, an ever new life springs from the bosom of the earth. Unceasingly prolific Nature unfolds her germs, regardless though sinful man, ever at war with himself, tramples beneath his foot the ripening fruit!　　　　　　　　　—ALEXANDER VON HUMBOLDT.

Infinite Spirit, You build the monuments of Your power in the rocks of the mountains, but You build the monuments of Your love in the hearts of men. When the bodies and the works of men have perished the rocks will abide and the trees will bear their fruit. But when the rocks have crumbled the souls of men will abide. If that which is seen is temporal, we thank You O Lord, that the unseen is eternal. We are awed by the majesty of the seas and the mountains. But we are inspired by the immortality of the soul. Heavenly Father, may we live today as if made for eternity. So may our lives be dignified and glorified. Amen.　　　　—GEORGE L. PERIN.

October 31

Turn from evil and do good;

seek peace and pursue it.

PSALM 34:14 (NIV)

God doth not need
Either man's work, or His own gifts, who best
Bear His mild yoke, they serve Him best; His state
Is kingly; thousands at His bidding speed
And post o'er land and ocean without rest—
They also serve who only stand and wait.

—JOHN MILTON.

O God, who did give to Your servant light in his blindness and music in the heart, grant that I may this day be swift to run on all errands of mercy and truth, or patient to wait for Your will, if You so command. Make me as unswerving as the stars above me, as trustful as the birds who sing at dawn, and fear not what the day may bring. May I be strong to resist all evil, and cleave to that which is good. May I be conscious that in the loneliest hour You are near, and in the most solitary place there is the communion of saints. May Your power flow through human weakness, and may all the trials and testings of life lead me constantly to the Rock that is higher than I. So may Your will be done in my life as it is in heaven. Amen.

—W. H. P. FAUNCE.

November 1

Mightier than the thunder of the great waters,
mightier than the breakers of the sea—
the Lord on high is mighty.

PSALM 93:4 (NIV)

I saw the long line of the vacant shore
The seaweed and the shells
   upon the sand,
And the brown rocks left bare
   on every hand,
As if the ebbing tide
   would flow no more,
Then heard I,
   more distinctly than before,
The ocean breathe and
   its great breast expand,
And hurrying came on the
   defenseless land

The insurgent waters
   with tumultuous roar.
All thought and feeling and desire, I said,
Love, laughter,
   and the exultant joy of song
Have ebbed from me forever!
   Suddenly o'er me
They swept again
   from their deep ocean bed
And in a tumult of delight, and strong
As youth, and beautiful as youth,
   upbore me.
—HENRY W. LONGFELLOW.

We give You hearty thanks, most Holy Father that You have not delivered up our souls to the emptiness and longing of despair. In Your mercy and wisdom You ordained that we may taste ever afresh the deepest joys of life and ever anew feel the thrill of its loftiest inspirations. Like the sea is our life for its largeness; like the sea in its ebbs and flows. O Father of Life, flood our souls this day with a tide from the ocean of Your own love lifting our lives to highest service and bliss. And Yours shall be all the honor and praise. Amen. —E. W. LUTTERMAN.

November 2

The bird, let loose in Eastern skies,
When hastening fondly home,
Ne'er stoops to earth her wing, nor flies
Where idle warblers roam.
But high she shoots through air and light
Above all low delay,
Where nothing earthly bounds her flight,
Nor shadow dims her way.

So grant me, God, from every care,
And stain of passion free,
Aloft, through Virtue's purer air,
To hold my course to Thee!
No sin to cloud—no lure to stay
My soul, as home she springs;—
Thy sunshine on her joyful way,
Thy freedom in her wings!

—THOMAS MOORE.

O God, who is both life and truth, the Author of our being and the light which lightens all, the source of our soul's life, and the goal towards which we strive, as cleaves the lark at dawn the heavenly blue, so may our souls be freed from sense, whose music siren-like would seek to draw us from our flight to You. As that same bird rejoices in the morning light, and sounds its note of praise, so may our souls be tuned to heavenly symphonies, and may the sunshine of Your love, resplendent in secure omnipotence, give glad assurance to our hearts, nor cease to guide our way, until we reach that central orb, our soul's true home, and find eternal rest in You. Amen.

—ALBERT B. SHIELDS.

November 3

There is ever a song somewhere, my dear;
There is ever a something sings always:
There's the song of the lark
   when the skies are clear
And the song of the thrush
   when the skies are gray,
The sunshine showers across the grain,
And the bluebird trills in the orchard tree;
And in and out, when the eaves drip rain,
The swallows art twittering ceaselessly.
There is ever a song somewhere, my dear,
Be the skies above or dark or fair,
There is ever a song
   that our hearts may hear—
There is ever a song
   somewhere, my dear—
There is ever a song somewhere!

—JAMES WHITCOMB RILEY.

O God, the Giver of all harmony and joy, before whom the morning stars sang together, by Whom the voice of the sparrow is heard, we thank You that we may serve You with gladness and come before Your presence with singing. Put Your new song into our mouths and help us to render the acceptable praises of the upright and pure in heart. Help us to love all Your creatures and to delight in the songs You have taught them. Especially enable us to bless our brother men, to hush their sighing and swell their singing, to strengthen the chorus of joy and praise with which You have ordained the world shall be filled. We ask with confidence because we know Your love. Amen.

—J. FRANCIS COOPER.

November 4

You will keep in perfect peace
those whose minds are steadfast,
because they trust in you.

ISAIAH 26:3 (NIV)

The snow has capped yon distant hill,
At morn the running brook was still,
From driven herds the clouds that rise
Are like the smoke of sacrifice;
Ere long the frozen sod shall mark

The ploughshare,
    changed to stubborn rock.
The brawling stream
    shall soon be done—
Sing, little bird! The frosts have come.

—OLIVER WENDELL HOLMES.

Almighty God, our Heavenly Father, You are the giver of all good gifts, and all that comes from Your hand is good. May we accept Your providences. In the dreary days of winter as in the pleasant summer season, Your mercies are new every morning and fresh every evening. Even when our hearts are chilled with grief and disappointment and failure, we would still put our trust in the eternal goodness. Help us, O God, to be truly grateful for everything that comes to us. In the winter of the soul may we learn the lessons of patience and resignation. Thus, with faith triumphant and with hearts full of gladness may we sing our songs of praise to Your holy name forever and forever. Amen.

—ARTHUR W. GROSE.

November 5

God has said, "Never will I leave you; never will I forsake you."
So we say with confidence, "The Lord is my helper; I will not be afraid.
What can mere mortals do to me?"

HEBREWS 13:5b-6 (NIV)

It is will alone that matters!
Will alone that mars or makes,
Will, that no distraction scatters,
And that no resistance breaks.
—HENRIK IBSEN.

No man can choose what coming hours
may bring
To him of need, of joy, of suffering;
But what his soul shall bring
unto each hour
To meet its challenge—
this is in his power.
—PRISCILLA LEONARD.

Infinite God, who perceives the destinies of worlds and of men; who brings to pass all that we enjoy, and who permits all that we suffer; may I this day be enabled to recognize Your Fatherly goodness, in the morning mists, even as in the noonday brightness! Should sorrow cloud my pathway, should disappointment make its keen thrusts, should temptation lay its attractive coils, may my soul be made aware of Your consoling presence, enjoy the compensations of Your grace, assert the potency of the wisdom from above! And may You reveal Yourself! So may be fanned to a flame the divine spark in my heart, whereby all are made partakers of the victory with and through our Lord, Jesus Christ. Amen. —ERNEST W. BURCH.

November 6

"Yes," she answered, lifting her eyes to his face; "I, too, have felt it, Hermas, this burden, this need, this unsatisfied longing. I think I know what it means. It is gratitude—the language of the heart, the music of happiness. There is no perfect joy without gratitude. But we have never learned it, and the want of it troubles us. It is like being dumb with a heart full of love. We must find the word for it, and say it together. Then we shall be perfectly joined in perfect joy."

—HENRY VAN DYKE.

Almighty God, forbid that we shall ever be satisfied with the rich gifts of Your land, or until the gifts have brought us, appreciative, humble, grateful, to You, the giver of them all. Help us to see that this is their high office, disregarding which the noblest of them becomes a stumbling block, accepting which the humblest of them becomes a means of grace and of surpassing gladness. Move us, then, to such acceptance of Your favors as shall bring us to You rejoicing, that we may need less the experiences which shall bring us to You weeping. And hallow all our human loves by lifting us to a common sense and acknowledgment of Your transcendent love, as shown especially in Jesus Christ. Amen.   —CHARLES R. TENNEY.

November 7

But when the kindness and love of God our Savior appeared, he saved us, not because of righteous things we had done, but because of his mercy.

TITUS 3:4-5a (NIV)

"What is the real good?"
I asked, in musing mood.
"Order," said the court;
"Knowledge," said the school,
"Truth," said the wise man,
"Pleasure," said the fool,
"Love," said the maiden,
"Beauty," said the page,
"Freedom," said the dreamer,

"Home," said the sage;
"Fame," said the soldier,
"Equity," said the seer.
Spake my heart full sadly—
"The answer is not here."
Then within my bosom
Softly this I heard:
"Each heart holds the secret;
Kindness is the word."

—JOHN BOYLE O'REILLY.

Oh, Father, we are in a world of wonder and of bountiful promise. We scarcely know which to choose. Of all life's quests we would seek the highest and best. You are a Lord gracious and kind. Grace is but another name for kindness. It is this which is pronounced as a benediction Sabbath after Sabbath, and for which we lift up our faces morning after morning, to receive. Crown us with Your loving kindness and tender mercies. But not for ourselves alone! As we meet the weary and heavy burdened in life, inspire us to show them the kindness of our God. As freely as we have received, so freely may we impart. Amen.   —W. G. RICHARDSON.

November 8

Humble yourselves, therefore, under God's mighty hand, that he may lift you up in due time. Cast all your anxiety on him because he cares for you.

1 PETER 5:6-7 (NIV)

What a blessed thing it is that we can forget! Today's troubles look large, but a week hence they will be forgotten and buried out of sight. Says one writer, "If you should keep a book and daily put down the things that worry you, and see what becomes of them, it would be a benefit to you." The art of forgetting is a blessed art, but the art of overlooking is quite as important. —AUGHEY.

Lord, we know not the path our feet must walk today; yet we are not anxious. "Your word will be a lamp to our feet," and what we need to know You will reveal just when we need to know it. Help us not to forget that we are under our Father's care; that He knows our frame, that He will not unduly burden us; that He will not "suffer us to be tempted beyond that which we are able to bear;" that He will make "all things work together for good to them that love Him." So may this day be one of peace to us, and through us may some troubled heart find rest. Amen.

—GEORGE SKENE.

November 9

A cheerful heart is good medicine,
but a crushed spirit dries up the bones.

PROVERBS 17:22 (NIV)

Learn to laugh. A good laugh is better than medicine. Learn to tell a story. A well told story is as welcome as a sunbeam in a sick room. Learn to keep your own troubles to yourself. The world is too busy to care for your ills and sorrows. Learn to do something for others. Even if you are a bedridden invalid there is always something that you can do to make others happier, and that is the surest way to attain happiness for yourself. —THE BEACON.

Father of all mankind, may the spirit of cheer mark this new day. May the smile of Your benediction rest upon us, and give courage to meet the duty and bear the burden. Help us each moment to know something of the highest joy of serving You. May that joy never be absent from our pain. May it consecrate every pleasure. May it lift us nearer the stature of the Christ, that the light of our life may shed its beams on the pathway of other lives—a light in their darkness, an assurance of sympathy in affliction, an inspiration to do and endure. So may all gladly go to their appointed duty, one with You, even as Christ, whose followers we aim to be. Amen.

—CHARLES T. BILLINGS.

November 10

Oh, the depth of the riches of the wisdom and knowledge of God!
How unsearchable his judgments, and his paths beyond tracing out!

ROMANS 11:33 (NIV)

Take whatever is good in man, and argue that God is not only that, but infinitely better than that. In fashioning your conception of God, make it as resplendent in justice, as august in truth, as noble and pure in love, as radiant and wondrous in pity, as enduring as you please. Never be afraid that you will overdraw the divine character. God is never better in your thought or imagination than He is in Himself.

—HENRY WARD BEECHER.

Almighty God, we thank You for the great thoughts and high hopes which lie deep in human hearts. We thank You for the visions of the perfect life which lead us ever toward the light. We long to follow those who lead the way to You. By faith and love may we be bound to them. As voices of Your spirit may they be to us. Bless us this day with hunger for righteousness. Feed us with the bread of life. Endow us with high hopes and determined wills, that we may be faithful. Amen.

—FREDERICK W. BETTS.

November 11

> May the righteous be glad and rejoice before God;
> may they be happy and joyful.
>
> PSALM 68:3 (NIV)

There was a man who smiled
Because the day was bright;
Because he slept at night;
Because God gave him sight
To gaze upon his child!
Because his little one
Could leap and laugh and run;
Because the distant sun
Smiled on the earth, he smiled.

He toiled and still was glad
Because the air was free;
Because he loved, and she
That claimed his love and he
Shared all the joys they had!
Because the grasses grew;
Because the sweet wind blew;
Because that he could hew
And hammer he was glad.

—S. E. KISER.

O Lord, who bountifully provides for us the necessities and comforts of life, and makes us glad in the enjoyment of the same; grant, we beseech You, that we may so use these, Your gifts, that in all our blessings we find You to be the source and author of all our happiness—of our health and prosperity, of our joys and hopes, and of the holy relations of friends and family; lest, resting content in that which is less, we fail to attain to that which is greatest—truly to know You and to love You, which is the very end of our being and the consummation of all bliss; through Jesus Christ our Lord. Amen. —WILLIAM H. P. HATCH.

November 12

I have seen
A curious child, who dwelt upon a tract
Of inland ground, applying to his ear
The convolutions of
   a smooth-lipped shell;
To which, in silence hushed, his very soul
Listened intensely;
   and his countenance soon
Brightened with joy;
   for from within were heard
Murmurings,
   whereby the monitor expressed
Mysterious union with its native sea:
Even such a shell the universe itself
Is to the ear of Faith;
   and there are times,
I doubt not, when to you it doth impart
Authentic tidings of invisible things;
Of ebb and flow, and ever-during power;
And central peace,
   subsisting at the heart
Of endless agitation.

—WILLIAM WORDSWORTH.

Father of Lights, with whom can be no variation or shadow that is cast by turning, give to me the joy of the love that endures as seeing Him who is invisible; that where Your speaking voice is, there may be my listening ear; that above the waste and clamor of the tasks that exhaust me in bodily strength, there may be supplied a power of will to do the right and a fellowship with all righteous men everywhere. Help me to remember that Life consists not in the abundance of the things I possess. Let my faith see through doubt, endure through temptation and privation, and cleave steadfastly to God, remembering that Love believing is Love triumphing. Through Jesus Christ our Lord. Amen.

—ADOLPH A. BERLE.

November 13

Do not store up for yourselves treasures on earth, where moths and vermin destroy, and where thieves break in and steal. But store up for yourselves treasures in heaven, where moths and vermin do not destroy, and where thieves do not break in and steal. MATTHEW 6:19-20 (NIV)

When Jeremy Taylor had lost all—when his house had been plundered and his family driven out of doors, and all his worldly estate had been sequestered—he could still write thus: "I am fallen into the hands of publicans and sequesterers, and they have taken all from me. What now? Let me look about me. They have left me the sun and moon, a loving wife and many friends to pity me, and some to relieve me; and I can still discourse, and, unless I list, they have not taken away my merry countenance and my cheerful spirit and a good conscience; they have still left me the providence of God, and all the promises of the Gospel, and my religion, and my hopes of heaven, and my charity to them, too; and still I sleep and digest, I eat and drink, I read and meditate—and he that hath so many causes of joy and so great, is very much in love with sorrow and peevishness, who leaves all these pleasures, and chooses to sit down upon his little handful of thorns." —SAMUEL SMILES.

Father of all mercies, who Yourself is more to us than the utmost of Your gifts; we thank You for those blessings of our life which come like the manna fresh every morning and pass with the passing day. Still more we thank You for the blessings which abide, like a pillar of cloud by day and fire by night, witness of Your own presence ever continuing with us. Give us grace and wisdom so to receive the ministries of this new day, that by means of them we may enter more fully into the Divine friendship and the everlasting habitations. Whatever may fail us, grant us such hold upon Yourself as shall be the having of all things, through Jesus Christ our Lord. Amen.

—JAMES FAIRBAIRN BRODIE.

November 14

Native goodness is unconscious,
    asks not to be recognized;
But its baser affectation is a thing
    to be despised.
Only when the man is loyal to himself
    shall he be prized.

*   *   *   *   *

If I live the life He gave me,
    God will turn it to His use.
        —BAYARD TAYLOR.

Live not without a friend!
    The Alpine rock must own
Its mossy grace or else
    be nothing but a stone.
Live not without a God!
    However low or high,
In every house should be
    a window to the sky.
        —WILLIAM WETMORE STORY.

Eternal God, who has neither dawn nor evening, yet sends us alternate mercies of the darkness and the day; there is no light but Yours, without, within. As You lift the curtain of night from our abodes, take also the veil from our hearts. Rise with Your morning upon our souls; quicken all our labor and our prayer; and though all else declines, let the noontide of Your grace and peace remain. May we walk, while it is yet day, in the steps of Him who, with fewest hours, finished Your divinest work. Amen.

        —JAMES MARTINEAU.

November 15

When Jesus spoke again to the people, he said, "I am the light of the world. Whoever follows me will never walk in darkness, but will have the light of life."

JOHN 8:12 (NIV)

I found it difficult the other night to cross a muddy street because of the deep shadow cast by my own body which stood between the electric light and the walk over which I was crossing. Not a little of the time, I fear, do we stand in our own spiritual light, making our own pathway black with ugly shadows cast by our own personality, while the light flashes all around us. If you would avoid the shadows, walk toward the electric light in the heavens and let its beams fall in your face.

—GEORGE L. PERIN.

Our pathway, Heavenly Father, is dark and lone. Sad and sinister suggestions born in our own hearts blind our souls and stay our steps. But with You there is no night. Light is Your shadow. Unto You, therefore, we would turn in the sweet surrender of the spirit. In our darkness which leads to death show us the way. Walking by Your guidance, intent upon Your will, may we rest with unforgetting memory upon Your sevenfold promise of life. Give us the gift of the morning star. With You by our side may this new day bring us a new vision of duty, a larger girding for life, the nobler hope, the truth that makes men free. And unto You be thanks, praise and glory. Amen.

—FRANKLIN HAMILTON.

November 16

The first principle of Christianity is to forget one's self. When Wilberforce was straining every energy to get his bill for the emancipation of slaves passed, a lady once said to him, "Mr. Wilberforce, I'm afraid you are so busy about those slaves that you are neglecting your own soul."

"True, madam," he said; "I had quite forgotten that I have one."

That remark contains one of the deepest truths of Christianity.

—HENRY DRUMMOND.

O Lord, give us the mind of the Master! We would look on our fellow creatures as he looked on them. We would be free from all taint of envy, jealousy, and sin. We would have his single eye and his hearing ear. We know that You are in man, for it is Your spirit which quickens within him every pure thought and moves to every unselfish deed. Give us a due sense of humility and appreciation that we may enter into the secret thought and understand the sincere purpose of all the toilers of this present world! Thus would we abide forever with the saints, the seers, and the singers, of all climes and ages! Amen.   —EBEN H. CHAPIN.

November 17

The Lord is my light and my salvation—whom shall I fear?
The Lord is the stronghold of my life—of whom shall I be afraid?

PSALM 27:1 (NIV)

Do we not know that more than half our trouble is borrowed? Just suppose that we could get rid of all unnecessary and previous terror; just suppose that we could be sure of final victory in every conflict, and final emergence out of every shadow into brighter day; how our hearts would be lightened! How much more bravely we should work and fight and march forward! This is the courage to which we are entitled and which we may find in the thought that God is with us everywhere.

—HENRY VAN DYKE.

O Gracious and Infinite Presence, You are the peace that dwells in the shade of night and the brightness and hope of this new day. We are gratefully conscious of the loving strength that stands ever ready to help. The call of the day's work is in our ears and the courage manfully to labor is in our hearts. Strengthen us, Father, when weariness of toil dissolves our noble resolutions; calm us when petty vexations distract from our holy purposes. May midday find us refreshed by Your grace and eventide solaced by Your benediction. And now as we go forth to duty let our hearts know no terror but the fear of wrongdoing and our minds no anxiety but the earnest desire to toil fruitfully. Grant that we may see beneath life's busy activities the great good You are working out among men and to this end learn to labor and to wait. Amen.

—CHARLES R. EAST.

November 18

And because we are his children, God has sent the Spirit of his Son into our hearts, prompting us to call out, "Abba, Father." Now you are no longer a slave but God's own child. And since you are his child, God has made you his heir.

GALATIANS 4:6-7 (NLT)

There is no thing we cannot overcome.
Say not thy evil instinct is inherited,
Or that some trait inborn makes
   thy whole life forlorn,
And calls down punishment
   that is not merited.
Back of thy parents
   and grandparents lies
The Great Eternal Will.

That, too, is thine
Inheritance, strong, beautiful, divine,
Sure lever of success, for him who tries.
Pry up thy faults with this great lever,
   Will,
However deeply bedded in propensity,
However firmly set, I tell thee firmer yet
Is that strange power that comes
   from truth's immensity!

—ELLA WHEELER WILCOX.

O Eternal Goodness, help us now, as another morning dawns, to readjust ourselves to Your purpose of blessing. We believe that the most certain, significant and permanent fact of the universe is that You are our Father. Thus we are the heirs of Your sufficient grace. There is no curse of ancestry for him who knows You as His parent. There is no weakness of the flesh for him who, through touch with You, becomes strong in the spirit. Help us all through this day to deny the chain of every earthly folly and sin, to stand erect and free as becomes children of the Infinite. So, finding and using the wisdom of our Master, who, most of all men, gained success, may we overcome the world. Amen. —GEORGE E. HUNTLEY.

November 19

If I say, "Surely the darkness will hide me and the light become night around me,"
even the darkness will not be dark to you;
the night will shine like the day, for darkness is as light to you.

PSALM 139:11-12 (NIV)

All things seem rushing straight into the dark—
But the dark still is God.

—GEORGE MACDONALD.

Love is and was my king and lord,
And will be, tho' as yet I keep
Within the court on earth, and sleep
Encompass'd by his faithful guard,

And here at times a sentinel
Who moves about from place to place,
And whispers to the worlds of space,
In the deep night, that all is well.

—ALFRED TENNYSON.

O God, our Heavenly Father, we thank You that You have led us into this new day. We thank You also, that, though its experiences are untried and its issues involved in uncertainty, we are unafraid, full indeed of glad expectation, because we know You as our King and Lord. Help us in obedience and love to keep close to You, so that, if ever quick darkness shall come upon us, we may still be undisturbed because of Your presence, to whom the darkness and the light are both alike. This we ask in the name of Him who loved us and gave Himself for us. Amen.

—CHARLES R. TENNEY.

November 20

May the God of hope fill you with all joy and peace as you trust in him,
so that you may overflow with hope by the power of the Holy Spirit.

ROMANS 15:13 (NIV)

Let thy day be to thy night
A letter of good tidings. Let thy praise
Go up as birds go up,
   that when they wake
Shake off the dew and soar;
   so take joy home
And make a place in thy heart for her,
And give her time to grow and cherish her;
Then will she come
   and oft will sing to thee
When thou art working in the furrows; ay,
Or weeding in the sacred hour of dawn.
It is a comely fashion to be glad—
Joy is the grace we say to God.

—JEAN INGELOW.

Our Father, we thank You for the blessings of night. In this new morning hour, we pray for stout hearts and strong to meet the day's work. May we go forth with a song on our lips and the joy of renewed youth in our souls. Amid the tumults of the day enable us to hear Your becalming voice. Then, though in dreariest labor, we shall have glad hearts, though pressed by dullest cares, we shall keep uncrushed hopes, though distracted by earth's din, we shall hear heaven's music. Abide with us, Benign Spirit. Inspire us to do our duty, and to learn that therein, alone, may true joy be found. Amen. —GEORGE RUNYON LONGBRAKE.

November 21

We can make our plans,
but the Lord determines our steps.

PROVERBS 16:9 (NLT)

The weather-prophet tells us of an approaching storm. It comes according to the program. We admire the accuracy of the prediction, and congratulate ourselves that we have such a good meteorological service. But when, perchance, a bright crystalline piece of weather arrives instead of the foretold tempest, do we not feel a secret sense of pleasure which goes beyond our mere comfort in the sunshine? The whole affair is not as easy as a sum in simple addition, after all—at least not with our present knowledge. It is a good joke on the Weather Bureau. "Aha, Old Probabilities!" we say, "You don't know it all yet; there are still some chances to be taken!"

—HENRY VAN DYKE.

Our Heavenly Father, You have covered us with the darkness and we have slept under the shadow of Your care. You have opened for us again the gates of the morning, and refreshed, we rise to praise You. The memory of mercies past inspires our hope for today. Reveal Yourself to us by Your spirit and through Your word; make nature to minister to us in the heavens above and the fields below; let every experience lead us toward Yourself. Help us to see Your face in those about us, and honor You in loving, helpful ministry to them. Bring to us today a fresh and larger sense of Your presence, forgiveness, and care, and so the assurance that all things are working together for our good. In the name of Jesus Christ our Saviour. Amen.

—SAMUEL H. GREENE.

November 22

I lift up my eyes to the mountains—
where does my help come from?
My help comes from the Lord,
the Maker of heaven and earth.

PSALM 121: 1-2 (NIV)

Peace is the message of the hills,
A peace that broods
Upon their mighty heads, and fills
Their forest solitudes;
The leaping mountain waterfalls,
As each unto the other calls,

Blend in a murmuring noise
Whose silver rushing music stills
The pretty play of human moods,
And bids the calmed soul rejoice
In the deep secrets of the woods,
The majesty of Nature's voice.

—PRISCILLA LEONARD.

Dear God and Father of us all, who makes Your sun to rise out of the sea and tints the hills with the rosy promise of the day, we look up when we awake and seeing the light upon the mountains know that the day is coming to fill the world with beauty and glory. With thankful hearts we praise You, and pray that to us may be granted that loftiness of nature, that stability of character, that repose of mind and heart and life that is prefigured to us in the natural world. Grant that we may each become mediums of Your love and hope to all who may chance to look up to us for guidance along the shores of life's tempestuous ocean. May the spirit of the Eternal find such expression in us and through us, this day, that all who come within the radiance of our joy may come into the consciousness of the joy of the Eternal. Amen.

—THOMAS J. HORNER.

November 23

He said, "Daniel, you who are highly esteemed, consider carefully the words I am about to speak to you, and stand up, for I have now been sent to you." And when he said this to me, I stood up trembling. Then he continued, "Do not be afraid, Daniel. Since the first day that you set your mind to gain understanding and to humble yourself before your God, your words were heard, and I have come in response to them."... Again the one who looked like a man touched me and gave me strength. "Do not be afraid, you who are highly esteemed," he said. "Peace! Be strong now; be strong."   DANIEL 10:11-12, 18-19 (NIV)

Our Heavenly Father, we thank You that You are not far from us at any time. We have only to look up reverently and to our imagination You are standing near. We have only to wait in the darkness of the night to feel Your presence with us. We have only to listen at any time to hear Your voice. You deign to stop and speak to us when we are in trouble, to guide our footsteps when we have lost our way, to renew our courage when we have become disheartened. O Lord, speak to us this day, saying to us, as unto him of old, "Peace be unto you, be strong, yea, be strong." Amen.

—GEORGE L. PERIN.

November 24

Then I heard every creature in heaven and on earth and under the earth and on the sea, and all that is in them, saying: "To him who sits on the throne and to the Lamb be praise and honor and glory and power, for ever and ever!"

REVELATION 5:13 (NIV)

Let star-wheels and angel-wings, with their holy winnowings,
Keep beside you all the way:
Lest in passion you should dash, with a blind and heavy crash.
Up against the thick-bossed shield of God's judgment in the field.
—ELIZABETH BARRETT BROWNING.

Be diligent and faithful, patient and hopeful, one and all of you; and may we all know, at all times, that verily the Eternal rules above us, and that nothing finally wrong has happened or can happen. —THOMAS CARLYLE.

Almighty God, our Father in heaven, the giver of every good and perfect gift, teach us, we pray, how to do Your will on earth as it is done in heaven, as the goal of our lives. Send down exceeding, abundantly above all that we can ask or think, the blessed influences of Your Holy Spirit, to transform each heart and all the world into the kingdom of heaven. Give us the Morning Star of Hope. Feed us from the Tree of Life. Teach us Your redeeming love. Grant that we may have some part with You in the redemption of the world, and be permitted to join with the whole glad earth in the chorus, "Blessing and honor and glory and power be unto Him that sits upon the throne, and unto the Lamb forever and ever." Amen. —F. N. PELOUBET.

November 25

Do you not know that in a race all the runners run, but only one gets the prize? Run in such a way as to get the prize. Everyone who competes in the games goes into strict training. They do it to get a crown that will not last, but we do it to get a crown that will last forever. 1 CORINTHIANS 9:24-25 (NIV)

What is the crown of the whole of life lived faithfully here? It is not a crown of gold or gems in another life; it is simply more life; a broader use of power, a healthier capacity, a larger usefulness. You are faithful unto death, through the misapprehensions and imperfections and absence of appreciation or gratitude in this preparatory world, and then there is offered to you inevitably and legitimately the crown of a larger, more serviceable, more effective life. —FRANCIS G. PEABODY.

To You, O Author of our lives, we speak thanksgiving and gratitude for Your gifts of love and trust. Help us to bring them into full exercise this day. By them may we know the experience of burdens made light and yokes made easy. With them, let us realize that we are effective workers with You. Because of them, show us how all our tasks are transformed to divine endeavors. Through them, set free all other of our highest impulses. So, O God, shall we know the fullness of life, we and all our loved ones. So shall we see doubt change to faith and blindness to vision. So shall our influence through word and work be the ministry of hope and of joy to any disconsolate, and to any who are a weak guide to the source of strength. For newness of life, for all the fruits of the spirit, whereby the heart is ever young and in joyous companionship with the Christ, for all this we pray now and ever. Amen.

—WILLIAM H. MCGLAUCHLIN.

November 26

As a mother comforts her child,
so will I comfort you.

ISAIAH 66:13a (NIV)

The child frightened in his play runs to seek his mother. She takes him upon her lap and presses his head to her bosom; and with tenderest words of love, she looks down upon him and smooths his hair and kisses his cheek, and wipes away his tears. Then, in a low and gentle voice, she sings some sweet descant, some lullaby of love; and the fear fades out from his face, and a smile of satisfaction plays over it, and at length his eyes close, and he sleeps in the deep depths and delights of peace. God Almighty is the mother and the soul is the tired child; and He folds it in His arms and dispels its fears, and lulls it to repose, saying: "Sleep, my darling, sleep! It is I who watch you."
—HENRY WARD BEECHER.

Blessed Master! We thank You that every tired and weary child may find rest in the bosom of the Father. Each morning brings with it new cares, new duties, new privileges, new responsibilities; for all these, we need Your protecting care, and pray for Your divine guidance. When wearied and burdened with the cares of daily life, help us to flee to You as the frightened child flees to the loving mother; and encircle us with Your arms of love, and whisper in our ears words of comfort and cheer and of forgiveness. Teach us to trust You in the morning, to walk with You through the day, and to commit our ways to You at all times. Amen.
—SAMUEL M. DICK.

November 27

> Truly my soul finds rest in God;
> my salvation comes from him.
> Truly he is my rock and my salvation;
> he is my fortress, I will never be shaken.
>
> PSALM 62:1-2 (NIV)

Certainly there never was a busier life than that of Jesus—His whole great mission bounded by three hurried years. Yet in the morning He says to His friends: "Let us come apart and rest awhile;" and again when the evening is come He is in the mountain apart, alone. That is the place of worship in a world of work. It is not a refuge from duty, or a shirking of it; it is the renewal of power to meet one's duty and do it. The work of life is not to be well done with a hot, feverish, overwhelmed, and burdened mind; it is to be well done with a mind calmed and fortified by moments of withdrawal; and it is to be best done by one who from time to time pulls himself up in his eager life and permits God to speak to his soul.

—FRANCIS G. PEABODY.

O Spirit of grace, who withholds Your blessing from none, take from us the tediousness and anxiety of a selfish mind, the unfruitfulness of cold affections, the weakness of an inconstant will. With the simplicity of a great purpose, the quiet of a meek temper, and the power of a well-ordered soul, may we pass through the toils and watches of our pilgrimage; grateful for all that may render the burden of duty light; and even in strong trouble rejoicing to be deemed worthy of the severer service of Your will. Amen.

—JAMES MARTINEAU.

November 28

For in him all things were created: things in heaven and on earth, visible and invisible, whether thrones or powers or rulers or authorities; all things have been created through him and for him.   COLOSSIANS 1:16 (NIV)

God gives to every man   That lifts him into life, and lets him fall
The virtue, temper, understanding, taste,   Just in the niche he was ordain'd to fill.
                                                      —WILLIAM COWPER.

Did you ever hear of a man who had striven all his life faithfully and singly toward an object, and in no measure obtained it? If a man constantly aspires, is he not elevated? Did ever a man try heroism, magnanimity, truth, sincerity, and find that there was no advantage in them—that it was a vain endeavor?   —HENRY DAVID THOREAU.

Holy Father, help us to be thankful that no life is beneath Your notice. If a sparrow cannot fall without You, how much more is Your eye fixed on Your child. Teach us, O Lord, that there is a divine purpose in each life. But may we not try to choose this without You. Show us how to wait upon You in holy silence till You make it known to us. O Master, say to us: "As the Father has sent me into the world even so have I sent you." When we have found at the Cross our little mission, O sustain us and help us to keep it steadily in view—let us share Your holy enthusiasm when You did say: "My food is to do the will of Him that sent me and to finish His work." O Father, when we are depressed whisper to us: "Your labor is not in vain in the Lord." May our mission transform us into the likeness of Jesus, and may we say with Him at evening: "I have glorified You on the earth; I have finished the work You gave me to do." Amen.
                                                      —L. P. JOHNSON.

November 29

The Lord is good to those whose hope is in him,
to the one who seeks him;
it is good to wait quietly
for the salvation of the Lord.

LAMENTATIONS 3:25-26 (NIV)

Though wrong may win,
its victory is brief,
The tides of good at first no passage find;
Each surge breaks, shattered,
on the sullen reef—
Yet still the infinite ocean comes behind.

The road of Right has neither turn
nor bend,
It stretches straight unto the highest goal;
Hard, long, and lonely?
—yes, yet never soul
Can lose its way thereon,
nor miss the end.

—PRISCILLA LEONARD.

We thank You, Heavenly Father, that awaking, we are conscious that You are near. Walk with us, through the untried path of this day's duty and service. We rejoice that You are in Your world. Within its striving is Your calm. Around its restlessness is Your rest. Your purpose fashions its achievements; Your love shapes its future. Help us to see it with clearer vision, to hold it fast with firmer faith. When wrong seems to triumph, may we know that it is already perishing, and hold hard by truth and love and faith. Give us grace to spend this day as becomes children of God in honor, in courtesy, in sympathy, in confident trust. When the way seems long and lonely, straight and steep, help us to sing as we march forward, since You are with us, who has said, "I will never leave you nor forsake you." Amen.   —CHARLES C. P. HILLER.

November 30

She was a droll little figure of a girl with a quaint old face, that showed too early the lines of care and work, and her clothing betokened a poverty-stricken home. Evidently not much of brightness had touched her life, but her face always lightened up when she mentioned her school or her teacher. "Why is it that you love your teacher so well?" she was asked one day.

Her eyes shone and her lips smiled happily as she replied, "Because she's glad to me!"

What a tribute was that! What an evidence was that of a happy heart that radiated its gladness! If we cannot bring other offerings of much value to the children and the poor among us, how blessed are we if we can bring gladness!

—ESTELLE M. HART.

Almighty God, teach us how to be glad. Put some gladness into our hearts. Show us where gladness is hidden in our little world about us, so that we may find it and use it. Give us the wisdom of Jesus, who, although a Man of Sorrows, yet spoke ever of His joy and His peace. We feel that the secret of things must be gladness, that somehow there is a covered joy even in what we call our sufferings. Let us find that. Keep our hearts pure of the soiling of evil desire, for we know that no gladness can come from the muddy fountains of sin. Let our hands be busy at some good part of the world's work, for we know that idleness never went hand in hand with joy. Let our minds be open to acknowledge, love and obey the truth, for we feel that truth alone can satisfy our hearts. And let us feel today the duty of gladness we owe to our fellow-creatures. Let us give to them what we would receive from You. Amen.   —FRANK CRANE.

December 1

O God, you are my God; I earnestly search for you.
My soul thirsts for you; my whole body longs for you
in this parched and weary land where there is no water.

PSALM 63:1 (NLT)

But winter has yet brighter scenes—he boasts
Splendors beyond what gorgeous Summer knows;
Or Autumn with his many fruits, and woods
All flushed with many hues, come when the rains
Have glazed the snow and clothed the trees with ice,
The incrusted surface shall upbear thy steps,
And the broad arching portals of the grove
Welcome thy entering.

—WILLIAM CULLEN BRYANT.

Our Father, we know that You will commune with us if only we truly seek You; You are the Infinite Consciousness and You include within Yourself our finite consciousness. We have our life in Your life. This morning we would be mindful of Your presence. The northern groves with snow-laden, bended branches bid us enter and worship. You send forth the rays of Your sun and touch them aglow with the reflected beauty of the snowflake. You have also created us. The flake reflects the sun, and may we reflect You, through living righteously. Help us to do the right and to forego the wrong. Amen.   —FRED ALBAN WEIL.

December 2

Jesus replied, "My light will shine for you just a little longer. Walk in the light while you can, so the darkness will not overtake you. Those who walk in the darkness cannot see where they are going. Put your trust in the light while there is still time; then you will become children of the light."   JOHN 12:35-36 (NLT)

"A commonplace life," we say,
　and we sigh;
But why should we sigh as we say?
The commonplace sun in the
　commonplace sky
Makes up the commonplace day.
The moon and the stars are
　commonplace things,

And the flower that blooms
　and the bird that sings,
But dark were the world and sad our lot
If the flowers failed
　and the sun shone not;
And God, who studies each separate soul
Out of commonplace lives
　makes His beautiful whole.

—SUSAN COOLIDGE.

Our Infinite Father, we open our hearts to You, for where You are heaven is. As the morning sun gives light and life to Earth, so You give light and life and joy to us. We say good morning to You, and as we listen Your good morning comes to us. As it comes we glow and expand like the opening flower. May this glowing spirit of love be in all we say and do and think this day, and still continue through all days to come. When we are vexed and weary with trials and labor, make us to remember this morning glow of Your Love that it may renew rest and peace within us. Help us, our Father, to enter the beauty of this day and this life by claiming our heritage as "children of light" and going forth to fulfill the common duties of the day as "children of God." Amen.   —WALTER DOLE.

December 3

If I could speak all the languages of earth and of angels, but didn't love others, I would only be a noisy gong or a clanging cymbal. If I had the gift of prophecy, and if I understood all of God's secret plans and possessed all knowledge, and if I had such faith that I could move mountains, but didn't love others, I would be nothing. If I gave everything I have to the poor and even sacrificed my body, I could boast about it; but if I didn't love others, I would have gained nothing.

1 CORINTHIANS 13:1-3 (NLT)

No matter! So long as the world is the work of eternal goodness, and so long as conscience has not deceived us. To give happiness and to do good, there is our only law, our anchor of salvation, our beacon light, our reason for existing. All religions may crumble away; so long as this survives we have still an ideal, and life is worth living. Nothing can lessen the dignity and value of humanity so long as the religion of love, of unselfishness and devotion endures; and none can destroy the altars of this faith for us so long as we feel ourselves still capable of love.

—HENRI-FRÉDÉRIC AMIEL.

Our Heavenly Father, we thank You for a night of peaceful rest, and we are glad to begin a new day with full assurance of Your loving care. We hope for pleasant ways and large success, but Your wisdom is better than our wishes and if it is appointed us to meet difficulties or temptations, we pray for strength to sustain a manly warfare. We have faith that whatever our condition You will still provide a way by which lofty purpose and resolute endeavor may use the circumstances of our life for a nearer approach to You and for service to our fellowmen. To this end be then the light of our way and the strength of our life, through Jesus Christ our Lord. Amen.

—J. SMITH DODGE.

December 4

He was a friend to man, and lived in a house by the side of the road.

—HOMER.

There are hermit souls
    that live withdrawn
In the peace of their self-content;
There are souls, like stars,
    that dwell apart,
In a fellow-less firmament;
There are pioneer souls
    that blaze their paths
Where highways never ran—
But let me live by the side of the road
And be a friend to man.

Let me live in a house
    by the side of the road.
Where the race of men go by—
The men who are good
    and the men who are bad,
As good and as bad as I.
I would not sit in the scorner's seat,
Or hurl the cynic's ban:—
Let me live in a house
    by the side of the road
And be a friend to man.

—SAM WALTER FOSS.

Our Father in Heaven, we come with thanksgiving for the light of another day and all the blessings which it brings from You. May the precious moments before us be filled with activity. Forgive us if we have been remiss in seizing our opportunities and so lead us this day that if we shall be called to You, the sweet voice of the Master may greet us with, "Inasmuch as you have done it unto one of the least of these my brethren, you have done it unto Me." In Jesus' name. Amen.   —J. E. CHARLTON.

December 5

Let all that I am praise the Lord; may I never forget the good things he does for me.
He forgives all my sins and heals all my diseases.
He redeems me from death and crowns me with love and tender mercies.
He fills my life with good things. My youth is renewed like the eagle's!

PSALM 103:2-5 (NLT)

One old lady kept a sighing;
Said she wasn't young,
Didn't look as sweet's she used to,
Times were all unstrung;
Troubles doubled aches, and favors
Went a flying past,
Wrinkles stung like thorns, and eyesight
Kept a failing fast.

One old lady kept a saying
Life was like the spring,
Brighter blossoms always coming,
Birds around to sing;
Troubles came—and went; she let 'em,
Didn't count the throng.
Thanked the Lord 'most every morning
She'd been young so long!

—JESSIE M. SHAW.

Our Heavenly Father, will You forgive us for the sighs and tears and frowns and doubts of yesterday? Especially will You forgive us for all that was little and petty and mean? May we begin again today with larger vision, higher hope and nobler ambition. May there be no sighs for lost beauty, no grief over faded youth and no lamentation over lost fortune. Thankful and glad for what we have, may we find our joy in using it for some high end. So may we conserve the youth of the heart and the light of the soul. Amen.

—GEORGE L. PERIN.

December 6

Trust in the Lord and do good.
>   Then you will live safely in the land and prosper.
Take delight in the Lord,
>   and he will give you your heart's desires.

PSALM 37:3-4 (NLT)

There is never a sky of winter
To the heart that sings alway;
Never a night but hath stars to light,
And dreams of a rosy day.

The world is ever a garden
Red with the bloom of May;
And never a stormy morning
To the heart that sings alway!

—FRANK L. STANTON.

O You who are the Love, the Light, and the Life in whom is no discord, no darkness, no disease nor death; but who is ever radiating sympathy, vision and health; we give You hearty thanks for the consciousness of Your abiding presence when we possess a humble and contrite spirit. May we ever remember that nothing but our own selfishness, pride, and forgetfulness can break this constant communion with You. Open our hearts just now for the inflow of the divine Love in order that we may pass it on to others today. Open our eyes today that we may see You everywhere striving against selfishness in the lives of all men. Fill us with Your Life today in order that there may go out to others a heavenly harmony, a song, a symphony, that will dispel discord, darkness and disease; that will overcome evil with good. Amen.   —E. J. HELMS.

December 7

Then they cried out to the Lord in their trouble,
and he brought them out of their distress.
He stilled the storm to a whisper;
the waves of the sea were hushed.

PSALM 107:28-29 (NIV)

As the bird trims her to the gale,
I trim myself to the storm of time,
I man the rudder, reef the sail,
Obey the voice at eve obeyed at prime;

"Lowly faithful, banish fear,
Right onward drive unharmed;
The port, well worth the cruise, is near,
And every wave is charmed."

—RALPH WALDO EMERSON.

Heavenly Father, keep our faces in the light and upward. Make us courageous in the storm. Help us to consecrate all our powers against the contrary winds and listen for the loving voice of Him who walks the rough waves and comes toward our frail barks. May we never be afraid; may we know peace and rest and trust. O Saviour, help us to know the reality of Your love and friendship, and hear You say in the darkest hour, "All is well." May no storm be too severe, no burden too heavy, no task too hard. So let us believe and live. Amen.

—CORTLAND MYERS.

December 8

Love thyself last: cherish those hearts that hate thee,
Corruption wins not more than honesty.
Still in thy right hand carry gentle peace,
To silence envious tongues. Be just, and fear not:
Let all the ends thou aim'st at be thy country's,
Thy God's, and truth's; then if thou fall'st, O Cromwell,
Thou fall'st a blessed martyr!

—SHAKESPEARE.

Father Almighty, we do trust in You, and we ask You for everything. You are pleased to give us everything. You give us the light by which we see. You give us this air which we breathe and with which we speak. Best of all, You have shown us that we are one family of Your children, alive in Your life and strong in Your strength. You give us the water that we drink and the food that we eat. Everything is Yours while it is ours. Now, Father, we are here to consecrate these gifts to Your service, to come and go indeed as Your children; when we speak, to speak the word that You shall teach; when we act, to do the thing that You would. Moreover, inspire us with Your holy spirit, that we may so come and go in our Father's service, and for the coming of Your kingdom in this world, that all men may be one, and may bear one another's burdens, and so fulfil the law of Christ. Amen.   —EDWARD EVERETT HALE.

December 9

Can a mother forget the baby at her breast
  and have no compassion on the child she has borne?
Though she may forget, I will not forget you!
See, I have engraved you on the palms of my hands.

ISAIAH 49:15-16a (NIV)

Each soul, alone unto herself, must bear
The heartache out of which man wins
  despair
Or hope according to his faculty.
Nevertheless one thing is certain;
  who hath known
Truth, beauty, goodness,
  shining in their sphere,
Shall not be lost through any lesser lure.
On black tempestuous waves
  he may be thrown;
Yet to the right port shall he surely steer,
And God Himself
  shall make his doing pure.

—JOHN ADDINGTON SYMONDS.

O God, with the dawn we would lift our grateful hearts to You! We know not what You have in store for us this new day, but we rejoice that we are in Your thought, and that we cannot pass beyond the reach of Your love. Helpless and weak, we pray for courage to be undaunted by the uncertainties of life, and that we may meet all its duties with a firm and tranquil mind. Grant that we may be helpful to all with whom we come in contact and forbid that we should judge others hastily or uncharitably. May our minds and hearts be open to the truth, that we may know and do Your gracious will. Guided and guarded by You, may the day be full of peace, purity and power. Amen.

—GEORGE M. HOWE.

December 10

There was never a song
    that was sung by thee,
But a sweeter one was meant to be.
There was never a deed
    that was grandly done,
But a greater was meant
    by some earnest one.
For the sweetest voice can never impart
The song that trembles within the heart.

And the brain and the hand
    can never quite do
The thing that the soul has fondly in view.
And hence are the tears
    and the burdens of pain,
For the shining goals are never to gain
But enough that a God can hear and see
The song and the deed
    that were meant to be.

—BENJAMIN R. BULKELEY.

Almighty God, our Heavenly Father, who has illumined the morning with the brightness of Your life, we rejoice in the potency of the influence that brings us into communion with You. For the blessed revelation of Yourself, for life and all things that nourish it, for the earth and the fullness thereof, for daily comforts and mercies and for the Light that lights every man who comes into the world, we give You thanks. We thank You too for the songs that we have sung and for the better songs that are in our hearts. We thank You for every noble deed and also for the dreams of nobler deeds that men have cherished. O Lord, bless our work and fill us with aspiration for nobler service. Bless the poor, the sick, and those that mourn. Hear this our prayer and answer our petition through Jesus Christ our Lord. Amen.

—FRANK D. SARGENT.

December 11

And let us consider how we may spur one another on toward love and good deeds, not giving up meeting together, as some are in the habit of doing, but encouraging one another—and all the more as you see the Day approaching.

HEBREWS 10:24-25 (NIV)

Love the spot where you are, and the friends God has given you and be sure to expect everything good of them. —JOHN ALBEE.

When do we lift each other up? Must we gain a height first or can we reach up our feebleness together to the Hands that do offer us a mighty help from on high? Near doing, and near living, and near loving; these life-particles make the great heaven, as the little polarized atoms of light, all magnetized one way, make the great blue in which the stars burn forever. —MRS. A. D. T. WHITNEY.

No discontent could harass us if we had a deeper faith in You and a broader love for those about us. We praise You, therefore, that we may be rooted and grounded in Christ. And that our little lives may glorify Him by bringing forth abundant fruit. You give us the holy privilege of being co-laborers with You in the salvation of needy humanity. Around us are the countless opportunities for ennobling and gladdening the lives of those whose courage burns low, or who have never known the transforming companionship of Christ. We would not forget that we are debtors to You and to that great Host whose love and service has inspired us. May we be not selfish takers only, but generous givers. May there be less gloom, fewer shackles, less guilt in the world because we are mastered by the spirit of Christ. Amen. —PHILIP L. FRICK.

December 12

No discipline seems pleasant at the time, but painful.
Later on, however, it produces a harvest of righteousness
and peace for those who have been trained by it.

HEBREWS 12:11 (NIV)

Have you learned lessons only of those who admired you, and were tender with you, and stood aside for you?

Have you not learned great lessons from those who reject you, and brace themselves against you? Or who treat you with contempt, or dispute the passage with you?

—WALT WHITMAN.

Help us, O God, always to be hopeful; teach us what it means to hope in You, and may we experience the truth of the promise which says: "He will strengthen your heart that hopes in Him;" but help us not to indulge in too fond hopes nor to be too easily elated by future dreams. May we see life clearly as it is and be ready to accept courageously whatever You send us. Help us to accept all our joys as Your blessings; all our duties as Your commands, and our sorrows as of Your appointment, and help us to believe that You will turn even that which seems to harm us, into everlasting good and everlasting joy. Amen.   —JOHN F. MEYER.

December 13

Do not conform to the pattern of this world, but be transformed by the renewing of your mind. Then you will be able to test and approve what God's will is—his good, pleasing and perfect will.

ROMANS 12:2 (NIV)

Life should be a giving birth to the soul, the development of a higher mode of reality. The animal must be humanized: flesh must be made spirit; physiological activity must be transmuted into intellect and conscience, into reason, justice, and generosity, as the torch is transmuted into light and warmth. The blind, greedy, selfish nature of man must put on beauty and nobleness. This heavenly alchemy is what justifies our presence on the earth; it is our mission and our glory.

—HENRI-FRÉDÉRIC AMIEL.

Our Father, this world is Your world, and this day is Your renewed gift of opportunity to learn life's lesson more perfectly. We need clearer insight into Your designs, that we may loathe every form of selfishness, and love devotion. Give us to know the Christ more intimately, and in the strength of His apprehended presence help us to employ this day in practicing the holy principles He taught. Assist us this morning to have, and throughout this day to keep, such an attitude of glad cooperation with Him, that work shall be shot through and through with joy in anticipation of its glorious result. So may this day be to us a time of real soul expansion; a wooing and a winning of that which is highest, even a purer, noble character. Amen.

—J. EDWIN LACOUNT.

December 14

> But the Lord said to Samuel, "Do not consider his appearance or his height, for I have rejected him. The Lord does not look at the things people look at. People look at the outward appearance, but the Lord looks at the heart."
>
> 1 SAMUEL 16:7 (NIV)

'Tis the mind that makes the body rich,
And as the sun breaks through the darkest clouds,
So honor peereth in the meanest habit.
What, is the jay more precious than the lark,
Because his feathers are more beautiful?
Or is the adder better than the eel,
Because his painted skin contents the eye?

—SHAKESPEARE.

In this world of mingled good and evil, amid the ceaseless struggle of the better with the worse, grant unto us our Father, the cheerful assurance that we are enlisted in the service of the good, bound for the better, and destined for the best. Reveal to us each day some task that we can do for You, some chance to bear with Christ the burden of another, some call to take the side of the right against the wrong. Help us to conquer hardship by patience, despair by hope, fear by courage, and hate by love; and may we find the peace, the power, the glory of Your perfect will and Your great kingdom reflected and reproduced in our hearts and lives. Amen.

—WILLIAM DEWITT HYDE.

December 15

Even to your old age and gray hairs
I am he, I am he who will sustain you.
I have made you and I will carry you;
I will sustain you and I will rescue you.

ISAIAH 46:4 (NIV)

Call him not old, whose visionary brain
Holds o'er the past its undivided reign,
For him in vain the envious seasons roll
Who bears eternal summer in his soul.
If yet the minstrel's song,
   the poet's lay,
Spring with her birds,
   or children at their play,
Or maiden's smile,
   or heavenly dream of art,
Stir the few life-drops creeping
   round his heart,
Turn to the record
   where his years are told—
Count his gray hairs—
   they cannot make him old!

—OLIVER WENDELL HOLMES.

Infinite Spirit of Life, in Your sight, there is no old age. The step may grow feeble, the hair may whiten, the eye may grow dim, but each human soul is still Your child. We gather about the tables of earth, families of children, some older, some younger, but all young in Your sight. We pause for a moment this morning to pray for the spirit of youth. Let us cherish the power of hoping and of believing. Let us have that fine quality of the child life which keeps it facing the future with glad expectancy. Let us not give over our toils till we must. Let us not relinquish our interest in life till the evening shadows fall, and even at the last, let us lie down like the child who sleeps with his hand in the hand of his mother. Amen.   —GEORGE L. PERIN.

December 16

> All hard work brings a profit,
> but mere talk leads only to poverty.
>
> PROVERBS 14:23 (NIV)

O toiling bands of mortals! O unwearied feet, travelling we know not whither! Soon, soon, it seems to you, you must come forth on some conspicuous hilltop, and but a little way further, against the setting sun, descry the spires of El Dorado. Little do you know your own blessedness; for to travel hopefully is a better thing than to arrive, and the true success is to labor.

—ROBERT LOUIS STEVENSON.

Our Father, we thank You for the work that You give us to do; for its joy, for its zest, even for its very task and weariness. We would interpret our labor by the highest good it brings us; through our brave and cheerful doing Your heaven of peace is found. We thank You for our diviner hopes, and for the Spirit that would complete them. They light our days with gladness, and set our feet in large places, and though the higher hilltops seem far away, yet meeting our duties faithfully, we do see them, and looking back we find the places of our departure lying far below. O blessed tasks! O blessed hopes! That lead us ever to our Father's love. Amen.

—ALBERT J. COLEMAN.

December 17

My sheep listen to my voice;
I know them, and they follow me.

JOHN 10:27 (NLT)

God speaks to hearts of men
   in many ways:
Some the red banner of the rising sun,
Spread o'er the snow-clad hills,
   has taught his praise.
Some the sweet silence
   when the day is done;
Some, after loveless lives,
   at length have won
His word in children's hearts
   and children's gaze;
And some have found him
   where low rafters ring

To greet the hand that helps,
   the heart that cheers;
And some in prayer,
   and some in perfecting
Of watchful toil through
   unrewarding years;
And some not less are his,
   who vainly sought
His voice, and with his silence
   have been taught—
Who bore his chains
   who bade them to be bound,
And at the end in finding not have found.

—ANONYMOUS.

O God, all voices of the earth are Yours, even when there is no speech or language, Your messages have many ways to reach the listening heart. Give us this day to hear at least some whisper of Your grace. If it may be, open our minds and attune our spirits to receive more than we could previously interpret of the assurances sent to us by elevated goodness and love. So let us be defended this day against wrong, and do our work in joy and peace through the knowledge that You are with us, our friend and helper even unto the end. Amen.   —HOWARD N. BROWN.

December 18

Teach me to do your will, for you are my God;
may your good Spirit lead me on level ground.

PSALM 143:10 (NIV)

Did you ever see a schoolboy tumble on the ice without stooping immediately to re-buckle the strap of his skates? And would not Ignotus have painted a masterpiece if he could have found good brushes and a proper canvas? Life's shortcomings would be bitter indeed if we could not find excuses for them outside of ourselves. And as for life's successes—well, it is certainly wholesome to remember how many of them are due to a fortunate position and the proper tools. —HENRY VAN DYKE.

Our Father, God, help us to begin this new day with the right spirit in our hearts—the spirit of love toward You and our fellowmen. Help us to begin the day if possible without mistake. If, in our human weakness we find that we have not succeeded, that we have erred or gone astray, help us not to despair, not to be discouraged; help us to know and to seek and to love the right. Help us never to forget what we owe to You, to our friends, and the beautiful world You have given us. Daily bread we have, opportunities open, like books on every hand. Greater than all life's bitter is its sweet. Ever ready is the Master to bless; ever ready is the spirit to comfort Your children look up and praise the Father eternal. Amen. —RANSOM A. GREENE.

December 19

For God so loved the world that he gave his one and only Son, that whoever believes in him shall not perish but have eternal life. For God did not send his Son into the world to condemn the world, but to save the world through him.

JOHN 3:16-17 (NIV)

I love You, O Son of Man! For Your strength and Your sweetness, for Your simplicity, Your courage, Your infinite tenderness, for Your glance which strengthens and pardons us, quickens us and lifts us up; for all that You have brought us of consolation, of peace and of warmth of heart. Abide with us! Teach us to see the divine spark imprisoned in every stone of the highway. —CHARLES WAGNER.

O Lord, our Heavenly Father, we thank You for all Your manifold mercies to us, for all Your constant care and watchfulness over us from the beginning of our lives to this day, for the revelations of Your presence in the world about us, in the shining sky, in the earth beneath our feet, and in the faces of our friends. Bless us, O Lord, this day, with health and strength and a good courage, and grant that we may show our gratitude for all Your goodness not only with our lips but in our lives, through Jesus Christ, our Lord. Amen. —GEORGE HODGES.

December 20

In every "Oh my Father!"
Slumbers deep a "Here, my child."

—THOLUCK.

This world, with its wonderful creations, its beauties, and mysteries may lead a child up to the father's throne, if his heart and mind are open to it. Fill the heart with goodness and there is no place for badness. Fill the soul with heaven, and there is no hell. And this delightful time will come when "God is all and in all."

—ABBIE E. DANFORTH.

Our Father, who is in heaven; we know that You have been good to us. We thank You for the daily witnesses of Your love. And we would walk worthily before You. But we are weak. Help us, O Father to see clearly what You would have us do! Give us strength. Fill us with Your spirit, that all the way we may be pure and patient. Help us to walk aright. In the name of Jesus Christ. Amen.

—CHARLES H. PUFFER.

December 21

The human spirit is the lamp of the LORD
that sheds light on one's inmost being.
PROVERBS 20:27 (NIV)

Grand is the seen, the light, to me—
  grand are the sky and stars,
Grand is the earth, and grand
  are lasting time and space,
And grand their laws, so multiform,
  puzzling, evolutionary;
But grander far the unseen soul of me,
  comprehending, endowing all those,

Lighting the light, the sky and stars,
  delving the earth, sailing the sea,
(What were all those, indeed,
  without thee, unseen soul?
Of what amount without Thee?)
More evolutionary, vast, puzzling,
  O my soul!
More multiform far—
  more lasting Thou than they.

—WALT WHITMAN.

O You, our Heavenly Father, in spirit we reach out to Your great spirit. Quicken within us visions of what things we may do this day, with You at hand, Your love abounding. Give us vision that we may rise to the opportunities of our daily task. Let Your holy spirit bear witness to the reality of our dreams and aspirations, that we may look not idly upon our opportunities, but rather that each new opportunity shall challenge us to nobler effort. O keep us this day full of faith in ourselves and You, each obedient to our vision, until full purposed, winning Your approval, we shall accomplish the thing for which You send us, and Yours be the glory. Amen.

—JAMES D. TILLINGHAST.

December 22

I see the wrong that round me lies,
I feel the guilt within,
With groan and travail cries
I hear the world confess its sin.

Within the maddening maze of things,
And tossed by storm and flood,

To one fixed stake my spirit clings:
I know that God is good.

I know not where his islands lift
Their fronded palms in air;
I only know I cannot drift
Beyond His love and care.

—JOHN GREENLEAF WHITTIER.

O You, without whose care a sparrow does not fall, who through the pathless sky guides the bird seeking its distant nest, Your trusting children are safe in Your dear love. We know not the way before us, but You do know; our feet may stumble in rough paths, but You will hold us up. Glad in this confidence, may we begin the day with song and finish it, whatever may befall us, in the calm assurance that all things work for good. Give us patience in perplexity, hope amid our fears, and faith to trust Your holy will as best. Thus walking in Your love may we reach home at last to see our Saviour's face. Amen.

—STEPHEN A. NORTON.

December 23

Wouldst make thy life
   go fair and square?
Thou must not for the past feel care;
Whatever thy loss,
   thou must not mourn;
Must ever act as if new-born.
What each day wants of thee, that ask;

What each day tells thee,
   that make thy task;
With pride thine own
   performance viewing,
With heart to admire another's doing;
Above all, hate no human being,
And all the future leave
   to the All-Seeing.

—GOETHE.

Dear Father, grateful for another new-born day, myself new-born, I greet You! Yesterday and all other yesterdays are in Your keeping. This day is mine! For the failures of the past I care not, nor do I mourn the losses of the days gone by. Today I am new-born! Indeed, aspiring to Your comprehensive wisdom, I may see my past and my present as one, and out of that past I may select—even from failures and losses— such experiences and lessons as will help me live the present—at least this one day which is mine!—more nobly, more fully, more usefully, more beautifully. May I, knowing myself to be Your Child, respect myself as a creative spirit able to look upon its own work and to say: "Behold, it is good!" And above all, I pray: that, today and always, I may grow in grace and loving-kindness—hating no one, but feeling, thinking, speaking, acting with good will towards all Your creatures! This day is mine! The future I leave to You, All-Seeing Father! But feel myself Your open-eyed and confident child. Amen.   —CHARLES FLEISCHER.

December 24

'Mid pleasures and palaces
   though we may roam,
Be it ever so humble,
   there's no place like home;
A charm from the skies
   seems to hallow us there,
Which sought through the world
   is ne'er met with elsewhere.

An exile from home splendor
   dazzles in vain,
Oh give me my lowly
   thatched cottage again;
The birds singing gaily,
   that came at my call,
Give me them, and that peace of mind
   dearer than all.

—J. HOWARD PAYNE.

O God, our Heavenly Father, we thank You for the blessings of home; for the shelter, safety, and hallowed associations of our domestic habitation; for the sympathy and helpfulness of family relationship. Help us we pray to make ours an ideal household, bright with cheerfulness, an exemplification of Christian faith and hope. May the happiness of all be the object of each. To that end help us to be patient toward one another, kind and forgiving. May we realize by many beatific experiences that it is better to give than to receive, better to serve than to be served. May we be disposed, as occasion may arise, to share, for a season, the comfort and inspiration of our home with those who are homeless. We thank You for the bright assurance that beyond the fading scenes and transitory experiences of this life, there is, awaiting us, an eternal abiding place in "a continuing city" whose maker and builder is God, where there shall be no more parting, and where the shadows of our present life shall forever flee away. Amen.   —CHARLES CONKLIN.

December 25

Today in the town of David a Savior has been born to you; he is the Messiah, the Lord. This will be a sign to you: You will find a baby wrapped in cloths and lying in a manger.   LUKE 2:11 (NIV)

That ever-vivid scene of Bethlehem.... A father, a mother, and a child are there. No religion which began like that could ever lose its character. The first unit of human life, the soul, is there, in the newborn personality of childhood. But the second unit of human life, the family, is just as truly there in the familiar relation of husband and wife and the sacred, eternal mystery of motherhood.   —PHILLIPS BROOKS.

"Glory to God in the highest, and on earth Peace." We take up the angel symphony and give it new breath, this gladsome day of days. You who did send Your Son in the likeness of a little child, that by His life of increase in love and beauty and wisdom and power He might give us courage to begin as children the obedience that alone leads at last to the measure of the stature of His fullness, accept our unutterable gratitude for all that gift. And oh, may He be born in us and formed in us, the hope of glory, that so we may share His peace, His victory, His exaltation, His union with You. Amen.

—C. ELLWOOD NASH.

December 26

Two are the pathways by which mankind can to virtue mount upward;
If thou shouldst find the one barr'd, open the other will lie.
'Tis by exertion the Happy obtain her, the Suffering by patience,
Blest is the man whose kind fate guides him along upon both!

—SCHILLER.

O You who has kept us safely during the unconsciousness of our slumbering hours, and brought us refreshed to this morning light, prepare us for the duties of this day by filling us with the assurance that we are Yours, and that You love us. Help us to be more like You, to love You more and serve You better. May we manifest our love to You by our willingness to be of service to our fellowmen. Make us warm-hearted and true, helpful and kind, reflecting Your love and doing Your will. We are glad to live in this beautiful world. And we pray that we may be faithful co-laborers with Jesus Christ, in being light, love and joy to all lives. Amen.

—CHARLES R. TENNEY.

December 27

And over all these virtues put on love,
which binds them all together in perfect unity.

COLOSSIANS 3:14 (NIV)

Stronger, and more frequently, comes the temptation to stop singing, and let discord do its own wild work. But blessed are they that endure to the end—singing patiently and sweetly, till all join in with loving acquiescence, and universal harmony prevails, without forcing into submission the free discord of a single voice.

This is the hardest and the bravest task which a true soul has to perform amid the clashing elements of time. But once has it been done perfectly unto the end; and that voice—so clear in its meekness—is heard above all the din of a tumultuous world: one after another chimes in with its patient sweetness; and, through infinite discords, the listening soul can perceive that the great tune is slowly coming into harmony.

—LYDIA MARIA CHILD.

Our Father, who is in heaven! We thank You that we are permitted to see the light, engage in the duties and enter into the experiences of this new day. We thank You for the order and harmony of this wonderful universe; that every force and law and being supports and balances every other force, law and being; that every life contributes to or may contribute to the welfare of every other life, and we pray, that each one of us may come into such relations with You, the great harmonizing soul of things, as to add our little note to the full anthem of perpetual and adorable praise. In Christ's dear name, we ask and offer all. Amen. —A. J. PATTERSON.

December 28

Sing to him a new song;
play skillfully, and shout for joy.

PSALM 33:3 (NIV)

It is said that a friend once asked the great composer, Haydn, why his church music was always so full of gladness. He answered, "I cannot make it otherwise; I write according to the thoughts I feel; when I think upon my God, my heart is so full of joy that the notes dance and leap from my pen; and since God has given me a cheerful heart, it will be pardoned me that I serve Him with a cheerful spirit."

Pardoned? Nay, it will be praised and rewarded. For God looks with approval and man turns with gratitude to everyone who shows by a cheerful life that religion is a blessing for this world and the next.　　　　　　　　　　　—HENRY VAN DYKE.

Our Father in Heaven, we awake this morning with a sense of thankfulness for the beauty and glory of Your creation. We praise You that as Your children we can be conscious of the kingdom of heaven always about us. So we pray for that attitude of mind and spirit of soul that will unlock for us the divine life. Help us to be conscious of You in all the varied experiences of this day. If it shall be a day of burdens, give us strength to play our part uncomplainingly, if a day of joy to accept it with true gratitude; and when the shades of night shall call us to our rest, may our memory of the day bring us peace. Amen.　　　　　　　　　　　—EDWARD C. DOWNEY.

December 29

As for God, his way is perfect:
The Lord's word is flawless;
he shields all who take refuge in him.

2 SAMUEL 22:31 (NIV)

Ah, don't be sorrowful, darling,
And don't be sorrowful, pray;
Taking the year together, my dear,
There isn't more night than day.

'Tis rainy weather, my darling;
Time's waves they heavily run;
But taking the year together, my dear,
There isn't more cloud than sun.

—ALICE CARY.

We thank You, heavenly Father, for the days just as they come. Nor would we measure the sunshine against the storm as if to test Your goodness by some petty form of bookkeeping. You preside over all our days, and whatever may be the face of nature we trust Your love. Let us go forth today, not in critical mood nor despondent mood but in the mood of high Christian faith, anxious, not to test Your providence, but ready to do our own part, taking care to hold our cup of blessing open-side up; so it can catch the manna when it falls. Then shall each passing day be full of blessing. Amen.

—GEORGE L. PERIN.

December 30

Fades the rose; the year grows old;
The tale is told;
Youth doth depart—
Only stays the heart.

Ah, no! If stays the heart,
Youth can ne'er depart,
Nor the sweet tale be told—
Never the rose fade,
   nor the year grow old.

      —RICHARD WATSON GILDER.

Dear Father, we thank You for the year now coming to its close, and for all that has blessed us in it. Help us to keep the good with which it has done us good in lasting memory. By the flight of time which its passing emphasizes, move us to earnestness in the labors committed to our hands. Beyond this, help us that we may be undisturbed, remembering that You are our dwelling place, and that we are the children of Your love and the sharers of Your everlastingness. So may we keep the vision of youth, the vision to which endings are but beginnings, the good leading to the better, and the best forever more. May Your blessing be upon all whom we love and should pray for in this and every day, in Jesus' name. Amen.　　—CHARLES R. TENNEY.

December 31

What shall we say about such wonderful things as these?
If God is for us, who can ever be against us?

ROMANS 8:31 (NLT)

Be not afraid, dear friend. What of sickness! What of sorrow! What of failure! What of misfortune! What of death! Is not this God's world? Are not you God's child? Go forth into the New Year with brave heart. When fortune smiles, smile with her. When fortune frowns, smile the more, and trust in God. —GEORGE L. PERIN.

Our Heavenly Father, we stand upon the utmost verge of the old year. Forgetting the things that are behind, we stand with our faces looking earnestly into the future. We do not despise the past, we do not forget its manifold blessings. We do not forget that You have been with us in the old year; for all this we would be grateful. With clear vision and earnestness of purpose, we would stand looking into the future expectantly, ready for its duties and its responsibilities; yet not ostentatiously nor with over-confidence, for we know our own infirmities, our own weaknesses. We would enter upon the New Year with confidence, not because of our own strength, but because of Your living presence. You are always with us, You are pouring out Your spirit upon us. O Lord, let us believe in You, and believing, let us have a heart for any fate. Amen. —GEORGE L. PERIN.

www.ingramcontent.com/pod-product-compliance
Lightning Source LLC
Chambersburg PA
CBHW060855120626
46553CB00001B/90